# HOW TO RECOGNIZE EMOTIONAL UNAVAILABILITY AND MAKE HEALTHIER RELATIONSHIP CHOICES

BRYN COLLINS, M.A., L.P

**MJF BOOKS**
**NEW YORK**

Published by MJF Books
Fine Communications
Two Lincoln Square
60 West 66th Street
New York, NY 10023

*How To Recognize Emotional Unavailability and Make Healthier Relationship Choices*
ISBN 1-56731-344-2
Library of Congress Card Catalog #99-75813

This edition published by arrangement with Contemporary Books, an imprint of NTC/Contemporary Publishing Group, Inc.

This book has also been published as *Emotional Unavailability: Recognizing It, Understanding It, and Avoiding Its Trap.*

Manufactured in the United States of America on acid-free paper
MJF Books and the MJF colophon are trademarks of Fine Creative Media, Inc.

10  9  8      7      6      5      4      3      2

*To Rod*

# CONTENTS

# ACKNOWLEDGMENTS

Just as it takes an entire village to raise a child, it takes a lot of experience and life learning to raise a therapist! I'd like to offer my thanks to the people who were my teachers on this journey. Although I may not have always enjoyed the lessons, I do certainly value them and carry them with me.

Special thanks to my agent, Jean Naggar, who is an exceptional teacher, an exceptional woman, and a very special friend; to my parents, Ron and Ellen Christgau, whose wisdom and innocence taught me the value of each; to my mother-in-law, Rose Collins, who taught me unconditional love with all its pain and glory; to my teacher, mentor, and therapist, Judith Barnitt; to my dearest friend, Molly Anderson, who taught me what real friendship is; to my brother, Jay Christgau, for infinite reasons; to my friends Roxanne Currie, Dave Estok, Jim Keenan, Brenda DeMotte, Donna Waldhauser, Leslie Lienemann, Dr. Mike Share, and Brian Hawkins, who supported and encouraged me; to my editor, Susan Schwartz, for her exceptional editing; to Bessie, Splash, Rosie, and Ranger for limitless enthusiasm and kisses; and to my husband and best friend, Rod, for things far too numerous to mention.

Finally, thank you to all of my clients and colleagues who keep on teaching me.

# INTRODUCTION

Imagine this: You've been invited to a party, but you realize on the day you're pretty sure the party is happening that you're not sure what kind of party it is or what time you should arrive. Well, you figure, you're smart and you'll just give it your best shot. So you dress in a kind of neutral casual-dressy style and show up at seven.

As you come up the walk, you can hear the sounds of a party: music, conversation, laughter, glasses clinking, and champagne corks popping, and you think, "This is going to be a great party." When you come up the stairs to the porch, you can smell delicious aromas coming from the house and again you say to yourself, "This is going to be a great party."

You ring the bell and your host emerges wearing a bemused, enigmatic smile . . . and a tuxedo.

"You're late," he says.

"I'm sorry. You didn't tell me what time the party was."

"I thought you'd figure it out."

"Well, I'm sorry. And I'm here now." You try a confident smile, which doesn't quite work.

Your host looks you up and down. "That may be true, but you're not dressed properly."

You look down at your elegant, if casual, clothing and then at his black-tie formal wear. "Yes, that's true. But I'm not that far from home. I can just go and change quickly and be right back before you even notice. I won't even be gone an hour."

You desperately think about what's in your closet that would fit with formal wear and how long it will take you to press it. You add up the travel time, wonder what you'll have to do to your hair to look right with whatever outfit you're going to put together, and try to think of how you can change your makeup without redoing it. After all, this still seems like it'll be a great party.

Your host shakes his head. "But then you'll be *really* late. Dinner will be over and I was *counting* on you to sit right beside me at the head table."

Your heart sinks. Your one chance and you blew it! Inside your head, you say several unflattering things about yourself, your abilities, your intelligence, and your potential, but out loud you declare, "Honest, I'll be back in forty-five minutes. I'll be perfect. Can't you wait? It's just forty-five minutes." You cannot imagine how you'll be back, but you want so badly to be the guest of honor.

Your host shakes his head. "Well, I don't know. But what are you planning to bring to contribute to the dinner? I've told you how much I like those special, individual nineteen-layer cakes you bake. I thought you'd know to bring one for every guest."

Behind him you can still hear the laughter and the music; you can still smell the exotic foods, and you can still see the champagne in his glass. And you still think it's the greatest party ever and you still want to be the guest of honor.

"Maybe I could be back in time for dessert. . . . How many guests are there?"

That's what an emotionally unavailable relationship *feels* like. You're just never quite good enough to get admitted to the party. You get seduced by the clear, often indirect and unspoken, message that something is just a little wrong. If you can fix that, the implied promise goes, you'll be the guest of honor and win the door prize: love.

But when you "fix" what was "wrong" the first time, something else is a little "wrong." And when you fix that, something else will appear.

Your host has no intention of making you—or anyone—the guest of honor. Your host also has no *ability* to make you the guest of honor—or even to open the door to let you in. Your host is suffering from **emotional unavailability**. This is the inability of a person to reach out and make a heart connection with another person.

What's so unsettling and painful is that you end up with

the clear belief that this is somehow your fault and that it's your responsibility to fix it by being perfect. If it isn't fixed, you're not perfect enough.

For the first of many times, let me say clearly to you:

YOU DIDN'T BREAK IT . . .
YOU DON'T HAVE TO FIX IT!

## What Was I Thinking?

You've just read the affirmation above (affirmation—a true and positive statement of the way things ideally are) and the metaphor about the party and said to yourself, "That's so obvious. I'd *never* get caught in any situation like that."

It seems obvious—until you're in the middle of it. It doesn't start out with unreasonable demands of perfection. If it did, you'd walk away after the first five minutes. We all get sucked into emotionally unavailable situations (I don't like to abuse the word *relationship* when describing something so one-sided) because the process is subtle and progressive. The demands move a little at a time, inching you away from your power base, shifting control of the situation to the emotionally unavailable person.

That's one of the keys to understanding emotional unavailability. The person who is not available doesn't want love as much as he or she wants control. Emotions are unsafe; control gives the illusion of safety.

It's perfectly reasonable to expect an emotional connection with someone with whom you have a relationship. We base a lot in life on expectations of certain behavior by others in given situations. That's part of the reason life's details don't overwhelm us. We use expectations as a guide to predicting the behavior of people around us. Otherwise we'd have to figure out every situation we encountered every minute of every day. Just imagine rush-hour traffic!

We expect police officers to enforce the laws and keep us

safe. We expect teachers to teach. We expect doctors to help us heal. We expect our partners in relationships to connect with us emotionally. These expectations put us into a particular mind-set when we're around those people.

Suppose that you are in a bank and a uniformed police officer is standing behind you in line. Someone comes in to rob the bank. You make decisions about what to do based on your reasonable expectation that the police officer will attempt to protect you and the others in the bank. People who have been in this situation where the "police officer" turned out to be a costumed accomplice of the robber have been more traumatized by the betrayal of the "police officer" than by the experience of being in a robbery.

If you are in a relationship with someone, you expect the relationship to grow and deepen over time; you expect a heart connection to be made and maintained. You operate your life from the basis of this expectation. When your partner in the relationship turns out not to be making an emotional connection, it causes trauma; that's why these relationships are so painful. The trauma then does further damage as it undermines your expectations about yourself and your abilities to make connections. As illogical as that may seem, it's human nature to look for flaws in ourselves when things don't go as we expect. We end up being traumatized twice by these relationships: once by the loss and abandonment and again by the loss of our own confidence in ourselves. That's why the end of these relationships can be so much more painful than the end of a fully realized relationship. We ruminate about what we could have done differently to make it work.

## A Road Map

One of the objectives of this book is to introduce you to emotionally unavailable types so you'll recognize them when they appear in your life. We'll do this in Chapter 1.

In Chapter 2, we'll take a look at some of the ways in which people become emotionally unavailable. We'll also explore emotions and mind-sets and some different ways to look at communication, which will help you spot emotionally unavailable people *before* you are hooked.

Chapters 3 through 16 focus on how the folks we met in Chapter 1 behave when they get into relationships. There are checklists and quizzes to help you identify these people, and some tools to understand how you get hooked in.

Chapters 17 and 18 give you tools to change the way you approach people and relationships. As you use these tools in daily life, you will attract other emotionally available people into relationships because you will be clearly emotionally available.

Chapter 19 helps you identify those people and relationships that go beyond emotionally unavailable into toxic. You'll learn how to recognize toxic people and how to get away and stay away.

My hope is that through reading and using this book, you'll learn to let go of emotionally unavailable people and relationships and find other emotionally available people with whom to connect.

❖

# Chapter One

# MR. WONDERFUL,
# MS. PERFECT,
# AND FRIENDS

*I* don't think I know anyone who has escaped having a relationship with someone emotionally unavailable at some point in their life. There's no particular time in life when the unhealthy relationship happens—some people have one in their teens, others in their senior years.

Some unlucky people I know have never had a relationship that *wasn't* emotionally unavailable! These sad folks can't seem to figure out how they keep getting into bad relationships. They don't realize it's a process of choice—and of education.

There's an old rule of thumb that people choose to be with partners who remind them of the parent with whom they had the most unresolved issues. As it turns out, that's usually true. It also leads a person to choose essentially the same type of relationship again and again. The partner might come in different packages, but the contents are emotionally similar. Part of the education process is to be able to recognize the type of emotionally unavailable person you've chosen in the past. That gives you a guidepost to figuring out what it is about that type that feels so familiar and entices you again and again.

Let's take a look at some of the personality types who

are emotionally unavailable. This is not an all-inclusive list, but it includes the major representatives. Recognize that all behavior falls along a range from pretty OK to extreme. These personality types fall along the same range: mild to unacceptable. Acceptable of course varies from person to person.

It's also worth noting that people can change. They do it all the time. Almost nothing is cast in stone. In each of these personality types save two there is potential to grow and change. It takes work and sometimes therapy, and it depends on where within the range the person is as to how much change he or she can make, but it can happen if the person believes it's important enough.

And the two who can't? Read on.

## Romeo/Romiette: Great Balcony, No Stamina

Ah, romance: Barry White is playing in the background, lights are low, the scent of roses fills the air.

Week One: "Baby, you are without a doubt the most gorgeous and wonderful woman I've ever met. I can't even look at you without wanting to sweep you into my arms."

You meet Romeo/Romiette and find yourself swept away. Sweet phone calls, endearing cards, flowers, special and thoughtful treats. When you're together, you are the center of attention.

Week Two: "I can't imagine how I survived without you."

You can't help it—suddenly you know you are *it*. Every love song was written for the two of you. Every romantic movie is about you. Romance novelists must have been hiding in your kitchen drawers, writing everything the two of you say and do into their books.

Week Three: "I can't stop thinking about you. You're making me get in trouble at work because I don't concentrate. I just want to spend time with you."

You begin to make plans. Words like *our* and *we* pepper your conversation. The distant echo of wedding bells rings in your ears. Your friends are sick of hearing about your perfect relationship.

Week Four: "Sorry I'm not here to take your call right now. Leave a number and I'll get back to you."

Week Five: "Sorry I'm not here to take your call right now. Leave a number and I'll get back to you."

Week Six: "Sorry I'm not here to take your call right now. Leave a number and I'll get back to you."

Suddenly, it's gone. Without so much as a by-your-leave or a go-to-hell, everything stops. There's no fight. There's no discussion. There's been no accident (you know because you've checked with every hospital emergency room in the state) and no funeral. Romeo/Romiette simply disappears.

You ruminate. You make up wild scenarios involving global amnesia or a terrorist kidnapping. You find yourself gracelessly leaping for the phone whenever it rings. You agonize about what it is *you* did to make this happen, and you leave desperate, unattractive, and unanswered messages at the phone numbers where you had reached Romeo/Romiette instantly only days before. Then you get sad. Eventually you might even get mad.

What you probably don't get is answers, even if you happen to run into Romeo/Romiette. What you will get then is a warm, superficial greeting and evasive answers to the questions you ask.

Before you completely trash-talk yourself, let's dissect this alleged relationship for a minute. When it first begins, the intensity of the connection is what hooks you. It feels deep and sincere, but that's in part because Romeo/Romiette is focused on you, and for most of us that's an unusual experience and the effect is heady.

Because the focus is on you, you don't find out much about Romeo/Romiette. Any questions of a personal or feelings nature get turned aside or converted into questions about you. This evasion serves Romeo/Romiette well because he or she has a wealth of information about what you want and what you like and what you believe; Romeo/

Romiette uses that to further engage you in the relationship. In return, Romeo/Romiette gets adoration, romance, and fulfillment—not to mention the thrill of the chase and the rush of the conquest—very sparkly stuff!

What doesn't interest this type of person is the dull patina of reality. As soon as any hint of repetition or familiarity appears—as soon as you push to know something about how Romeo/Romiette *feels* about something—alarms begin to peal and Romeo/Romiette begins to look for a new conquest. Remember those wedding bells you heard? That was the alarm going off.

Romeo/Romiette has made no emotional investment in the relationship. The connection you felt is with yourself because Romeo/Romiette focused his or her attention—and your own—on you.

It's one-sided but doesn't feel that way because most of us are so grateful and flattered to be the center of someone's total attention that we don't see it—sometimes not until years afterward!

Gratitude and flattery are not acceptable substitutes for love and real emotional connection. That's what causes the pain of this kind of abandonment. Essentially, it's as if you're being abandoned by yourself. Meanwhile, Romeo/Romiette remains emotionally distant, emotionally unavailable, throughout the course of this relationship, so when it ends, he or she has no pain and no sense of abandonment. Instead, Romeo/Romiette's drawn to the thrill of the chase with someone new.

Why would someone do this? Although it seems really mean and manipulative, it comes from a place that's sad and empty. People like Romeo/Romiette are so numbed and at arm's length from themselves that it's impossible for them to connect on any real level with another human.

While you're emptying that box of Kleenex and downing that quart of triple fudge cookie dough ice cream, it's important to remind yourself that this isn't about you. You have been treated like a precious object that, once acquired, is no longer desirable.

Being *objectified*, treated like an object, is one of the hallmarks of abusive relationships. It's not OK and it's not nice and you didn't deserve it. Healing comes from being able to let yourself off the hook and from identifying the lesson you learned or the unfinished business you might have finished from the encounter. Before you jump off that balcony that Romeo/Romiette left you on, finish this book, finish the ice cream, and try to remember how good it feels to feel good about yourself! That's the biggest gift Romeo/Romiette has to offer.

## Indiana Jones: The Dangerous Man

The sound of the howling Alpine winds almost drowns out his words, but you can make out, ". . . gorgeous in this . . . feel so good to be . . . adrenaline feels just like love."

You most often meet Indy in high-intensity situations: he's the ski instructor; the cliff diver; the race-car driver. His conversation is filled with references to exotic places and exciting events. There's nothing he won't try "just for the fun of it." He might come in a uniform: cop, firefighter, jet pilot. The unflappable, cool rescuer who can take on anything and still keep his head. He also keeps his heart—and his emotions!

What he gives is a steady stream of adrenaline-by-association as he tells you the tales of his exploits. Sometimes you even find yourself following him out the door of a perfectly safe airplane, down a dangerous ski run, or to the bottom of a shark-patrolled reef without really knowing how you got there. Indy is all adrenaline. Even when it's just the two of you sitting cozy in front of the fire, the room is filled with his sky-diving, bad-guy arresting, firefighting electricity. Where Romeo is completely focused on you, Indy is completely focused on events and excitement. He casts himself in the central role, but it's all action—and no interaction.

As long as you continue to be the awed spectator/supporter, the relationship continues. But should you look for any emotional content or try to share any emotion beyond, "Wow! You're amazing!" you will find yourself abandoned on a dead-end road while he's off to the remote wherzis to whatzis with whozis. When the adrenaline dissipates, Indy disappears.

So why are women attracted to Indy? Adrenaline and excitement are a turn-on. What happens is that the event and the person doing the event get jumbled together so the person becomes the excitement of the event or the action. Indy probably got tuned to that style early in life when he was praised for things he did but not for who he was, or when he got a strong reaction from peers and parents (probably about 180 degrees apart!) for pulling off some crazy stunt. Suddenly he was in the action spotlight. He didn't have to make any emotional connections or commitments, take any emotional risks, or make himself vulnerable to get attention.

Think of a high school sports hero who gets lots of positive attention for his athletic achievement without having to put any of his self or his soul into it. I'm not saying all athletes are Indys, but a lot of Indys were star athletes whose careers ended with graduation. When that spotlight went out, they went looking for another way to plug it back in. Sometimes the military provides the spotlight; sometimes being a punk or gang member; in other cases it might be a hobby or interest that's fraught with risks—rock climbing, scuba diving, white-water rafting. In all these situations, the message is the same: Indy's value comes from what he does, not who he is. You'll notice that in his chosen fields of activity there's no incentive to explore emotions and there might even be a disincentive because then Indy would have to be vulnerable, and tough guys don't do vulnerable in their view.

When you finally tire of the war stories and want something more in the way of an emotional connection, Indy will grab the next plane to Timbuktu—or the local equivalent—and go on to the next adventure appreciator.

Just as all athletes are not Indys, neither are all scuba divers, bungee jumpers, cops, firefighters, and so on. The love of a particular sport or sports or an exciting hobby doesn't preclude a person's making emotional connections. Where Indy makes his appearance is when the sport or activity takes the place of real emotional connections— where the activity is the connection.

Where Romeo slips away silently, Indy disappears in a cloud of activity. He just gets busy and you're not on the schedule. He might go off on an adventure or take up a new activity you're not interested in or he might find a new group of adventure buddies. Just ask for a commitment and watch the activity burst forth!

This breakup involves not so much ice cream as a garage sale as you get rid of the scuba gear or ski boots. Because the relationship was not with the person but with his action and behavior, the end is not so much pain as it is adrenaline withdrawal. The residual these people leave in our lives, however, is a taste for the jazz of excitement. This fallout is dangerous because it can lead you right to another Indy. Another ride on the great roller coaster of dangerous men (or women).

Take heart. You *can* learn to be comfortable with a person whose idea of excitement is a movie and McDonald's. All it takes is a real emotional connection.

## Tens and Other Trophies

JFK Jr.'s double, Claudia Schiffer's doppelganger, Cindy Crawford's twin, Brad Pitt's look-alike. Where Indys rely on their excitement quotient, Tens rely on the power of their physical beauty to enchant without connection. The underlying dynamic is much the same. The Tens got the message early in life that looks were a better asset than anything else they had to offer—a *terrible* message—and reacted by developing that asset. What they learned is that it's a low emotional risk to have an adoring person captured by their looks. They have the illusion of connection without having to give anything back.

"What do you think about this shirt on me?"

"Looks great. It's really you."

"Does my hair look all right?"

"Looks great. I think this cut is the best ever."

"I only drink Evian water because I want to keep my skin perfect."

"Let me just get some of that for you."

"I think I'll take up horseback riding because I think I'd look good on a horse."

Your role in the relationship is clearly defined from the first contact. You are in charge of admiration and adoration. It's your job to complement and compliment, to display and step out of the way while your Ten basks in the glow of the spotlight.

In a sense it's another form of objectification but this time the object is the Ten and it's a role he or she takes voluntarily! This is key to understanding how low the Ten's self-esteem is. If you believe your only value is as a trophy or an object for others to admire, that's self-victimization. So, you're asking yourself, if I have a relationship with a Ten who chooses to objectify himself or herself, does that make me an objectifier?

Good question. It looks right at the heart of objectification because this voluntary offering of a person as an object also objectifies the person to whom the object is offered. In other words, as the Ten is self-victimizing, he or she is also victimizing you. What a no-win situation that is.

It takes a while for the admiration to wear off, but eventually the reflected glow of the spotlight isn't enough and you ask for something from the heart. What you're offered instead is more beauty. There's nothing wrong with beauty, but it's not enough when your heart needs attention. Beauty is not emotion.

Sometimes Tens will attract trophy hunters. These relationships are mutually parasitic and unfulfilled emotionally but each person's agenda gets met so we're not going to focus on those combinations. Think of them as emotional unavailability squared.

The person who is attracted by the beauty of the Ten gets a different kind of rush than the adrenaline-by-association of the person who chooses the Indy. It accesses feelings of pride and accomplishment by association; they can't miss the glances of appreciation and jealousy coming their way. Don't misunderstand, however. Just as all action-oriented guys aren't Indys, all beautiful people aren't Tens. What distinguishes the Tens is the emotional distance they keep from anyone who tries to connect and be a part of their lives. Sounds pretty lonely to hold the world at arm's length, doesn't it?

The breakup with a Ten is painful because it attacks *your* self-esteem. If you've been getting a glow-by-association from being the partner of a Ten and suddenly you're replaced, you have to be a very grounded, centered person not to wonder if it might have happened because you're not attractive enough. That speculation leads down a very rocky and negative trail, a trip you should avoid at all costs. It's hard to remember that love and beauty are not the same thing, but that will help you avoid getting stuck in negative rumination. A little positive self-talk, some reality checks, and the use of emotional dark glasses to block out the glare of the reflected spotlight and you'll be ready to find a genuine heart link with someone else!

## Mama's Boys and Daddy's Girls

"Well, my mom always knew what I wanted without my having to tell her. Why can't you figure it out? Why do I always have to tell you what I need?"

"If my daddy thought I was unhappy, he would buy me something to make me feel better. What are you going to do for me?"

They grew up secure in the belief that they hung the moon. Mom and Dad gave them everything—except emotional connections. When you enter a relationship with a Mama's Boy or a Daddy's Girl, you are expected to take over where Mama and Daddy left off. The problems with this expectation are legion.

First, it's unlikely that Mama and Daddy are going to be willing to relinquish any presence in the life of the Boy or Girl. Instead, their expectation is for you to join the admiring audience, but not as a full member. Instead you are to remain in a subordinate role to them and to the Boy or Girl—a satellite.

The second problem will arise as your love is compared, generally unfavorably, to the love Mama and Daddy offered. Often this will be measured in material goods or money ("Daddy would have gotten me the . . .") or in terms of boundary-free acceptance ("I don't know why you're upset. Mama never got upset when . . .").

Which leads me on a small side trip. We seem to have gotten confused about the difference between unconditional love/acceptance (desirable) and boundary-free acceptance (dysfunctional). Unconditional love/acceptance says, "I love you because you exist. I accept you for who you are. However, you must act right and be a good citizen of the world or you will have consequences."

Boundary-free acceptance says, "I know Junior shouldn't be doing drugs, sleeping with everything that moves, and stealing from us and his employer. But I don't want him to suffer consequences. He needs treatment. It's society's fault. It's his teacher's fault. It's his therapist's fault. You don't understand him. He's special."

Junior may be a lot of things, but he's no fool. It takes very little time for him to catch on to this scam. "I'm special. Rules don't apply to me. If I get consequences, Mama will fix it." Most elementary schoolteachers can tell you the effects of this parenting style as they struggle with classrooms full of kids who believe they can do anything they please whenever they want.

Many of my fellow clinicians and I have practices filled with adolescents we're supposed to "fix" because they got the message when they were little that their Mama or Daddy would make consequences go away. In order to function in the world and in a relationship, kids—people—need structure and an understanding that consequences will result from a violation of that structure. When you are in a relationship with someone who's never had to take ownership of his or her behavior, you are expected to take over the job Mama and Daddy started and make consequences go away.

This relationship gets even messier when you try to establish some structure. Let's say your expectation, stated clearly, is monogamy. Your partner becomes attracted to someone outside your relationship. What decision do you imagine she'll honor: your expectation of monogamy or her own pleasure? And how do you imagine she'll react to your pain, outrage, anger, or any attempt to set consequences?

"Mama would never . . ."

"I'm going home to Daddy!"

Mama's Boys and Daddy's Girls were protected by their parents from all potentially painful and therefore *learning* experiences. They never had to feel their feelings. Before that little lower lip even had a chance to quiver, Mama was there, making the hurt go away.

It's a no-win situation to be in a relationship with someone who is at arm's length with his or her feelings. It's worse when the original protector is lurking around waiting for any hint of pain in the Boy or Girl before swooping down upon the source of that pain—you—and once more rescuing her or his little one.

In a relationship with Mama's Boy or Daddy's Girl, you can expect a negative return on your emotional investment. This leads to enormous frustration. The relationship will abruptly end if you even ask for any completion of the circle of emotion or suggest that behavior has consequences or hint that you are displeased about anything your partner has done or said. It will be a loud and stormy ending; the wail of the thwarted child is quick to surface and will be enhanced by the chorus of protection from Mama or Daddy. You are left bruised and confused, your reasonable expectations shattered and scattered, second-guessing yourself and your belief system.

The sad thing for the Boy and Girl and the good news for you is that they will not learn, but you will recover.

## 'Holics: Alca . . . , Coca . . . , Spenda . . . , Sexa . . . , Worka . . .

Soapbox Alert! Before plunging into this topic, let me jump on the soapbox for a minute to make the observation that I do not subscribe to the current theory that everything is an addiction, a model that dominates a lot of therapeutic approaches. I believe addiction should have a very narrow definition, which only includes physical dependence on a substance. I do not believe a person's negative choices or behavioral responses to his or her experiential history constitute an addiction. Calling negative behavioral choices addiction confuses making an explanation with taking responsibility.

An explanation is not an excuse. People need to own their behavior—warts and all. Everybody makes bad choices once in a while. You grow from the experience and try not to make the same bad choice again.

Using the addiction model allows a person to use an explanation as an excuse and not own the behavior. "It was the addiction. I'm powerless." Bull feathers. Own your behavior, keep your choices, and be powerful. End of soapbox.

'Holics are people who get focused on one behavior to the exclusion of anything else—including their relationships. At the same time, they demand your unconditional and absolute devotion to them and their obsession. This expectation helps the 'holic stay in control of you without having to exert much effort.

> ## Good judgment comes from experience.
> ## Experience comes from bad judgment!

You, on the other hand, get the clear message that if you do everything perfectly, you might get the loving connection you hope for. The problem with this setup is multi-dimensional: the 'holic is getting everything he or she wants *without* having to give anything back; the 'holic is not able to make that loving connection with you as promised because he or she is focused on the behavior. Therefore his or her primary relationship is with the obsessed behavior.

That's an important point. With a 'holic, the obsession is the primary emotional focus. It means you will never be the primary emotional focus for this person. That position is filled—permanently! It's not satisfying to be second banana. My friend Connie Day paraphrased Shakespeare on this subject: "Hell makes no music like a woman playing second fiddle!"

For the sake of this discussion, I'll use the words *addiction* and *obsession* to cover the same turf as "repetitive behavioral choices that reflect obsessive focus." It'll just be simpler. It doesn't mean I'm giving up my soapbox!

We can divide 'holics into two groups: behavior 'holics and substance 'holics. There is some common ground between the two groups. First, the obsessive focus on getting the addiction met overrides everything else. Second, the addictions are rarely apparent on first contact. It's not until you know the person more intimately that the addiction begins to show up, and by then you're involved. Third, the obsession takes a lot of psychic and emotional energy, leaving little for anything else.

Let's look first at the behavior 'holic group. Into this category fall the worka-, sexa-, shopa-, fooda-, sportsa-, and so on. I'm not talking about people who *like* to do certain things or who really enjoy their hobbies. A hobby, just for the sake of clarity, is something you enjoy doing, talk about with people of like interest (and sometimes with people who only *pretend* to be interested because they are your friends), but which does not drive your life. When I say 'holics, I am talking about people who can't think of much else but their obsession. Every conversation either is about the obsession or gets manipulated to be about the obsession or doesn't occur at all because the person is attending to his or her obsession and is therefore absent from you.

Let's use a workaholic for an example, though this will apply, with obvious variations, to all the behavior 'holics. There are both male and female workaholics. These folks work every day, either in the office, at home, or on the road. When they are not working, they are thinking about work or on the phone or sending a fax or at the computer. If you ask them what they do for a living, either you get an evasive answer reflecting that they believe their job is much too complicated for you to understand, or you get a flood of unintelligible information designed to dazzle you. In either case, the answer reveals the passion.

It also reveals the focus. But there is something fascinating about someone so focused and that fascination is the (misguided) belief that you will be able to distract the workaholic and get that same focus transferred to you. That might not be a conscious thought on your part, but it's there.

Another component of the fascination is the implication of power. The reasoning goes like this: if someone is important enough to have to work endless hours like this, he or she must be some kinda wonderful! Not necessarily. Workaholics are far more likely to be middle-level managers, women trying to shatter the glass ceiling, or persons in their own business where it's work or perish. Or maybe all that backbreaking work is really because the person owes money to everyone on the planet!

With behavior 'holics, the person is completely obsessed with the chosen behavior, which means the maximum slot you could hope to occupy is number two. It might be seductive for a while to be in the second spot to the career of a rising workaholic because you see the potential financial rewards and acclaim and you enjoy the feeling of being part of it all. But money and acclaim are no substitute for presence and love. A checkbook isn't much of a cuddle!

"Sure, we can go to Ralph and Judy's for dinner. Do you think we should take a bottle of booze?"
"I'm sure they'll have wine with dinner."
"Do you think they'll have enough?"

The second group is the substance 'holics. If you've cast your lot with someone using alcohol and/or drugs (the true 'holics of my definition of 'holics), you are competing on a very unlevel field. Read this and believe me: *There is nothing on the planet or off more important to the substance 'holic than the drug. Period. No exceptions.*
Of course, the 'holic is not going to admit that. The 'holic is going to tell you that you are the center of his or her world. As long as you continue to support the habit, you will get that message. But if you set limits, keep your boundaries tight, and refuse to support damaging behavior in any way—emotionally, financially, or behaviorally—suddenly the center of the world shifts for the 'holic. Until you do set limits, however, your contributions to the negative behavior of the 'holic keep you in the relationship—in your subordinate position to the habit, of course.
If you are in a relationship with a person who is addicted to a substance, there are two things you cannot afford to forget. They are absolute truth, unchanging and immutable:

1. You will always play second fiddle to the substance.
2. You are not now and never will be powerful enough to cause your addicted partner to change, give up the substance, behave in a responsible way, or treat you in the way in which you deserve to be treated.

*You cannot earn what does not exist.* Make this your mantra. Chant it whenever you have the urge to do something to attempt to earn the love of the 'holic by preserving the relationship between the 'holic and the substance.

In your supporting role with a behavior or substance 'holic, you are expected to make the same kind of sacrifices your 'holic makes for his or her obsession/addiction—without any probability of reciprocity. And should you point this out, you risk losing your second-place status or being accused of disloyalty (which is for most substance 'holics grounds for abandonment). A few threats like this and you learn not to object to your lot in the relationship. Once you are firmly in your role, it's possible the 'holic will spend even less time or energy with you because now he or she can "count on you to be there," which is 'holicese for "take you for granted." When you finally lose your tolerance for getting only a small piece of the emotional pie and end the relationship, you will also carry the burden of the sadness and pain because the 'holic still has his or her primary relationship and has lost nothing.

Here's the heart of what keeps 'holics in the behavior: they are locked in a relationship with an emotionally unavailable love object, which they believe they can capture if only they work hard enough. Sound familiar? It's layers of emotional unavailability.

# Emotional Einstein: The Thinking Person's Love

"Charles, how do you feel about me? We've been exclusively together for about six months now and I'd like to know where I stand."

"Clarissa, I think we have many mutual goals that fit well together. I think you are very bright and I think we have a great deal of fun together."

"I agree, but how do you feel about me?"

"I think you are enchanting—very charming and quite delightful."

"Thank you. But how do you feel about me?"

"I think you have so many good qualities. I think you'll be an excellent mother and wife."

"Thank you. But how do you *feel* about me?"

"Clarissa, I don't understand you. What more do you want to hear? I've been *telling* you how I feel!"

Love is not an intellectual exercise and emotional connections are not made through the brain. You have to have a brain to make emotional connections, but your brain is not where the hook happens.

If you were an Emotional Einstein, you would now be telling me, "There is no such thing as feeling with your heart. Your heart has no capacity to have emotional feelings because it is primarily muscle." Which would be completely missing the point.

Emotional Einsteins are characterized by their amazing capacity to put everything in intellectual terms. For an Emotional Einstein to experience anything, it must be analyzed, dissected, quantified, qualified, categorized, and tied into a neat little package. Emotions don't do any of those things very well, so the Emotional Einstein dismisses them.

"I love you."

"Do you mean love in the romantic sense or in the universal sense of . . . "

That's it in a nutshell.

Being in a relationship with an Emotional Einstein means that nothing will go unanalyzed. There will be careful planning, thorough assessment, and no emotional surprises. Even the most emotional moment will be carefully controlled so it doesn't break loose and get, well, emotional.

To the Emotional Einstein, the only thing in the world that's safe is thought. Emotions are turbulent, unpredictable, and uncontrollable, and therefore they must be avoided at all possible costs.

If you want any of that turbulent, unpredictable, uncontrollable emotional stuff and you spring it on your Emotional Einstein, he or she will freeze up like a deer in headlights, then rush like mad to get back into the safe intellectual world that can be controlled. As long as you don't demand an emotional, nonintellectual relationship and you march to the drum of the Emotional Einstein—a very measured pace—things will proceed with logical steps from one stage of life to another.

This modus operandi fits the bill for a lot of people and if it works for you and you can get through life's most intensely emotional moments without someone to share them—your wedding, the birth of your children, a really good sunset—then read no further. If, however, you like a little emotion in your life and you are in a relationship with an intellectualizer, it will have to come from you without much help from Emotional Einstein. You can ask for what you need emotionally and the Emotional Einstein will try to give it to you, but it will be as an intellectual exercise and not from the heart.

When you finally get frustrated with the head and demand the heart, the Emotional Einstein can't provide it. The breakup will have a lot of tears and sadness on both sides. Your tears will fall because you can't get what you need; Emotional Einstein's tears will fall because he or she can't understand what it is you're not getting. Even the breakup, however, will be intellectualized as Emotional Einstein tries to figure out what happened and fix it.

Emotions can't be categorized, evaluated, assessed, quantified, and analyzed. And they can't be fixed because they're not broken!

# The One in the Mirror: Narcissists and Other Self-Lovers

I have a buddy, Pete, who's a narcissist. If I'm not in contact with Pete and I see a story on TV about a terrible plane crash, I think to myself, "What an awful thing. The poor families of the victims must have to deal with so much after this tragedy." If I am in contact with Pete and I see the same story, I find myself thinking, "What an awful thing. I hope Pete's not bummed!"

Narcissists have that effect on you because they firmly believe the center of the universe is located just behind their own eyes and they expect you to share that belief without question or qualification.

As with all the personality types, narcissists fall along a continuum from mildly offensive to pernicious. There is a special brand of narcissist that is predatory. These people are to be avoided at all costs. They are human sharks, unable to feel anything or connect with anyone. Consult the last chapter of this book, "Dumping the Toxic and Moving On," for further details. What we'll discuss in the current chapter are the more mainstream sorts of narcissists.

Narcissists have an aura of grandiosity—they're special and can only, in their view, be truly understood by other special people. But since they believe there really isn't anyone quite as special as they are, they can't be truly understood by anyone but themselves. Narcissists have a tendency to overstate their accomplishments and understate their challenges. They also have a highly exaggerated sense of entitlement; not only do you owe them everything they want but you should be delighted to give it. Couple that entitlement with the narcissist's lack of empathy—the ability to feel the pain another feels—and you have someone who is completely unable to reach out to anyone but wants everyone to reach out to him or her. And if you could read minds so the narcissist wouldn't ever have to wait for anything. . . .

A relationship with a narcissist is fraught with frustration because no matter what you do, it isn't good enough. While you're stinging from each rejection, new demands are being made that you won't be able to adequately meet; not to mention your own needs, which are in mothballs . . . in the back of the deep freeze . . . in an abandoned warehouse . . . in another country . . . on another planet. . . .

There's an old saying in show business: you're only as

good as your next booking. The relationship with the narcissist has that same quality.

So what's the hook? First, people who are full of themselves can be very appealing because at first it looks like confidence, and confident people are magnetic. Confident people who are not narcissistic, however, share their confidence with people around them. You are enriched by the contact. Where confident people enjoy building your strengths, narcissists are focused on building their own strengths and will draw from you in a parasitic fashion. The hook comes from the illusion that you are a partner in something special and wonderful—the narcissist's view of himself or herself in the world. What you get back is the satisfaction of making the narcissist feel good about himself or herself, a condition that requires constant maintenance.

If the narcissist doesn't feel constantly attended to, he or she will withdraw from you. You get the strong message that if you don't get on the train you will be left at the station without a backward glance. Narcissists choose people who are pleasers by nature, so the threat of abandonment produces a flurry of restorative activity on the part of the pleaser. It's the control mechanism the narcissist uses. When you finally tire of pleasing the narcissist and meeting his or her every need without appreciation, acknowledgment, or emotional connection, you are left with lots of frustration and self-blame. You weren't good enough to be in a real relationship, goes the tape the narcissist has planted in your head.

Recovery comes with reality, which creeps back with the help of therapy and time. Part of that therapeutic process is erasing the tapes. The danger is that until those tapes are erased, you're very vulnerable to a rerun with another narcissist.

If you're tired of holding the mirror for someone else and making appreciative noises while getting nothing back, begin the process by giving yourself some good, strong positive talk—it's the only thing that drowns out the whine of the narcissist!

# Eels and Other Slippery Critters

"I don't know if I'm ready to make a commitment."

"Marriage is an obsolete institution invented by the _____." (Possible fill-ins include: old folks, conventional society, church, government, socialists, conservatives, or parents.)

"I think we should still keep living our own lives. I don't want to get too involved, even though we're living together."

Ah, the mating call of the Slippery Critter—the type that just can't quite commit to much of anything. Or at least much of anything you want. A Slippery Critter can come close. He'll move in with you. She'll share a checkbook. A Slippery Critter might even bring a kid into the world with you. What the Slippery Critter won't do is give you his word and keep it.

You might get a halfhearted promise about an eventual commitment at some later date when some unnamed conditions are right or when a certain goal is reached, which may or may not be something the Slippery Critter actually plans to do. In other words, the devil will have a hockey team before you get what you want.

In the meantime, you are stuck to the unfulfilled relationship by the magnet of hope. The distant goals of your Slippery Critter become your focus because you think they are the way in which you will get what you want. If by some accident the Slippery Critter actually achieves the goal that stands in the way of commitment to your objective, somehow another goal will always appear. Naturally, the new goal must be reached first before your commitment can be honored.

Satan's slapshots!

You're hooked by the great and powerful maybe. How do you get unhooked? You set limits, ask for what you want with specific timing, and then brace yourself for the probable departure of the Slippery Critter because he or she cannot tolerate solid expectations, clear limits, and adult relationships.

Recovering from this type of relationship involves rebuilding trust—trust in others and trust in yourself. And that's how you get rid of that hockey team!

## James Bond: Spies and Lies

"Rick, who's Jennifer?"

"Jennifer who?"

"I asked you first. I found this note in the pocket of your jeans. It's from someone named Jennifer who sounds as though she knows who you are."

"What are you doing snooping in my stuff?"

"I wasn't snooping. I was doing your laundry. So who's Jennifer?"

"She's just this girl . . ."

"Just this girl what?"

"Why are you bugging me? Don't you trust me? What's the matter with you?"

He won't tell you where he lives. She will give you only a work number. He's evasive about his history, friends, job, and background. A year after you marry her, you find out she's been married before. A mistress shows up. You find bills for credit cards you didn't know you had.

Secrets and the lies that support them make it very hard for a person to make an emotional connection. In part that's because the secrets create a wall. In part it's also because the secrets take a lot of energy to maintain and that energy is stolen from having a relationship with a person.

James Bonds are secret-keepers who withhold information from people with whom they are in a relationship. Sometimes this is because they believe the secrets give them power or an illusion of mystery and excitement; other times

# THE DIFFERENCE BETWEEN SECRET AND PRIVATE

**Private matters** are those traits, truths, beliefs, and ideas about ourselves that we keep to ourselves. They might include our fantasies and daydreams, feelings about the way the world works, and spiritual beliefs. Private matters, when revealed either accidentally or purposefully, give another person some insight into the revealer.

Secrets, on the other hand, consist of information that has potentially negative impact on someone else—emotionally, physically, or financially. Secrets, when revealed either accidentally or purposefully, cause great chaos or harm to the secret-keeper and those around him or her.

PRIVATE:  I believe in reincarnation.

SECRET:  I have a wife and a mistress and neither knows about the other.

PRIVATE:  I got terrible grades in high school.

SECRET:  I forged my medical degree.

it is because the revelation of the secrets will end the relationship and they won't get what they want—the reason for keeping secrets in the first place.

When you get into a relationship with a James Bond, you may enjoy the mystery at first. It's kind of exciting not to know when he or she will suddenly appear to sweep you into whatever passes for his or her Aston Martin or private jet and then just as suddenly disappear again.

As the relationship moves along, however, predictability becomes more important and desirable to you, but the James Bond has no interest in being trapped by your rational expectation of continuity in the relationship.

You begin to snoop. Bond leaves you alone in the car or

the apartment for a few minutes and your fingers stray to the glove compartment or desktop. You hate yourself for what you're doing, but you can't stop. Bills, letters, scraps with phone numbers—a flood of information without explanation. What you're looking for are the missing pieces of James Bond's life that you don't get to know. The problem is that you have no threads to weave into a fabric of truth. All you have is scraps that have no clear meaning.

Or, worse perhaps, you *do* find something: a breathless love letter you didn't write, a sexy card you didn't send, a photo that isn't you. Now what do you do? Now you have information and a whole new conundrum. In order to confront James Bond with the information, you have to admit you've been snooping. Then Bond has the perfect out: he or she can get mad at you for snooping and never have to own up to the rest of it.

The other thing that happens is that you lose trust completely. Being in a relationship with someone you don't trust isn't being in a relationship at all. It begins to undermine your trust in yourself as well and that undermines your self-image, which makes you more vulnerable, which undermines your self-confidence—you can see the descending spiral here.

Meanwhile, James Bond isn't making any changes. The secrets and lies continue, surrounded by denials and protestations of honesty or indignation that you would even suspect him or her of not being completely truthful.

James Bond has difficulty with both truth and honesty, which makes trust impossible. The sad thing is that even if he or she changes completely, it's still really hard to build trust because of the history. So you get more and more suspicious and less and less trusting while James continues along the self-focused path of getting his or her needs met above all else.

When the situation finally blows up—and these relationships almost invariably blow up rather than fade away—your ability to trust anyone blows right with it. The next

## THE DIFFERENCE BETWEEN
## TRUTH AND HONESTY

Truth is empirical, demonstrable fact. Your bank balance, today's date, whether or not you're married.

Honesty is about feelings. If you're honest, you are open and clear about how you feel. You can be truthful without being honest, and you can be honest without being truthful (the latter a little more difficult). The best relationships, stating the painfully obvious, are both truthful and honest. Trust is built on both truth and honesty, tempered by the proof of predictability and reliability.

person who comes into your life will be under the microscope, and that is a very uncomfortable spot for anyone. The new potential partner often departs to avoid being distrusted at every turn.

Your recovery comes first from reestablishing a trusting relationship with yourself because that's the foundation of a trusting relationship with anyone else. And, yes, you have to turn in your decoder ring.

The categories in this chapter reflect many of the emotionally unavailable types of people you might meet. There are certainly others I haven't looked at. The important thing is to recognize that when you feel as though you are doing all the work in a relationship or you're with someone who just won't commit or you figure out you're never getting your needs met, perhaps you'll realize that the other person just might be emotionally unavailable. Believe me, it's better to find that out before you begin blaming yourself for every problem in the relationship. When someone is holding you at arm's length, it's not your fault! Remember: You didn't break 'em, you can't fix 'em.

## *Back to the Party*

One day, after spending countless hours either on the porch or desperately trying to be perfect enough for your gracious host so he'll let you into the party, you happen to catch a glimpse of what's going on inside when he carelessly lets the door swing open for just a moment.

What you discover then is that the music is all on tape, the conversation is coming from the television, the people you thought you had seen are only cardboard cutouts, and the food is Dinty Moore in a crockpot.

You only get a glimpse, but when you see it's all just a sham, I hope this book will help you walk away. Or better yet, I hope you can avoid finding yourself on the porch in the first place!

# Chapter Two

# BACKGROUND

## *Feelings/Emotions: The Basic Four*

If we're going to talk about emotional availability, we need to begin by talking about emotions and feelings. One thing that's hard to do is to define what is or isn't there if we don't have some clear, common language on the subject.

So what are feelings and emotions, besides two different terms for the same concept? Feelings/emotions are the *nonintellectual content of experiences.*

When we have an experience it registers in two different realms. One is the intellectual realm and into that part goes empirical information—that which we can observe, touch, taste, and document. The other is the feelings realm and into that part goes the emotional response to the empirical information—the nonintellectual content.

Let me give you an example. Let's say you are standing in a bank when suddenly a masked person enters, brandishes a gun, demands money, gets a bagful, and leaves. That list of events would go into the intellectual slot—empirical, observable on the videotape, verifiable truth. The feelings realm would contain your internal responses to the events—fear, excitement, confusion, maybe even rage.

While the intellectual content would probably be at least somewhat consistent across the people who saw the same event, the feelings content could be very different. There might be some people who thought the whole thing was fun and exciting while others might be outraged and still others terrified.

Emotions, then, are nonintellectual, subjective, individual, reactive, and immediate, which is why they are so hard to define and talk about. Each of us experiences emotions in our own way and defines the common words of emotion by our own inner responses. So if you can't exactly explain or clearly define an emotion except on your own internal terms, how can you tell what you are feeling much less talk about it with someone else?

The answer comes in two stages. Step one is to learn how to connect what you feel with a name. The second step is to learn how to detect and interpret those emotions in other people. Following steps one and two will make the final step, talking about emotions, easy and logical. But first, let's look at an important difference: I think vs. I feel. It's important to make this distinction. When you're dealing with the emotional part of your life, thinking has little to do with it—feeling is everything. When you're talking about emotions, the phrase to use is "I feel." When you're talking about truth, or at least the truth as you perceive it, the phrase to use is "I think" or "I believe."

People often use "I feel" when they really mean "I think." "I feel you're a jerk" is not about emotion, it's about a belief and that is intellectual. "I think you're a jerk" would be the clearer way to express it. "I feel sad that I believe you're a jerk" would be one way, on the other hand, to talk about the emotions and the intellectual content within the same statement.

Therapists talk about *intellectualizing*, another example of the difference between "I think" and "I feel." When people aren't certain about their emotions—what to call them, how to feel them, how to talk about them—it seems far easier for them to keep the emotions inside the head. That means staying with the fact content of events and analyzing *what happened* rather than looking at *how you feel about what happened.* Big difference. It becomes an even bigger difference when one partner is intellectualizing and the other partner is emotionalizing.

The first step toward making strong emotional connections, then, is to make sure both people are talking about the emotional content of events and not using the words "I feel" when what they mean is "I think."

One way to begin connecting with emotions is to learn the names and the feelings that go together.

Let's start with the building blocks—what I call the basic four. If the language of emotions is familiar to you, this will serve as a refresher and clarifier.

One thing to remember is that everything you feel is connected with an external or internal event and usually both. In all emotional situations, there are both external (the situation in which you find yourself) and internal (how you feel about it and what you remember from past experiences about being in a similar situation) events. You add the internal physical cues such as a racing heart or butterflies in your stomach and you have a full-blown emotional picture! So how do you connect what you feel with a name?

There are hundreds if not thousands of words in English to name feelings; some of them are pretty obvious and simple and others are much more subtle and confusing. The basic four are the foundation for almost all other feelings. They are *mad*, *sad*, *scared*, and *glad*. We'll look at them one at a time.

## Mad

Mad covers those emotions that occur in situations in which we feel maligned, used, lied to, let down, and so on. Mad can be as mild as irritation or as explosive as rage but it can also be tied up with confusion, aggravation, frustration, etc. What mad is *not* is anger.

What? True. Anger is a mind-set, not an emotion. Let me explain. Mad, the emotion, is time-limited, situation-focused, and reactive. Someone steals your car. For a while you are really mad. Then the cops arrest the guy, you get your car back, and you begin to cool off. Eventually the thief goes to jail, your insurance company pays for the repairs, and you are no longer mad.

Anger, on the other hand, is a mind-set from which you operate in all areas of your life. It's like a blanket of fire, covering all other emotions and all situations. It is general, long-term, and nonspecific. Anger becomes the glasses through which one sees all parts of the world. It seems to arise in a childhood filled with unfairness and a belief that things never will be fair.

But anger is not an emotion. The emotion is mad. The confusion may have arisen from a bout of political/social correctness when someone who dictates manners decided that mad was a bit too aggressive and encouraged us to be angry instead. Well, it might sound less offensive but it muddies the emotional waters.

## Sad

Sad covers the emotional territory of grief, melancholy, loneliness, and hopelessness, among many others. Like the mad/anger distinction, what sadness is *not* is depression.

Depression is the mind-set, a gray fog that covers everything, sucking all the joy out of life and replacing it with gloom. Sad, like mad, is situation-focused, time-limited, and reactive. Depression is general, global, and long-lasting because it is a mind-set, not an emotion.

Someone you love dies. You feel intense grief at first but as time moves along you are able to broaden your emotional horizons and your grief turns to deep sadness, then to acceptance. Eventually, sadness no longer dominates your emotional landscape. None of that is depression. Grief may be an ingredient in an episode of clinical depression but depression and grief are not the same thing because grief is specific, reactive to a particular situation, and time-limited.

Depression extends beyond grief and touches all the corners of your life. Unless it's treated in some way, it can last for months or years and get worse. As anger seems to stem from the belief and experience that life will be unfair, depression seems to come from a focus on the past. If depression can be expressed in a phrase, it would be, "if only. . . ."

## Scared

Scared includes the feelings that grip us when we are edgy, nervous, frightened, or even terrified. The mind-set companion for scared is anxiety and the same distinctions apply as for mad/angry and sad/depressed.

The anxiety mind-set presents as emotions such as fear, terror, and tension, or experiences such as panic attacks, which suddenly overwhelm a person with a pounding heart and a sense of impending doom often disproportionate to what's going on in the person's life.

Scared is definitely connected with something you can point to in a very specific way—"lions and tigers and bears, oh my!" are only the beginning. People are scared of specific, individual things. Many fears are based on indirect or direct experience combined with imagination. By the time you are an adult, you often can't remember much about the origin of the fear, but nevertheless the fear is deeply imbedded.

Some common fears involve spiders, flying, snakes, dogs, strangers, thunderstorms, and the dark. Some other fears I've heard people talk about are clowns (more common than you would think), rodents, showers, water, sponges, and vacuum cleaners. Whatever anyone fears produces both emotional and physical responses when it is encountered.

Anxiety, the mind-set, could be viewed as living in the future. Its roots are mistrust of the way things might work out and a belief that the world is a very scary place.

One hallmark of the anxiety mind-set is worrying. Worry is the projection of a future filled with terrible things, a place that you travel to by means of your imagination. Once there you try to fix what isn't even happening. The phrase that goes with anxiety is "what if . . ." as in "What if I lose my job and can't pay my mortgage and they come and repossess the house and then I have to live on the street . . ." and so on. You can see how quickly anxiety sends you down a steep slope!

## Glad

Glad includes the full range of joyful, happy, delighted, and the many other words used to express those moments of happiness, peace, and contentment in our lives. It is also the only case in which the emotion and the mind-set have the same name as well as the same effect on the mood and behavior of the glad person.

I have been lucky enough to have several people in my life who truly live in the glad mind-set. They keep the troubles of their lives in perspective, accept reality with grace, eschew worry, and are mad when it's appropriate but don't allow mad to become anger. They are not doormats, but are often first to extend a hand to others in trouble. They're emotionally connected with the people in their lives and emotionally available. I always smile when I think of these people.

A person's mind-set is a part of his or her identity, one facet of what makes up his or her personality. It's the perspective from which a person generally views the world, the filter through which he or she processes new (and old) information.

It's difficult to change a person's mind-set because it's entwined with personality. What can change is one's ability to be more situation-focused and less globally reactive, which helps the person work within the context of mind-set and personality. The job of change is not to make a person over but to make him or her broader and more adaptable: in other words, more emotionally available.

People who live primarily in a particular negative mind-set tend to be much less emotionally available. As you look at the different types of persons we talked about in Chapter 1, you can begin to put them into various mind-sets and see how living in the mind-set prevents connecting on an emotional level.

Romeos, for example, are probably anxious, as are Indiana Jones types. 'Holics are usually depressed, as are Mama's Boys and Daddy's Girls, although they can also be scared. Emotional Einsteins and Narcissists usually have anger mind-sets, while Slippery Critters and James Bonds are often anxious.

The problem with living in a mind-set is that it soon dominates your emotional landscape by not allowing you to be in touch with your emotions but only with the mind-set. Knowing your emotional triggers and signals lets you stay with your emotions no matter what your mind-set.

Here's a quiz to help you figure out where you stand.

## WHAT IS YOUR MIND-SET?

Read each scenario and choose the answer that most closely fits your reaction. Be brutally honest. As you answer each question, make a dot on the grid in the box containing the letter that matches your answer. In other words, if your answer to question 1 is A, put a dot in box A.

| A | B |
|---|---|
| C | D |

1. *If I'm stuck in traffic, I'm most likely to*
   A. drum my fingers on the wheel and worry about being late.
   B. brood about my rotten luck.
   C. get up really close to the car in front of me and blow the horn.
   D. listen to the radio.

2. *When the phone rings in the middle of the night, I*
   A. grab for it, my heart pounding with fear.
   B. expect bad news.
   C. curse the caller and slam the phone down if it's a wrong number.
   D. answer it.

3. *If a cashier shortchanges me, I*
   A. worry that the manager won't believe me if I complain.
   B. just accept it as typical of the world.
   C. slam my fist on the counter and demand to see the manager.
   D. mention it to the cashier.

4. *If I hear a whispered conversation, I*
   A. assume it's about something I've done wrong.
   B. don't have the energy to care.
   C. know it's going to be trouble for anyone telling secrets.
   D. assume it's not my business.

5. *If the TV remote stops working, I*
   A. get very flustered and believe I've broken it.
   B. think it's just one more thing going wrong.
   C. throw it at the TV.
   D. check and replace the batteries and/or read the manual.

6. *If someone is sitting in the seat I have tickets for at a game, I*
   A. worry about confronting the person because he or she might get violent.
   B. assume my tickets are wrong.
   C. get a cop to throw the bum out.
   D. ask the person to check his or her seat number.

7. *If the dog eats a plant in the garden, I*
   A. worry that it might be poisonous and call the vet.
   B. talk to my friend who had a dog die from eating a strange plant so I'll know what to do if the dog dies.
   C. kick the dog.
   D. try to identify the plant and then call poison control while petting the dog.

8. *If my child gets a D in algebra, I*
   A. lie awake worrying that she won't get into college and will have to take menial jobs all her life.
   B. remember how bad my grades were in high school.
   C. ground her for the rest of high school.
   D. offer to help and if she refuses, let it go with words of encouragement and empathy.

9. *Every year on April 15, I*
   A. worry about getting audited.
   B. believe I'll be audited and it will come out badly.
   C. grouse about the government.
   D. file my return.

10. *If a neighbor's stereo is too loud and I can't sleep, I*
    A. lie awake and try to decide how to ask them to turn it down.
    B. lie awake and think about my rotten luck to live next to this idiot.
    C. pound on my neighbor's door and threaten violence.
    D. phone and politely ask the person to turn it down.

11. *If I find a scratch in the side of my new car, I*
    A. run around trying to find matching touch-up paint so it won't hurt the trade-in value.
    B. expect it.
    C. leave a really nasty note on the windshield of the car next to it and write the license number down so I can file a police report.
    D. make a note to get some touch-up paint and repair it.

12. *I believe the lottery is*
    A. a possible way to solve all my money worries.
    B. rigged.
    C. always won by some jerk who never bought a ticket before.
    D. fun to dream about winning.

13. *If my neighbors borrow my lawn mower, I*
    A. worry that their kids might get hurt and that I'll get sued.
    B. assume they'll return it broken.
    C. track them down to make sure I get it back right on time.
    D. am glad to loan it and glad to see them.

14. *I have a strange pain in my back. I*
    A. agonize about making a doctor's appointment, then worry.
    B. assume it's cancer.
    C. feel really put out that I have to take time off from work.
    D. make an appointment and have it checked out.

15. *I get a phone call from a company saying I've won a prize. I*
    A. feel suspicious that it's a scam.
    B. believe it's a wrong number.
    C. know the jerks are trying to rip me off.
    D. get the details.

16. *My spouse is late coming home from work. I*
   A. assume he or she has been in an accident.
   B. assume he or she is up to something.
   C. am really mad.
   D. am happy to see him or her when he or she arrives.

17. *There's a flu going around. I*
   A. call the doctor's office to find out if it was covered on this year's flu shot.
   B. begin to feel achy.
   C. really yell at the guy who sneezed in the elevator.
   D. hope I don't get it.

18. *I get a speeding ticket. I*
   A. wonder how long it'll be before my insurance rates go up.
   B. assume the cop has been waiting for me.
   C. go ballistic and tear it up where the cop can see me.
   D. pay it.

19. *A high school acquaintance dies. I*
   A. try to find out as much as I can about what caused it.
   B. believe life is short.
   C. presume the person lived a bad life.
   D. send a sympathy card to the family.

20. *The bank bounces a check. I think it's their error. I*
   A. spend hours trying to find the mistake and fix it.
   B. assume it's going to end up costing me money.
   C. storm into the bank and really chew out the manager.
   D. call and attempt to figure out what happened and how the situation can be rectified.

Now look at the grid and see where most of your dots have fallen. If most are in the A square, you have an anxious mind-set. Most dots in the B square indicates that you have a depressed mind-set. If most of your answers fall into the C square, you have an angry mind-set. If most of your dots are in the D square, you are a person whose mind-set is glad.

The more dots you find in one square, the more strongly you are in that particular mind-set. If the distribution is about even among three or four of the boxes, you are a person of many moods, but none constitutes a mind-set. That means you are fairly adaptable, depending upon the situation, or that you have not been clear with yourself about your feelings. Your mind-set, remember, is how you look at the world. It's hard to change it, but it's very possible to learn how to moderate its influence on you.

## So Where Do Emotions Come From?

Emotions are a combination of cues, events, and memory.

We learn our emotions in childhood, which is why they sometimes feel both larger-than-life and childlike, particularly those emotions that seem important by virtue of their connection with big events. The refinement of emotions continues throughout our lives. We learn subtler versions of the bigger emotions of childhood and we learn how to measure and control our emotions. Unfortunately, this is a lesson some people have trouble learning; instead of controlling their emotions within a range of behavior that is agreed to be socially acceptable, they allow their emotions to rule the day. For example, you can high-five your buddy after you watch your team score a goal, but it's considered bad form to high-five your buddy after listening to an aria at an opera. At the opposite extreme are people who try to limit emotional impact by shutting down their emotional states or constricting them to a tiny band so as not to be overwhelmed.

When people react with the maximum emotional response to every experience, they actually limit their emotional connection. That's because such excessive responses make a person difficult to predict or evaluate emotionally.

The result of both too little and too much emotion is to shrink the person's true emotional range. In other words, a person's emotional availability is constricted. People can learn to open up emotionally, but it takes a willingness to try.

Now that we've had an overview of emotions and mindsets, it's time to tie that information together with the concept of emotional availability.

*Emotional availability is the ability of a person to reach out and make an emotional connection with another person.* This presumes that a person already has an internal connection with his or her own emotions, is clear about what he or she is feeling, and is able to identify what someone else is feeling. If any of these factors is missing, an emotional connection can't be made.

Emotionally unavailable people are cut off from their own and others' emotional processes, isolated from the emotional content of their lives. It's a lonely way to live. It's also correctable, but first we need to understand how it arises.

## *How Did This Happen?*

As a culture we like having someone or something to blame. It makes a nice package: "Such and such happened and it's Marvin's fault." We feel good. Marvin is the bad guy so we know who's to blame and we can all get together over a cup of self-righteousness and point out just exactly what a rotten guy Marvin is. By contrast we are the good guys, and we like that too. Blame, therefore, gets a big workout.

An explanation is not an excuse. Let me add to that: An

explanation is not a license to blame. It's just an explanation. People who need to blame others are looking for a superficial, quick, zero-responsibility fix for a situation instead of being willing to explore the deeper interactions that may be at work.

Explanations are important to understanding the process. People who commit odious acts against others deserve to have a trial either by jury in a formal legal setting or by public opinion. As part of that trial, their explanations deserve to be heard and considered with the rest of the evaluation of behavioral choices. If there are consequences, they must be taken. Blame might be part of those consequences, but so must an apology by the offender, which should, logically, follow.

In an effort to understand emotional unavailability, we need to look for some explanations of where this behavior comes from. This search is an effort not to blame but to explore the deeper origins of emotional unavailability with an eye toward understanding both the emotionally unavailable person and the person who chooses to have a relationship with him or her.

One hallmark of emotionally unavailable people is that they are unconnected not only with the emotions of other people but also with their own emotions. This disconnection manifests itself in a number of ways. We'll look at just a few of them.

## The Gray Zone

Emotionally unavailable people have almost completely lost touch with their emotions. This disconnection can happen to anyone temporarily after a traumatic event when the emotional system is stunned; it's the emotional version of hitting your elbow and having your arm go numb. People who suffer temporary disconnection eventually recover their feelings bit by bit. Emotionally unavailable people come from another perspective entirely: the Gray Zone.

The Gray Zone has its origin in childhood experiences. People who are in the Gray Zone learned not to trust their emotions in childhood; consequently, they have trouble making emotional connections in their adult lives.

The process works like this: Kids believe their parents are perfect, no matter how imperfect the parents really are. So if a child is growing up in a family where there is emotional inconsistency—Dad says, "I'm only beating you with a belt until you're unconscious because I love you," or Mom is an alcoholic and is tightly connected one minute but very distant the next—the kids assume they are the ones who are wrong, not Mom and Dad.

Using kid logic, they say to themselves, "Dad says love is a beating. I thought love was kissing and hugging and safety. Well, Dad's Dad, so he must be right."

Experience stacks up and pretty soon the child has decided all his or her emotional cues are wrong and stops trusting them. Thus the Gray Zone is born—an emotional area of dense fog into which the person puts all subtle, smaller, daily emotions, not feeling them because he or she has learned not to trust them.

People who live in the Gray Zone do feel some emotions, but only the really big ones. Great highs and deep lows. No love, only passion. No irritation, only rage. No sadness, only despair. Their emotional state looks like this:

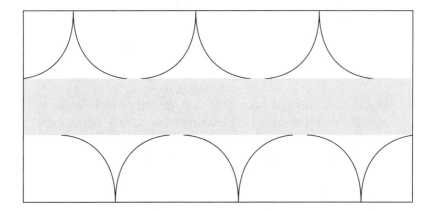

If you are not a Gray Zone person and you're in a relationship with someone who is, you'll notice that he or she seems to be very flat emotionally one moment and suddenly will blow up with an emotional outburst that seems out of proportion to the situation as you experience it. Life around a person living in the Gray Zone is like riding a roller coaster. It's not hard to see how difficult it might be to connect emotionally with people whose feelings are unavailable in the Gray Zone.

First, the subtle daily fluctuations of mood and emotion are lost to them and lost on them. They think people who have more normal emotional lives are not to be trusted and that goes back to their old childhood stuff of not being able to trust the emotions they saw in others.

Second, if you are in touch with your own emotional ebbs and flows, it's draining to be around someone who is always either flying or crashing. Just when you have adjusted to jubilation, you suddenly have to deal with a deep blue mood.

Third, it's impossible to predict where that Gray Zone person will be at any time around any issue. You get jumpy even thinking of asking for emotional input or feedback or starting an emotion-based conversation for fear of the response it will provoke.

Meanwhile, on the part of the Gray Zone person, your subtle fluctuations of mood and response to daily life are suspected of being manipulative or dishonest. He or she has no idea how to read your emotional state, predict your behavior, or interpret small behavioral changes. As a result, the Gray Zone person often tries to provoke large emotional responses.

This is known as button pushing; it comes from the same place as the original emotional damage. When children stop trusting their emotional experiences, they have to find something else to trust and very often that ends up being the very emotional chaos that is damaging them. They quickly learn how to get an emotional connection with the inappropriate parent(s) through instigating chaos. Mom and Dad, probably Gray Zone people themselves, react quickly to the chaos, and a connection is made. Never mind that it is wildly dysfunctional—the whole family recognizes the connection, and that reinforces the Gray Zone and builds mistrust of less volatile emotions.

The child who has been beaten and told this is love might actually try to create enough anger in Dad to get another beating. After all, to the damaged kid, the beating represents love, and kids really want to feel an exchange of love with their parents. The child learns quickly how to push Dad's buttons. There's just nothing quite like getting arrested for shoplifting or auto theft or assault to jump Dad up out of that emotional fog and into the visible, connectable, emotional mountain peaks.

As this child grows into adult relationships and cannot make emotional connections as most people do, he or she quickly learns to identify buttons in friends and partners to make Gray Zone emotional connections. Often the button pushing comes in the form of an attack—verbal abuse or insults. It's an attempt to make an emotional connection with a significant person in the only way the Gray Zone person knows. But this often has disastrous consequences. Persons who are *not* in the Gray Zone find themselves being mysteriously attacked inside what they believe to be a safe relationship. Often they will assume they are doing something wrong, something that provokes their partner to this behavior. They may attempt to change to please the attacker.

The attacker can't recognize these subtle changes except as threats to the emotional connection he or she has made. The attacker will increase the button pushing in a desperate attempt to keep the emotional lines open on his or her own terms. It's not hard to see how these relationships can escalate from verbal abuse to physical abuse as frustration levels rise for the Gray Zone person and emotional unavailability continues for the partner.

The Gray Zone is a major contributor to emotional unavailability because it is such a comfortable hiding place for the person who has lived there most of his or her life. Think of it this way: if you grew up in a family where everyone walked backward and spoke French and you suddenly emerged into a world where everyone walked forward and spoke English, which would feel more safe and comfortable to you? Gray Zone people are, essentially, backward-walking French speakers who will work very hard to stay in that space even when everyone around them is turned in the other direction and speaking another language.

When something is familiar, even if it is horrendous and uncomfortable, a person will tend to choose that over something that promises to be more comfortable but is unfamiliar. When people ask why a battered woman returns again and again to her batterer or why an abused child longs for contact with the abusive parent, the answer is the Gray Zone. To coin an old expression, "Better the devil you know than the devil you don't."

Although they may feel numb, people who have hidden in the Gray Zone for a long time will cling to that feeling until something makes them uncomfortable enough to choose another place to be. What makes people get that uncomfortable? Usually it's emotional pain. In the case of Gray Zone people, emotional pain elevates them to the high spike levels and that's where they can make a connection.

The help of a therapist is important as the person begins to look around in that fog to see what's really going on. A therapist's job is to help the person connect with his or her old emotional pain and reexperience it in manageable form. This process allows the Gray Zone to become much less foggy and much more clear, thereby opening the person's emotional life and experiences. Remember, however, such exploration requires a leap of faith on the part of the person who is closed and a willingness to experience the scary possibility of opening up old wounds. It's important to honor that leap of faith when someone makes it!

## Anger: The Universal Cover-Up

So much of our emotional lives is dictated by cultural rules and patterns—called *mores* by sociologists. The mores for any society evolve over time and experience and are passed from one generation to the next through cultural institutions such as the family, the religious and educational systems, the media, and peer modeling.

In our culture, people have been given the clear message that being emotional is something that should somehow be limited to certain, well-defined circumstances. It's interesting that although we have shifted the paradigm somewhat, the rules have stayed intact. Let me give you an example.

It used to be, not so very long ago, that the social rule that men should not cry had very few exceptions: birth, death, and extreme moments of patriotism were pretty much it. Our culture has now loosened up somewhat so it has become acceptable for men to weep far more freely. However, prohibitions continue to exist and they are, if anything, more rigid in their narrower cast. One primary rule is that men do not cry in an office or professional setting. Another unwritten rule seems to be that women can cry in a professional setting but only once before credibility begins to slide rapidly.

The prohibitions around emotions in office settings are broader than eschewing tears. The rule, unwritten to be sure, puts everyone into the Gray Zone in a sense by sending the message that too much of anything is too much. Too much joy, too much sadness, too much laughter, too much warmth, too much confusion, too much frustration—none is appropriate in a professional setting. Constraint is everything. This isn't a bad rule in general but the application is often harsh and "too much" can sometimes become "any."

There is one emotion that has carte blanche in almost any setting: anger. If a man cries in his office, he's seen as weak or inept. If he gets angry, he is feared or respected or seen as somehow powerful. Tears on the football field would be surprising and uncomfortable. Anger is seen as almost a necessity to the game.

In essence, anger is the universal emotional cover-up for real feelings. My colleague Jim Keenan has a way of explaining this that I really like:

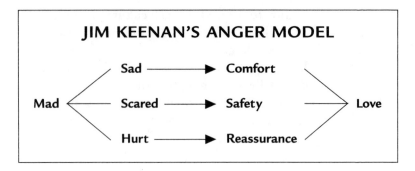

So what does this mean? Jim's theory is that when you are little, and you are feeling sad, you want comfort so you go to a significant adult such as a parent or a teacher. The same is true of when you're scared and seeking safety or when you're hurt and needing reassurance. Those responses are loving. Essentially, then, when you express your feelings in a true way to a caring adult, you are actually seeking and receiving love.

When you get older, you get the clear message that there are lots of circumstances in which it is impossible or uncomfortable to let your true feelings show. At that point, the one universally acceptable emotion—anger—comes up. Therefore, says Jim Keenan, when a person is angry, he or she is really asking for love.

If you think about a circumstance in which a person of significance to you has been angry, and you think about what's underneath the initial, superficial response, I bet you'll find there was really another emotion. Frequently that hidden emotion is some permutation of scared: "I'm scared you're going to abandon me," "I'm scared you're not going to be able to forgive me," "I'm scared you won't value me anymore."

Bradley and Marsha married when they were just out of high school. Each went on to college, accumulating student loans that began to look like the national debt as each got a master's degree and Bradley went on to pursue his Ph.D. Meanwhile, they tried to juggle the responsibilities of being parents, professionals, and members of the community. The pressure cooker was at full boil.

Bradley's biggest relief from the pressure was to play baseball on the local team. He lived for the league and worked out in a batting cage during the off-season. Bradley came to see me one March; he was devastated because although he could hit the cover off the ball and was an excellent shortstop, he wasn't drafted by his team and no other team had picked him up.

"Yeah, I'm aggressive. Yeah, I yell. So what? I'm still the best player around." Bradley then proceeded to tell me the story of the previous season when he had been suspended for six games for six different infractions, each of them involving an angry outburst in response to something that had happened in the game. Once he threw a bat into the opposing dugout when he heard a comment from the other team he thought was directed at him. Another time he pushed an umpire. He told me the worst thing he'd done was to leap into the crowd and punch out a fan. He did have the grace to look embarrassed as he admitted this, but only because he believed he'd punched out "the wrong guy—not the one I thought said something."

He admitted that he'd been arrested for getting into a fight in a restaurant two weeks prior to our first session and that he'd hit Marsha "a couple of times when she didn't listen to me."

Bradley's universal emotional response was anger, but when I began to ask him about how he felt about not being drafted, his words said "angry," but his eyes said "miserable, sad, scared, abandoned, lonely, devalued, isolated, left out." When I pointed this out to him, he got mad at me. "What do you know?"

It took Bradley a while to be able to peel back the layer of anger that he hid in, but eventually we were able to use Jim's anger model to work down through the anger to find the real feelings underneath. Bradley discovered he was a much more emotionally complex person than he'd thought. His mind-set will probably always be anger, but as Bradley was able to connect with his other emotions, anger became less able to lock him out from everything else. The angry hiding place is the perspective from which Bradley views the world. Bradley chose anger to be his sole response to all emotional circumstances.

There's an old expression among therapists: "If the only tool you have is a hammer, the whole world looks like a nail." In Bradley's case, his only tool was anger, so he pounded on everything with his anger hammer. Once he began to expand his toolbox of emotions, he was able to feel many emotions besides anger. The result? He was angry a lot less often.

He also learned how living in one mind-set made him emotionally unavailable to himself and everyone he loved. I knew he had made the connection with himself when he was able to spontaneously and emotionally apologize to Marcia for his past violence and constant state of anger and to ask for her forgiveness without using manipulation.

If you're in a relationship with someone who uses anger as a universal emotion, it's hard to work down through to connect with the real emotions underneath. Certainly one thing you want to do, if you believe the relationship can work, is to be true to your own feelings and not respond to the anger you get by giving mad in return. Relationships fraught with constant fighting are ones where you can certainly suspect an anger mind-set exists.

I'm not one of those therapists who thinks everyone needs a therapist living in the garage to fix everything, but having anger as your universal emotion is a situation in which working with a therapist can speed the process of getting out of hiding and into the full light of emotions.

## Powerlessness

Another source of emotional unavailability is the victim experience. What being victimized removes is personal power. When we talk about personal power, it's not power in the sense of dictatorship but *empowerment*, which is the ability to retain your choices.

# POWER = CHOICE!

The message from the abuser is clear: "You have no right to make the choices that impact your life. I have all the power, you have none." The experience of disempowerment comes from a wide variety of sources, but in each case the outcome is the same: the victim has his or her power diminished or removed. Alternatively the victim may offer up all his or her power to the perpetrator in voluntary surrender. People can choose to remain in a victim position if that's where they believe they want to be, or they can choose to work actively on the victimization and its effects on their lives. They can then move forward as survivors. Choosing to be a victim is choosing to surrender your power. Choosing to be a survivor is choosing to take it back.

The experience of powerlessness is a terrible teacher, and its lessons are long-lasting. It can come from a single experience or it can be the culmination of many negative experiences that feed into a sense of loss of control in circumstances. The result is the person who is being victimized gets the clear message that he or she has no power. People with no power have no voice. People with no voice believe themselves to be invalid. Persons who are invalid can't trust their emotions and must instead negate them. That's how victims become emotionally unavailable.

Let me give you two quick examples.

## BECKY
Becky had a childhood unimaginable to most people. Her grandfather treated her as a sexual being beginning when she was an infant and continuing until his death when she was an adolescent.

Sexual victimization is a quick route to powerlessness through the process of objectification—the treatment of a person as an object. When you get in the car, does the car decide where you are going? Does your oven decide what you will have for dinner? Does your sewing machine determine what you will wear? Obviously not. Those are objects and they have no power. When a person is objectified, he or she has no power to determine what will happen. Sexual victimization is a very powerful kind of objectification, though it is far from being the only kind.

Not only did Becky's grandfather abuse her sexually on a regular basis but her mentally ill mother essentially gave him permission to do so by refusing to stop him even after she was confronted by Becky's father. In fact, Becky's mother divorced her husband when he insisted on limited contact between Becky and the grandfather. So the abuse continued with no adult intervention.

When she was ten and again at fifteen, Becky was gang raped. Her mother blamed Becky for the grandfather's death. Becky's mother punished her by sending her to live with an uncle. The uncle also abused Becky sexually. Not surprisingly, Becky began to act out against herself by means of an eating disorder and many suicide attempts. Becky firmly believed she had no value as a person and was treating herself as though she were disposable. In effect, she was objectifying herself.

What Becky lacked was personal power. Her choices had been taken away so often that by the time she came to my office in her middle twenties after being sexually harassed at her job, she had no idea how to make choices or how to accept power. Becky was completely disempowered by other people making choices that took her options away. Becky's accumulation of victimization experiences taught her that she had no power and took away her ability to make emotional connections with herself or others. Her self-attacks were, in a sense, an attempt to gain power over her situation by being able to choose whether to live or to die. Becky's story is an extreme example of trying to find empowerment.

## SYLVIA
Sylvia had what she described as an idyllic childhood. She was the baby of the family and much adored by her six

brothers as well as parents and grandparents. Her father was a highly successful businessman who was not often present at home, and when he was, she said, she spent little time with him. However, she quickly assured me, she knew he loved her though she couldn't say how she knew. She was well educated and popular with many friends.

She met Jim at a church function and was attracted to him, she later told me, because he was "so different." Jim was a drifter with no particular credentials other than his Vietnam military service, which he wore like a hair shirt—his burden and other people's guilt. He had been working for a government contractor and had come into Sylvia's town on a temporary assignment.

Sylvia was fascinated by him. Her family and friends were horrified, but Sylvia pursued Jim with fervor. In hindsight, Sylvia realized she saw a lot of her father's distance in Jim, but at the same time she pursued him because he felt "familiar" on an emotional level. It's not unusual for people to marry a copy of the parent with whom they have the most issues and try to fix the relationship with that parent by fixing the spouse.

After their marriage, Jim became violent with Sylvia, first verbally and then physically. Sylvia told me she stayed with him because she believed he would eventually "come around and be nice." She also saw herself trying to push Jim into being the man in her life her father had never been. This desire kept her in the relationship. While she waited for him to be nice, she had three kids whom Jim also abused.

After twenty-six years of abuse, Sylvia came to my office not to work on the effects of Jim's abuse but because she was grieving over the loss of her mother a few months before. Jim came to the first few sessions with her, not to support her but to make sure that we "stuck to the subject and didn't waste his money."

When I was finally able to bore him enough to evict him from the therapy sessions, Sylvia was able to say only that she didn't know how her life had turned out the way it did. When I asked about abuse, she immediately told me about her wonderful childhood and denied any possibility of abuse.

She was adamant that no one had ever touched her sexually and that her brothers, father, grandfathers, and uncles were all great guys. She was stunned to hear I also meant abuse as an adult and that abuse is more than inappropriate sexual behavior.

It took Sylvia a long time to understand that Jim's behavior had as much impact on her as childhood abuse would have had. It also took her a long time to begin to see how much of her power she had surrendered to Jim in an effort to please him while waiting for him to come to his senses.

Powerlessness, then, comes from a real or perceived inability to make choices. So how does that connect with emotional unavailability? Someone who takes your power away in order to make a connection is not healthy and not emotionally available. That person is much too focused on gaining control over you to participate in the give-and-take of relationships. That's pretty obvious.

What might not be so obvious, however, is that a person who is victimized by a power grabber learns a particular kind of emotional-connection system, one that involves submission to someone else as a basic condition of connection. The connections made by this sort of person are not real connections but warped through the power system, almost as though there were a third person in the relationship through which all emotions had to be filtered.

People who have been abused, who have been disempowered, have special challenges with emotional availability. Not only is trust difficult or impossible but their understanding of how connections are made begins with a warped definition of what constitutes a relationship. This damaged understanding of how relationships should work explains the mystery of why abused persons often choose an abuser for a partner even in a new relationship: familiarity is more comfortable, even when it's uncomfortable.

Emotionally available relationships require both partners to be available. When a victimized person chooses an abuser as a partner, neither is emotionally available and the relationship is based on power losses and gains rather than emotional exchanges.

These relationships often are hallmarked by score keeping. The person with more power keeps score to be certain the person with less power doesn't acquire power; the person who has been disempowered will keep score to evaluate the relationship. Neither person is being emotionally available.

## Internal and External Feedback Systems

When you make an important decision about something in your life, how do you go about evaluating your choices and making a final decision? Most people use a combination of both internal and external feedback.

Let me give you an example. Let's say you're thinking about moving. The first discussions are usually internal. You say to yourself, "I would like more closet space. And I'm tired of hearing the neighbor's stereo. Besides, with a baby coming, we're going to need more space."

The next discussions usually occur with your partner. "What do you think? Can we afford this move? What neighborhood do you like? What do you think about a townhouse?" These discussions are information-gathering events that give you input to add to your own feelings and ideas.

The next round of conversations occurs with friends and family. You're again gathering information, opinions, and ideas to factor into the decision.

"You know, your mom and I really like townhouse living. I never have to think about painting, cutting the grass, or shoveling snow."

"When Mark and I moved to Hidden Valley Hills we were even more pleased with the neighborhood than we had expected. It's a safe, clean, nice area."

"I hate townhouses. You can't do what you want with your own property without some busybody intruding. A hobby farm is the ticket!"

"The property taxes in Hidden Valley Hills have gone up every year for the past six years. It has the highest tax level in the state."

Finally you're ready to make your decision. You consider all the information you've gathered, then negotiate a decision with your partner.

The process of *external feedback* involves asking friends, family, business associates, your banker, your attorney, and others whose ideas and opinions you trust and who have some appropriate connection with your process of decision making for their input and ideas, then putting it all together into a reasonable, appropriate decision.

The *internal feedback* system measures the options against your own internal yardstick. That yardstick is made up of your own values and beliefs, your experiences, your education, and your self-knowledge. Most people combine, in weighted averages, internal and external feedback to make choices.

Some people don't have an internal feedback loop and focus their behavior around input only from the external loop. One place therapists often see this external loop at work is in adolescents who are still constructing their internal feedback system. Accessing the external loop only is how kids talk themselves into purple Mohawk haircuts; pierced faces, navels, and other spots; and tattoos of various sorts. Unfortunately, it's also the system kids use for more dangerous behaviors. Drugs, gangs, alcohol, and promiscuity, for example, are reinforced by the external feedback loop. In formal psychiatric terms, this is known as *external locus of control.*

Hypothetically, as a person proceeds through the trials of adolescence, he or she begins to develop that internal loop—an *internal locus of control.* Usually this development parallels the refinement of a personal value system on which adult morality is based. An adolescent brings childhood belief systems, usually those of his or her parents, into the cauldron of adolescent turmoil and stirs them with the beliefs and values acquired through school, religion, community, and friends. What emerges at the end of the teens or in the early twenties is an internal feedback loop that the person uses, with refinements and adjustments, throughout the rest of his or her life.

Some people get stuck, for whatever reasons, in that adolescent spot of looking only outside for feedback about life decisions. Instead of working to develop an internal system of feedback, they focus only on input from others. This use of outside feedback wouldn't be a huge problem if all of the outside sources were idealists with perfect, selfless morals and only the highest good for others as their motivation. It becomes a huge problem, however, when the external sources are human, complete with faults and selfish motives.

If someone has an internal feedback loop and is exposed to humans with faults and selfish motives, an internal process monitor measures the input, *including* the faults and the selfish motives, and allows the person to make a clear decision. If, however, a person has not developed an internal feedback loop, he or she does not possess a way to evaluate the input. Instead, this person tends to take things completely at face value and go along with the crowd.

Without an internal feedback loop, this person has no idea what his or her own feelings, ideas, and values are on any particular subject. Worse, this person has no way to predict possible consequences for behavioral choices because he or she has not evolved a value system that signals right from wrong.

I think most mainstream people assume criminals know that what they are doing is wrong and that they will be caught, and choose to do things anyway from some sort of misplaced sense of adventure. The reality is that the great majority—maybe 95 percent—of criminals have no internal feedback system and have no concept of the possible outcomes of their behavioral choices. They are, generally, reacting only to impulse with no forethought at all.

Of course, not all people who lack an internal feedback loop are criminals. However, all people who lack an internal feedback loop are unconnected from their emotions and unable, therefore, to make a connection with anyone else. Thus anyone who lacks an internal feedback loop can be characterized as emotionally unavailable, criminal or not. Obviously, the folks who choose to be in criminal activities have more complex problems in their lives than just emotional unavailability, but for the sake of our work here, that's one consideration.

People with no internal feedback loop are most identifiable by their focus on the opinions and ideas of others. They'll ask what you think, what the guy at the gas station thinks, what the woman at the pharmacy thinks, what their friends think, and then give all input—good, bad, or indifferent—the same weight while making a decision. You will find yourself no more or less important to them than the stranger on the commuter bus, which is pretty disheartening if the decision being considered happens to be about your life.

It also means your input will be no more or less valued or important than that of anyone else. Thus, if your partner's buddies are pushing him to take a week off and go hunting in Montana during the same week you were planning a romantic cruise, his decision about which to choose will not be based on what is best for you as a couple. It will more likely be based on whichever opinion he heard last. The recognition of this kind of decision-making process can be pretty uncomfortable.

One client whose husband had consistently made awful, externally focused decisions described it this way: "I felt as though he were surrounded by a brick wall. Every time he'd make a decision, I'd be there, banging my head against the brick wall, trying to find the hidden doorway that would enable him to hear my input and make a good decision that had some consideration of my and the kids' lives in it." What she finally came to realize was that the only way that door was going to open was from the inside.

In this case, the husband had an epiphany—a major realization that helped him connect with himself. He was at home alone with his three kids. As was his practice when he would "babysit" (just a little side comment here—fathering is parenting and parenting is *not* babysitting!), he was focused on his Internet explorations. He heard a scream, but decided it was just the kids playing. He ignored the second scream as well. Suddenly his eight-year-old burst into the room, crying and frantic. "Billy's dead!" she screamed over and over.

He rushed out to find his son unconscious in the driveway, blood pouring from a gash on his forehead. He later reported that at that moment he saw clearly and for the first time how his selfishness had impacted his family. He decided to change his ways, and over time he not only opened the door but tore down the brick wall!

The development of an internal feedback loop takes more than just an epiphany, however. It takes a lot of work to construct and maintain the system, and that commitment is hard for people to make if they don't see why they need it. Working on an internal feedback loop is another situation where a partnership with a good therapist can facilitate the process and keep it focused.

People who remain externally driven only—and that condition can last a lifetime—can never make satisfying emotional connections with others because they have no connection with themselves. Making a self-connection is the place to begin.

## Attachment Theory

Another explanation (which, you'll remember, is not an excuse) for people being unable to make emotional connections goes all the way back to birth. This theory was explored in the work of John Bowlby, a British researcher; Harry Harlow at the University of Wisconsin; and Mary Ainsworth at the University of Texas. All three of these researchers have studied how parents, primarily mothers, bond with their infants and children. While Bowlby and Harlow studied attachment in monkeys, Ainsworth worked with human mothers and toddlers. All three have written extensively about the effects of attachment in early life on later attachments—which is a facet of emotional availability.

Here, in brief, is an overview of Dr. Ainsworth's conclusions. Her experiment focused on a group of mothers and their one-year-olds. They were brought into a room where they could be observed through one-way mirrors. The room had a chair, sometimes two, in the middle where the mom would sit. Sometimes the other chair would be occupied by a stranger. The room was ringed with toys. The mom would sit in the chair and put the child on the floor. After a time, the mom would get up and leave the room, then return in a short time. If there were a stranger present, the stranger would remain when the mom left. Everything was observed and carefully recorded, then data were compiled.

From the experiments, Ainsworth identified three types of babies: the first type she called "securely attached." These babies would explore the room in sort of a daisy-petal pattern—check in with mom, check out the toys, back to mom, back to the toys. When the mom would leave, the securely attached child would fuss or cry. When the mom returned, the baby would greet her, be comforted, then go back to exploring.

These kids have a belief that they would not be hurt or abandoned by significant adults and they trusted the world they live in. Ainsworth reported about 25 percent of the babies she studied were securely attached. As adults, securely attached people make securely attached relationships hallmarked by love, trust, communication of emotions, and predictability. They are emotionally available.

The second group was made up of babies that Ainsworth called "insecurely attached" (what a friend of mine calls Velcro babies). These babies would cling to the mom and not explore the room. When the mom left, they were inconsolable. When the stranger offered comfort, it was rejected. However, when the mom returned, the baby would reject her angrily, still crying, and cling to the stranger. Insecurely attached babies accounted for about 50 percent of the children Ainsworth saw in the experiment.

Insecurely attached babies grow up to be insecurely attached adults, alternately clinging to or rejecting their partners but unable to connect on an emotional, trusting level. They may invest trust naively, then not trust people who really should be trusted. They fear abandonment. They may lack the ability to be assertive and act helpless in order to get attention and be cared for.

The third group Ainsworth identified as "unattached." These babies ignored the mom and were unconcerned when she left or returned. When the moms held these babies, the babies often arched their backs and leaned away. You can imagine that when they get older, these people have little or no ability to make an emotional connection with anyone else. Beyond that, however, they can also be dangerous.

The unattached child often grows into an adult who is aggressive or destructive. He or she may have an extensive criminal history or involvement, beginning in adolescence or earlier. Unattached people reject anything that seems like control or authority and so have frequent conflicts with their parents and teachers, bosses, and the police. They have a poor relationship with the truth and seem to have no conscience. They get what they want by manipulating others.

Dr. Ainsworth looked at the first few days of life as a key to what forms a person's attachment style. Some of that can come from the personality of the child and some from the emotional availability of the mom. If the mom is not emotionally available to the baby, if she is afraid of the baby and doesn't trust herself as a mother, the baby will pick up on that and the result will be a person who is not securely attached. That child frequently grows up to be an emotionally unavailable person.

Looking at the distribution in Ainsworth's experiments, can we leap to the conclusion that only 25 percent of the population is ever going to be emotionally available? No. That's because people can and do learn, grow, and change. Many insecurely attached kids grow past that style either through therapy or life experience.

Other researchers have looked at what they call resilient children. These are people who might have had horrendous childhood experiences but because they have also had a significant relationship with an appropriate, loving adult, they end up with little or no emotional scarring. The same could be said for insecurely attached children; if they have a father or grandparent or aunt or neighbor or teacher who helps them form trusting and appropriate attachments, they are not as likely to continue in an insecurely attached style.

The core issue of attachment is one of trust. Obviously, if this is, as Ainsworth believes, an early infancy–created style, trust must be something instinctive and very basic to the human condition. In truth, this theory is what Harlow and Bowlby affirm with their monkey studies—attachment/trust is at the core of the relationship between child and mother in all primates.

A person who is unattached may lack the ability to learn to trust. We're not sure where complex emotions such as trust arise in the brain, so we can only observe their presence or absence by virtue of behavior. People who don't attach early to mom will have trouble learning how to trust anyone. This kind of global mistrust is a version of emotional unavailability. Trust, after all, is at the core of good emotional connections. Naturally, someone who cannot form a basic trusting relationship probably isn't a good bet for a partner.

So what do these folks look like as adults? Securely attached children grow up to be people who can reach out emotionally. They are able to trust without jealousy and suspicion. They think with their heads but feel with their hearts and know the difference between the two. They are able to express their emotions and seek out people who do the same.

Insecurely attached people are likely to be clinging and jealous. An insecurely attached partner doesn't trust that you will do as you say, so he or she tends to check up on you and give you tests to see if you are telling the truth. Meanwhile, he or she isn't necessarily being trustworthy. An insecurely attached person is likely to have a large external feedback loop. At the same time he or she doesn't necessarily trust the external loop. That's because insecurely attached people have trouble trusting anyone—not just their partners.

Unattached people are not present emotionally. They make promises they don't keep, and they rarely apologize.

They frequently use other people without remorse and are often characterized as cold, distant, and angry. Sadly enough, however, they are seen by many people as a challenge—"I can break through that and find the real person underneath."

Forget that. It rarely happens. What usually does happen is that you end up frustrated, hurt, damaged, manipulated, and worse.

## The Problem of Low Self-Esteem

We therapists talk a lot about self-esteem—how to raise it, how it impacts behavior and choices, where it comes from—but I'm not sure we define it clearly for ourselves or our clients. By my definition, and at risk of stating the obvious, self-esteem is the ability of a person to see himself or herself in a realistic, positive light; to set limits that protect his or her boundaries; to form meaningful, reciprocal relationships; and to trust both head and heart.

A person with low self-esteem sees himself or herself in negative terms. For example, women often value themselves more for body shape and looks than for their internal qualities. We're not here to tackle these demons—volumes have been written on this subject. But, put simply, when we value the package more than the contents, that's low self-esteem. Furthermore, when we believe other people value the package more than the contents and then we act accordingly by obsessing over being thin enough, young enough, or pretty enough, that's even lower self-esteem.

Sometimes people who have low self-esteem give just the opposite impression. They may brag about accomplishments or inflate their own importance. They might also attack others verbally with criticism or devaluing. People whose self-esteem is low often compare superficial traits and possessions to make themselves feel more powerful or richer or better. What they do not do is accept themselves or others.

People who have high self-esteem aren't threatened by the achievements, accomplishments, possessions, physical attributes, or assets of other people. They don't judge, and they accept others unconditionally. When they talk about their own accomplishments or achievements, they keep them in perspective and are able to be proud in proportion to the achievement without diminishing other people. People with healthy self-esteem make appropriate emotional connections with other people. Those relationships are clearly defined, emotionally available, head- and heart-connected. People with healthy self-esteem also *trust* their heads and their hearts. They have the ability to recognize truth and honesty in others and are able to be truthful and honest themselves.

Perhaps one of the most central features of healthy self-esteem, however, is the ability to set boundaries. Good boundaries are integral to good relationships and, conversely, bad boundaries make for terrible relationships.

## Boundaries

Robert Frost once said, "Good fences make good neighbors," and that is the essential message of good boundaries. Boundaries between people are behaviors that show respect for the individuality, privacy, personal space, and time of another while keeping one's own individuality, privacy, personal space, and time.

For example, Judy was my boss on a special project I did for a company in New York. It was common knowledge that Judy had been put in the position she was in for political reasons within the company, not for her knowledge and understanding of the project. Judy made no effort to learn the project but made many efforts to control and intimidate the people doing the work.

Judy demonstrated boundary problems in many ways. She would go through the desks of the people who worked for her while they were out of town, take documents that were irrelevant to the situation and, by the time the employee got back into the office, have made a terrible, synthetic mess that the employee had to clean up. Judy would then use this mess to victimize, criticize, and undermine the employee. It was her way of staying at the center of everything.

Judy's personal relationships were brought into the office with embarrassing and intimate detail. She was incapable of keeping anything to herself, so all of our salaries were revealed as were any personal details of our lives she was able to glean from our files. It was a constant challenge to keep a strong sense of self in the face of her intrusions.

Judy was a walking example of bad boundaries. Each of us who worked for her had to work twice as hard to protect ourselves from her attacks as we did to actually do our jobs, so it created a terrible work environment in which no one felt safe.

Safety is at the heart of good boundaries. It's one of those core issues like trust that has lifelong impact on a person's ability to make good connections.

If you come from a family with good boundaries, you will have grown up in an environment where you felt respected, valued, honored, and able to control your own destiny. If you come from a family with bad boundaries, you were never given the opportunity to develop a sense of individuality and separation from your parents, so you may have trouble letting anyone else have a sense of separateness or individuality. Bad boundaries encourage invasion of someone else's personal space and turf, and that behavior undermines the ability to make a true emotional connection.

If you are in a relationship with someone with bad boundaries, you probably lack a sense of safety because you never have any privacy. You aren't able to trust your partner to respect your space, time, person, or property. At their most extreme, boundary violations are violent—aggressive physically or sexually—and frightening. At their most common, boundary violations are disrespectful. What boundary violations never are is acceptable.

Bad boundaries make people emotionally unavailable because, in a sense, they are too available. A person with no boundaries retains none of the Self everyone requires in order to be whole. People who have no sense of Self themselves also have no sense of Self of anyone else. Therefore, they are unable to recognize another person's emotions or to recognize their own emotional position in any contact.

What emerges instead is a totality, an immersion in an uncomfortable pool; once you are in, you drown in the agenda and needs of the boundaryless person. That's not a place where a person could be emotionally available with any safety or openness.

## Control

In some emotionally unavailable people, isolation comes from a need to control the behavior of the people around them, both emotionally significant persons and strangers alike.

This need to control extends beyond behavior to thinking and belief systems, and it is dangerous to both parties. The person who wants to control is miserable most of the time, needing to check and recheck on the partner to be certain that the control is holding. The person who is being controlled is miserable most of the time because of fear of the possible consequences of not living up to the expectations of the controlling partner, even though those expectations may never be clearly laid out or detailed and even though the consequences are equally undefined.

Charlotte was fifteen when she first started coming to see me. Her parents were mystified by the fact that she had suddenly stopped turning in her homework, stopped going to her job, and stopped seeing her friends. All she seemed to want to do was play with her cat.

We spent a number of sessions talking about her relationship with her cat—how reliable and safe the cat was, how the cat loved her without reservation or qualification, how the cat had reasonable expectations of their relationship, how the cat respected her. The cat was the silent spokesperson for what else was going on, but it took a while for us to get there.

Charlotte's parents were both teachers and they had high expectations for their only daughter. She had some dreams of her own that her parents thought were great— she was an Olympic-quality diver—and had her eye on medical school. She had also been one of the most popular girls in her class before the cat became the focus of her life.

After a time of building trust with me, Charlotte began to talk about the life her parents didn't know she had. Charlotte had met a boy at a swim meet in Iowa. This boy, Mark, was a senior in a high school about thirty miles from Charlotte's school. He, too, was the focus of his family's expectations, so much so that they pushed him relentlessly to succeed, demanding that he be at the top of his class, the president of the school council, and the captain of every team he went out for (he had lettered in four sports). In short, he was their perfect showcase son. Mark was kept very busy living up to all those expectations, which didn't match his dreams for himself.

When Charlotte met Mark, he was stressed not only by the expectations of his parents but also by the expectations of his coaches, advisers, and various college and professional athletic recruiters who were pressuring him with options for his future. Charlotte was immediately attracted to Mark because he was "so cute" and such a good athlete. He was attracted to her because of her soft, trusting nature.

Charlotte knew her parents wouldn't be happy with the age difference between herself and Mark or even that she was dating at all, so she kept the relationship a secret, telling lies to her parents so she could sneak off for dates.

Soon Mark began to make demands of Charlotte. He asked her to phone him at specific times to check in with him. He also insisted that she end relationships with friends he didn't know. He wanted more sexual involvement than she could handle, but because she had lied to her parents, she couldn't get their help and advice about how to manage Mark. He had effectively cut her off from her friends and her family. Charlotte was left believing that she had to do everything Mark told her because he was her only ally and her only friend. She told me he didn't feel very much like an ally or a friend, but she didn't know what else to do.

Mark's controlling behavior became more and more burdensome for Charlotte. He convinced her to have sex with him, manipulating her so she believed she had agreed, but leaving her feeling that she had been raped. She began to retreat into the world of her cat to escape from Mark's control and the tyranny he had created with her. Charlotte's retreat, however, had increased Mark's efforts to control her, and she had become increasingly depressed and fearful as he became more demanding.

I've seen many adult relationships in which control was the central issue, but parents need to know that Charlotte's situation is not uncommon among adolescents. Charlotte is only one of several young patients in my practice who have been victimized by controlling boyfriends.

Charlotte brought Mark into one of our sessions and we talked about what he hoped to gain from controlling Charlotte. His answer? He wanted to be sure she didn't get hurt by "some creep." He wasn't very flattered when I pointed out to him how creepy his own behavior had been toward her. He had trouble seeing that what he had done was abusive.

When Mark began talking about the pressures he felt from his family, school, sports, and personal goals, he became agitated, so I asked him what he was feeling. "Controlled," he blurted, "and I hate it!" He then looked at Charlotte and shook his finger in her face. "Don't you see that you made me do this? If you had told me no, I would have quit." With that he stormed out of my office.

Charlotte decided not to continue dating Mark—a courageous decision for a young girl—and was able to talk to her parents about what had happened. She managed to get her homework turned in—she had been doing it all along—and get herself back on track with her friends, activities, and family. Charlotte was one of the lucky ones!

People who need to control don't trust their world to be safe without constant monitoring and intervention. They don't believe in their own ability to create safety internally. They are extremely externally focused and often have little insight about their own feelings or the feelings of anyone else. All they can focus on is getting their own needs met, even if that comes at the expense of someone else. It's a miserable, isolating kind of spot to be in and makes for complete emotional unavailability. You can't be available to someone else if you're not connected with yourself.

## The Toxic Balloon

If you blow up a balloon and don't tie the neck, then let go of it, what happens? It flies around the room in unpredictable ways making an unattractive blatting noise and finally jets to the floor in an unanticipated spot, flat and deflated. That's a similar result to what happens when you stuff all your emotional trash into a "toxic balloon" without working on it and processing it. Eventually, it rips out of your control and runs amok. You get overwhelmed and your careful internal system of controls breaks down. Everything spills out willy-nilly and creates a scary internal environment.

Now think about what happens if you blow the balloon up again but this time you continue to hold the neck between your thumbs and first fingers then open the neck just a little bit. The balloon still deflates, but it doesn't fly all over the place. When it's deflated, it's still under control and predictable. That's therapy.

The toxic balloon is part of emotional unavailability if it continues to receive all the emotional content of a person's life. Everything gets dumped into the toxic balloon— good feelings, bad feelings, scary feelings, happy feelings—the whole mess all jumbled together into a blob of the unfeelable.

It's confusing enough to feel the emotional effect of one thing at a time and harder still to feel the effects of two or more. But it's just about impossible to feel all the emotions of a lifetime all at once. This crush of life emotion is what a person fears he or she will have to experience if that toxic balloon is ever allowed to let things come out. The person fears being overwhelmed by the accumulation of feelings gathered over the years, all of which were individually overwhelming. In response, he or she makes what seems to be an obvious choice, stuffing everything into a personal toxic balloon and feeling nothing.

People who choose to feel nothing, to guard those emotions and experiences and let no one in, are certainly emotionally unavailable. They have no idea what's in the toxic balloon and no interest in finding out. Furthermore, if you want emotional contact from such a person, you are seen as a threat to his or her protective balloon.

I had a client who was a real movie fan and talked about his life by referring to various movies he'd seen. He had been filling a toxic balloon with years of abuse by his alcoholic father and emotionally absent mother. He'd married a woman who was physically and emotionally abusive to him and to their children and who was from a family of abusive people herself. He'd been unable to achieve his personal goals and had a lot of anger and resentment about those losses but never revealed a bit of it. He stayed safe by remaining hidden and by keeping his emotions locked away.

During one session we were talking about his childhood experiences with learning how to trust in the context of his family and suddenly he got a horrified look on his face.

"Sorry, but that's behind the grid," he said.

"The grid?" I asked in my best therapist-neutral tone.

"Remember in *Ghostbusters* when the pollution control inspector came to the firehouse and shut off the grid? Do you remember what happened?"

I told him I remembered that all the ghosts suddenly escaped.

"Well, I have a grid too, and whenever we talk about emotional issues, I feel like you're going to come in and shut off the grid and everything bad in my life is going to come out at once." He looked truly scared at the prospect of being overwhelmed. What he didn't realize was that being in the therapeutic setting would help him avoid being overwhelmed. We worked on that puzzle for a long time before we turned off the grid—section by section in a safe and manageable way.

Having a grid or a toxic balloon might initially feel safe, but after a while it takes all of a person's emotional energy to maintain the lines of defense. There is no emotional

## TOXIC BALLOON DETECTOR

Circle True (T) or False (F) for each of the following.

1. I rarely cry.       T     F

2. If I feel like crying, I do everything I     T     F
can to stop myself.

3. I rarely saw my family express any     T     F
emotions when I was growing up.

4. Emotions are embarrassing.      T     F

5. There are many things from my      T     F
childhood I don't want to talk about.

6. I think people who express emotions     T     F
are weak or silly.

7. People who get emotional at work risk     T     F
ruining things for all of us.

8. Emotions are a waste of time. People     T     F
do much better when they use logic,
not emotions.

9. If my friends want to talk about their     T     F
relationships, I change the subject. It's
just boring.

10. When I hear people talking about how     T     F
they feel, I'm not sure what they mean.

The more True (T) answers you have, the more likely it is that you are harboring a toxic balloon.

energy left over to form relationships, feel feelings in the present moment, or learn new emotional techniques or experiences. This state clearly creates emotional unavailability. It can be reversed, but it requires that the person who's isolated from his or her emotions be willing to find out that he or she doesn't have to shut off the grid or release the balloon all at once!

## Big Family Secrets

People who come from families that have big secrets have a lot of trouble making emotional connections because they have learned in their families that things are often not what they seem to be.

For a long time our culture believed that the adoption of a child needed to be kept a secret from that child. Families went to great lengths to keep the secret, sometimes even when the child had figured it out and begun asking questions. The secret took on a life of its own that took priority over the emotional needs of the people in the family. It became the focus of family emotional energies.

Many things go into the family-secrets hopper. In my family, it was the early divorce of my mom's brother that we were forbidden to talk about, even though all of us knew. All the cousins would gather at the little table—what did our parents *think* we were talking about over there in isolation from the big table?—and whisper about how mystified we were by why it was a secret when it wasn't a secret. Even my *adopted* cousins thought it was strange!

Some family secrets are a great deal more pernicious than divorces or adoptions. It often seems that the worse the secret, the more elaborate the scheme the family creates to protect it. An extreme example of this is incest.

It disgusts me when other members of a family know that incest is going on but choose to protect the sickness in the family rather than to protect the victim or victims of the incest. The clear message to the victim(s) is that they are far less important than some public perception of the family. This message creates emotional scar tissue for the victim(s). Those victims carry not only the terrible burden of the damage incest does but also the burden of being the *reason* the family has to have a secret. It's a difficult enough burden for an adult. It's an impossible burden for a child.

One of my clients came from a large family that had lived in an isolated area in North Dakota. Her mother was also from a large family in the area and much of my client's social life was centered around interactions with her mother's family. Unfortunately, the mother's brother was a pedophile who preyed on all of his nieces and nephews at family gatherings. At least *thirty* people of various ages had been victimized by this man and at least five of them had told their parents. Nothing, however, happened, because the parents were all afraid of what the matriarch of the family would think.

Therefore, Uncle Pedophile was allowed to continue his behavior while the family spent its emotional energy containing the secret. The outcome of this behavior was horrendous. My client and three of her female cousins began putting the information together and discovered not only that he had abused at least thirty people in their family but that there was more to it than that. The uncle and his wife ran a day-care center in their home. He also led a Boy Scout troop and coached a Little League team. He was a leader in the local church and everyone had always been impressed with his interest in children! He received, along with the rest of the family, many condolences when three of his nephews committed suicide and two of his nieces attempted suicide within two years.

When the grandmother died, my client and her cousins decided it was time for Uncle Pedophile to be confronted. They chose to confront him at a family reunion. Unfortunately, the outcome they had expected was not what came to pass. The four women had expected that they would confront the uncle and that others of the cousins and community who had been victimized by him would step forward immediately to join in the confrontation. Instead, they found themselves at the center of a storm of controversy and anger. Other cousins they knew had been victimized came to the defense of the uncle; the four were shunned and scorned for attempting to bring down this pillar of the community. It was at this time my client began seeing me, and we worked hard to restore her faith in herself or anyone else as the storm continued around her. Even my client's mother chose to side with the uncle.

But, two months later, after my client and her cousins had been through a terrible time of turmoil, some positive things began to happen. First, a young woman who had been victimized by the uncle at the day-care center stepped forward and filed a lawsuit against him. Then a young man who was in the military and who had been on one of the uncle's sports teams came forward. Several others from outside the family opened up and told their stories. These revelations seemed to give permission for other family members to speak out; a few additional cousins admitted they too had received his unwelcome attentions.

There were still other members of the family who chose to try to protect the crumbling secret by attacking the four women who had made the original allegations. Today those women are struggling to make the family realize that they told the truth and did the right thing. Each is still battling the emotional energy drain of this terrible family secret.

You can see how a secret can suck all the emotional life out of the family as a unit and out of the individual members. It undermines the ability of courageous survivors like my client to make an appropriate emotional connection.

Big family secrets do big emotional damage and create emotionally unavailable people! If you can't trust the emotions in your family to be safe, how can you trust the emotions anyone else might offer? It seems safer to the emotionally damaged person to simply continue to hide and not connect, even though that is a lonely and isolated way to live.

Making this situation even more complicated, memories that are frightening or painful may be repressed—hidden away by the psyche in an effort to protect the self. If you suspect that you are burdened by a family secret, you can do some observing and questioning. Ask the member of the family most likely to chat about it. Talk to family members in an emotion-based, nonjudgmental way about the *effect* of the suspected secret. Process the ways in which secrets can safely be brought into the light. If the secret is something that has done damage—such as sexual abuse or family violence—you may want to work with a therapist to help manage the emotional fallout.

If you are partnered with someone whose family is burdened with a pernicious secret, remember the importance of good boundaries. Families have difficulty tolerating their members revealing secrets. In general, families will have even less tolerance for an outsider stirring things up. Your role will be one of supporting your partner's quest. This support requires finesse and balance to keep your partner, his or her family, or both from seeing you as a threat.

If your partner's family secret is of the "don't tell anyone Uncle Harry declared bankruptcy" variety, it's better off left alone. If, however, the secret is a dangerous one—incest, violence, drug abuse—that could have an impact on your married life or the lives of your kids, your partner will require appropriate support from you in the form of a compassionate ear, reinforcement of the decision to uncover, and action, such as going with your partner to therapy or being present at confrontations. Remember, keep your boundaries tight and don't do the work *for* your partner—just do it *with* your partner.

In summary, a lot of the things that create emotional unavailability come down to core issues that begin in our families of origin or in our earliest relationships and carry forward into the rest of our lives.

These core issues most often revolve around trust and safety. If people don't learn how to trust—and that's trust in the sense of predictability, dependability, and emotional presence—they don't develop the tools to create relationships that have a trust element later. Instead they find maladaptive ways to create the illusion of trust. An example of that would be the person who tries to create what looks like a trust relationship by exercising complete control over his or her partner.

If people don't feel safe in their families or with their parents, they have a hard time learning how to feel safe with other people and how to help other people feel safe with them.

In order to make a relationship, the people in the relationship have to be emotionally available. If they're not, the relationships will be damaged. In the next chapters, we'll take a look at how some of these relationships form and how to recognize them.

# Chapter Three

# THE DEEPLY DESPERATE
# Unrequited Romance
# Novels

*N*ow we'll take a look at how emotionally unavailable people look and act within the context of relationships; but first we'll go over some introductory ideas.

Relationships. We spend a lot of time in our lives talking about them, worrying about them, predicting them, autopsying them, defining them, and trying to adjust them to fit our needs.

We have relationships with our partners, parents, kids, coworkers, therapists, bosses, church, subordinates, government, celebrities, and strangers. Relationships can be passionate, passionless, fulfilling, draining, one-sided, mutual, manageable, out of control, predictable, or random.

Relationships are the energy at the core of our lives. They are the engines that drive us and often the way in which we define ourselves as successful or not. They have huge power to help us or harm us. Mysteriously, they are often the facet of our lives over which we feel we have the least control or power.

People initially connect with one another for a constellation of reasons but stay together for entirely different reasons. Between getting together and staying together is the turf of a mystical question—what is there about you that fits with me?

This is a good spot to observe that everyone has some degree of emotional unavailability. It's human nature to have some reserve. This reserve enters into all relationship patterns and helps create the ways in which people connect with one another. The degree of each person's reserve determines the degree of dysfunction in each relationship. If you're a person who is 95 percent available and you are with someone who's 60 percent available, you can immediately see how much more work you are going to have to do to maintain a connection. If each of you is at 90 percent, you may be doing things to keep your distance, but the energy spent by each of you to maintain the connection is about equal. That doesn't necessarily mean it's a healthy relationship but more that you're starting out at the same spot.

It's important to be able to assess these availability differences as well as the types of relationships they create. This evaluation involves a good hard look at who we are. One time in our lives when we are vividly aware of ourselves and our dreams is when we get into a relationship with someone we think might turn out to be significant. Suddenly the bright spotlight of wishes and futures makes everything in the world seem all the more intense.

We examine ourselves in great detail. Unfortunately most often we look for those flaws and faults that may doom our relationship and drive the object of our dreams away. We become hypervigilant about even the most subtle nuance of inflection or behavior in ourselves or the object of our attention.

If the person with whom we are entering this new emotional landscape is available to love and be loved, each person is treading carefully, thinking, paying attention, and assessing the relationship as it grows. Each is also having his or her private moments of fear, doubt, and reassessment to make sure this is the right place to be at this time of life. This process is appropriate and necessary to the formation of healthy, growing, living relationships.

However, it's misleading to use the word *relationship* when talking about associations formed by more extensively emotionally unavailable persons. These are more often contacts made for the convenience, enhancement, or enrichment of the emotionally unavailable person, with little thought for the partner other than how the partner's presence can provide what the emotionally unavailable person needs.

For most emotionally unavailable persons, none of this is a conscious process, even though to a potential partner it might feel something like this: "Let me see, how can I make Julie my willing slave and just plain use her for my own needs while giving her nothing in return but pain and grief?" That sort of manipulation is reserved for only the most odious of perpetrators. Those folks certainly exist—see Chapter 19, "Dumping the Toxic and Moving On"—but most emotionally unavailable people don't intend to be malicious or to cause pain. They are simply operating out of a place that is not connected with anyone else—or even with themselves.

As a matter of fact, many suffer great guilt pangs when they find out they've hurt someone. They just don't have the ability to recognize the emotions they feel or those that they cause others to feel. The emotionally unavailable person tends to stay away from emotional content in anything because it is much too complex and mysterious and often because it is much too threatening. Before you drop into that caretaker role and react to protect the poor thing, however, remember that *this is an explanation, not an excuse.* You don't deserve to be in a relationship that's not reciprocal no matter how reasonable the explanation may seem.

If you are in a relationship where you are the 95 percent partner and your beloved is operating at about 50 percent, you are faced with some decisions. There is obviously a wide horizon of choices to consider but three seem pretty obvious: you can resign yourself to the status quo and continue doing all the work—and having all the grief when the relationship ends; you can end the relationship; or you can take a deep breath and plunge into the process of change.

This third choice takes courage, and you will find you and your partner both have to make changes in the way you approach the relationship. Sometimes, but not always, therapy is part of the process. As we look at the different types of relationships, I'll note where therapy would be a helpful tool. Other contributors to the process of change are open communication, the development of trust, higher self-esteem on both parts, and, most important, a *willingness* to change. We'll explore more about changing and growing in Chapters 17 and 18.

Now let's look at the first of the relationships in which you might find yourself.

## The Deeply Desperate

My friend Connie Day made an observation several years ago that has stuck with me. She noted that dating seems to have become an end in itself. It used to be that marriage was the objective of dating. You began dating someone and as you moved along, the relationship either ripened and began to become more complete or it withered and each of you tried again with someone else. If the relationship began to grow, it proceeded through "going steady" to engagement to marriage. It may not have been a perfect system, but it worked pretty well to get people together.

Now the rules have changed. Change in itself is not bad, but it certainly impacts how people go about the business of their lives, and for some people, confusion arises. I get confused, for example, when two people who own a home together, have two or three kids and a dog and cat but are not married refer to one another as girlfriend or boyfriend. Those terms are woefully inadequate to express the realities of the relationship at hand.

The confusion for some single people becomes more intense as they struggle to define relationships under the new paradigm and to alter their expectations.

Social contracts are based on expectations and experience. Experience teaches us what society expects of us. Expectations are built around what we hope to experience in the context of society. That's where we get in trouble. If our expectations are unrealistic or unachievable, frustration and disappointment follow and people who are frustrated and disappointed don't make great connections.

It would seem as though people who are desperately searching for love would be among the most emotionally available, but I don't believe that's true. The very desperation of their search overpowers the ability of anyone to connect in either direction as the force of the need for a connection takes up all the psychic energy available.

Patricia is in her early twenties. She's finished a couple of years of college while working. She lives in an apartment complex known for its high percentage of single people. When she first came to see me, she was tearful and anxious because her roommate had just become engaged and was planning to move in with her fiancé. Patricia and her roommate had been friends from first grade. They'd shared an apartment since high school graduation and Patricia was overwhelmed at the thought of having to find another roommate. She was also, as it developed, overwhelmed by the thought of being single and alone. Her roommate's engagement brought all that emotion to the surface.

Patricia couldn't think or talk about much else than finding the right man and settling down. She tried the bar scene, dating services, singles clubs, networking, the produce department at the local upscale grocery store, even singles ads in the paper. In each setting, she followed the same pattern: she would meet someone and instantly begin talking about what a great husband he would make. When he didn't instantly propose, she would begin casting about for someone else immediately—and desperately.

I asked her if she were saying the same things to the men she met as she was to me about their husband potential and she admitted that she probably was. We worked on playing things a bit cooler and she finally met a man, Jerry, who seemed interested in her and inclined to stick around.

I continued to encourage Patricia to live in the present

and enjoy the moment and she managed for a while, but when her roommate's wedding approached, Patricia began to lose ground. Jerry was invited to the wedding and Patricia was maid of honor. Patricia later told me it was a most romantic evening and, as they danced, she had told Jerry that she loved him. Our session was ten days after the wedding and she hadn't heard from him since.

"I'm sure he's just really busy," she said, her voice tremulous. "He has such a responsible job." I gently pointed out that he had been able to find time for her before and suggested that she might have pushed him a bit too much.

"But I want to be in love," she said plaintively. "And I want someone to be in love with me."

Patricia turned Jerry into a mission. She pursued him with relentless determination despite his clear statements all along that he was not interested in a capital-R relationship and in spite of my attempts to help her save some of her self-esteem by stepping back. Patricia became focused only on being in a permanent, committed relationship with Jerry, even though he was clear it was not what he wanted.

She would talk at length about her feelings for Jerry, but when I asked her to tell me how it felt to be in love with him, she could talk only about what she needed. Patricia was unable to see that her feelings were not for Jerry but were internally focused on herself and her needs. Thus there were no real emotions with which to make a connection.

Many people confuse needs with feelings because the two are indeed intertwined, even though they are also independent and very different. Basic needs fulfill internal, survival goals of the person and include things like food, shelter, safety—things without which a person cannot survive. Emotions and emotional connections are on a different level—those things that make life full but are not mandatory for survival. People can survive without emotional connections, though the lack can make life flat and empty. Emotions such as love and friendship add warmth and texture to our lives and help us thrive. Emotions enable us to connect with others who bring additional gifts to the richness of our lives.

The difficulty for people like Patricia, who classify love as a need, is that rather than enriching their lives, the quest for love narrows their world so much that they end up living on a survival level—food, shelter, safety—and eliminating the many other sources of enriching emotion available through friends, family, and community. Instead, the only thing they can think about is finding love, ignoring the irony of how much love they're passing up!

Patricia cut herself off not only from Jerry, who retreated quickly from her desperation, but also from meeting anyone else who might be able to mesh with her more effectively. Patricia, instead, chose a dysfunctional relationship with herself to fill her life, obsessing about something that would never be and keeping herself isolated from healing and from a real connection.

If you are the object of unrequited love, you know it is a very uncomfortable position. I'm certain Jerry, a decent and nice man, was actively squirming at Patricia's inappropriate attention and pursuit. Meanwhile, Patricia kept wanting me to tell her Jerry was emotionally unavailable because he wouldn't respond to her demands. It took a lot of work and a long time before Patricia could see that *she* was the one who was emotionally unavailable in this situation because her relationship with her unreasonable expectations blocked out any other options.

People who are so focused on the process of getting love usually believe the object of their attention is the one who is deficient in emotional potential. They see themselves as overflowing with love that is just waiting to be tapped by the right partner. Instead of finding Mr. Right, Patricia found a series of Mr. Right Nows, all of whom she bemoaned as emotionally unavailable without realizing that she was the one keeping love at a distance.

Making it all the more complicated, people like Patricia will sometimes attract someone who is also emotionally unavailable—a joining of two 50 percent commitments. Then the games begin as the two jockey for the position of being the one who is in control. The deeply desperate get the reinforcement of their belief system that no one will ever return the love they believe they are pouring out.

The deeply desperate keep the potential partner at arm's length with impossible standards of emotional attachment and exaggerated expectations of what love can do in their lives. When the potential partner, emotionally available or not, doesn't live up to those standards and expectations, the deeply desperate person feels double the rejection because it is a rejection of the core self.

If you see yourself in Patricia, it doesn't mean you are condemned to a life of hopeless questing and constant rejection—unless that's what you choose to do. The empty well in your life can only be filled by one person—you! As you develop a healthy relationship with yourself, you will be more open and as you are more open, there will be room for someone else in your life.

## DEEPLY DESPERATE CHECKLIST

☐ Unrealistic expectations of the potential partner

☐ Poor boundaries

☐ Constant quest for the "perfect mate"

☐ Fall in love instantly—and tell the potential mate

☐ Belief that love is a need

# Chapter Four

# SHALL WE DANCE?
## Cha-Chas, Tracks, Chains, and Tangos

he Deeply Desperate aren't the only ones who create elaborate patterns of attachment and unattachment to protect their own emotional unavailability. The intricacies of the patterns some people fall into would make Arthur Murray sit up and take notice, but the dances they create do only negative things to the people involved.

The chain relationship is a series of highly intense contacts interspersed with periods of distance during which each partner tries to figure out what the other will do next. The outcome of this pattern is that the contact periods are brief and the distances comprise more of the substance of the relationship. The focus, however, continues to be on the times of contact, which is unrealistic. By focusing on the closeness and using that to define the relationship, the partners set themselves up to be disappointed. It's not the relationship that's the problem but where they are looking to define it.

Let me tell you a story to illustrate what I mean. I had the unique opportunity to talk with the great jazz trumpeter Miles Davis in a completely casual, informal setting. From this conversation came one of the best pieces of wisdom I've ever heard. We were talking about music (what else?) and he said, "What you gotta realize is that music is as much about the silence as it is about the notes. Without silence, music is just noise. The silences are what define music."

In the case of the chain relationship, the distances define the relationship, not the brief moments of contact. Almost anyone can sustain an intense relationship for a short time. The trick is to sustain an intense relationship over the long haul. If someone is emotionally unavailable, the thought of long-term close contact is not appealing at all and that person will work hard to maintain a tolerable distance.

The brief moments of intensity help to keep the other person hooked while still maintaining an emotionally safe distance for the unavailable person. A friend of mine in New York was the mistress of a famous (and married) man. He supported her financially while she pursued a theatrical career. He paid for her apartment, car, clothes, expenses, and classes. His only demand was that she be available when he called. Sometimes this meant she would go to meet him where he was performing. Her preparation for these trips was always elaborate, filled with great bursts of shopping and hours in the beauty salon so she would be even more gorgeous when they met. They would then spend an idyllic time in some exotic location, filled with intense passion and connection. Between these visits, there was little contact. When I asked my friend how she felt about this, she said, "It's much easier to sustain a relationship in short bursts than to have to work at it every day."

My friend is a stunningly beautiful woman who is as bright as she is pretty. She has talent, money, looks, and brains. She also had precisely the relationship she wanted because it enabled her to remain focused on her real attachment—her career. The man was able to have the intimate company of a beautiful, articulate woman, which fed his ego without distracting him emotionally from his marital relationship. The problem arose when my friend developed a life-threatening illness and needed consistent emotional support of the kind a partner supplies. At that time she began to realize how much she had denied herself when she remained emotionally unavailable to any relationship that could have been more complete. My friend took the difficult step of returning to her family in Florida and ending the relationship with her married lover. She recovered from her illness and in the process met a physician to whom she is now married and with whom she has a very connected relationship.

Somehow, probably from early relationships with parents, the emotionally unavailable person (A) has come to believe that letting someone get too close is risky, so when anyone (B) gets close, alarms go off and A backs away. But that's not the end of it because when B gets too distant, that's just as scary, and A again approaches the intimate connection, which scares A enough that he or she backs off again. This approach-retreat-approach-retreat pattern makes up the chain dance.

The connected person, B, stops being able to trust or predict the relationship. Instead, he or she lives in constant insecurity and questioning. Most often, however, the commitment B questions will be his or her own.

Remember, we assume our relationship partners are coming from the same place we are. From that assumption, it seems a logical leap to presume that if the connection isn't working it must be something we're doing. We then set about taking all sorts of corrective actions to fix something we didn't break. That creates a lot of frustration and few rewards!

A relationship pattern where *both* partners are unable to approach each other would look like railroad tracks winding through hilly country. When one partner approaches, the other feels threatened and backs off but only to the exact distance that keeps the partner at emotional arm's length—not too close and not too far. If the partner then backs off, the other will approach but just to the distance that they have nonverbally agreed is mutually safe.

This pattern keeps the relationship in neutral—not too close and not too distant—and unable to grow. The emotional energy in the relationship is spent on maintaining the perfect distance, not on making the relationship develop.

Harry and Linda are both professionals with high-power

careers. They work for competing firms and are highly competitive with one another in the professional arena. In their personal lives, they fill their time with professional association activities and sports. Harry is a golfer with near-professional scores and Linda is a tournament-quality tennis player. Their lives are carefully scheduled and planned. They indulge in very few events that don't have planned outcomes either professionally or personally.

Harry came to therapy to talk about his growing frustration with Linda's reluctance to consider having a child—something he stated she had known was one of his primary goals for his early thirties. I pointed out to him that his language didn't sound like his objective was a child to love so much as a goal to be met. Harry was indignant.

"Of course we'll love a child. That's a given."

"That's not as easy as you'd like to believe. Babies demand a lot and rely heavily on cute in return. You sacrifice sleep, time, energy, money, and worry, and they still turn into adolescents!" I told him. "Are you prepared to give up golf for T-ball? Are you ready to come home early from work if the child is running a fever? Is Linda holding off because she knows the sacrifices and isn't willing to make them?"

Linda joined us after a few sessions and it became clear that each was locked firmly on to the tracks—career and personal—they'd chosen. As long as the calendar was two-dimensional, the business nature of their relationship wasn't a problem. Adding the third dimension, the needs of a child, would mean their tracks—both parallel and separate—would have to change and adjust. They may have been able to keep one another at arm's length, but babies have no tolerance for that sort of distance.

Linda and Harry had to work first on re-creating their carefully separate connection before they were able to welcome a child into their world.

If you find yourself in a relationship that doesn't seem to be growing, perhaps it's because you and your partner are keeping it at a tolerable distance. Breaking the mold requires taking a risk to move closer and stay there while encouraging your partner to join you in a closer space. You can't do this too quickly or unilaterally, so the first step is to open communication with your partner about the state of your relationship and where it might be able to grow. If your partner is not willing to follow this trail with you, perhaps it's time to change tracks!

A relationship that has the same quality of approach-retreat but feels more like a push-me-pull-you is the cha-cha as first one partner and then the other either retreats or chases. Unlike the chain, in which there is more distance than closeness, or the track, in which the objective is to keep the distance, the cha-cha is a constant, alternate seeking of intimacy that's always in motion.

Each partner believes he or she wants the intimacy but when it approaches, the person gets overwhelmed and backs off. The other partner then comes forward until that partner reaches his or her own tolerance point and backs off.

Rob and April came into therapy after dating seriously for about eight months. April wasn't particularly interested in therapy, but came because she wanted me to tell Rob he was wrong and she was right.

Rob explained that he wanted to go forward with the relationship but felt as though April didn't. When he asked, however, she would tell him that she was committed to the relationship and just thought he was stalling.

For several sessions I tried to help them use better communication skills with one another, to speak clearly and with feelings and to try listening more carefully, but I had to agree—their relationship was stalled. I was stuck, too, until a session or two later when April asked, "Rob, why do you move away from me a little bit when I sit next to you?"

"Like you don't," was his answer. So much for communication skills.

"Aha!" I said, surprising both of them. "How often does that feeling happen for each of you?"

Rob said, "Any time I try to get close, April backs up. Then I have to move again and she backs up again. Finally

I get tired of chasing her and stop. She always comes after me then."

"And that's when you back away," April said quickly. "Then I come close to you and you back away again. In order to get you close to me, I have to stop."

Cha-cha-cha. I said, "That's true physically. How about emotionally?"

Both nodded in agreement. "Always. I just get tired of it."

With Rob and April, as with other dancers, the energy flow in the relationship is consumed by the advance-retreat. Consequently nothing is left on which to build. Each partner is afraid to let go because both believe the relationship is viable. After all, it's so active! Unfortunately, it's active laterally and not expanding because neither party is willing to be the first to take the risk to get close.

If you reach out for your partner and reach out and reach out and then suddenly he or she feels much too close so you back up and back up and back up until he or she feels so far away so you reach out and reach out and . . . cha-cha-cha . . . then you are in this dance. To break the pattern, you need to develop a tolerance for intimacy, which takes practice and trust.

The tango is an intricate, passionate, and highly formalized dance that originated in Argentina. Tango relationships have that same feeling of a never-ending pattern of stylized footwork and predetermined poses that represent feelings and positions in the relationship. The energy flow is like a whirlpool that holds the two people in the relationship and keeps it twirling without growth or change.

Anita married Ron when they were finishing graduate school. They began a business together in a suburb of a major city. Ron had some severe physical problems but hadn't told Anita about them before they were married, even though the disability impacted his ability to father a child, which Anita desperately wanted. When Anita began pressing for a pregnancy, Ron tried to sell the business to a competitor. When Anita objected to the sale, Ron had a very public flirtation in their small community. Anita then got a job outside their business. In response, Ron took a partner into the business, which led Anita to open a competing business. When Anita's business became successful, Ron had an affair with her secretary.

Every move had a countermove, which had a countermove, which had a countermove. All the moves and countermoves kept the relationship spinning long after the love and connection had gone. Both partners were so busy with the tango that they lost the ability to see either themselves or each other. All either could focus on was the intricacy of the dance itself.

If you are in a tango, you will feel consumed by the relationship's need to keep fueling the dance with more and more steps and moves. To stop the dance, stop reacting. Instead of reacting, think, communicate your feelings, and demand that your partner do the same.

In all these dances, both partners have some degree of emotional unavailability and that leads me to repeat my earlier comment that there is no one who is completely emotionally available all the time. Everyone has some level of availability that's less than 100 percent in one or another situation. There are also people who are completely emotionally unavailable. They are dangerous and toxic because they are unable to make any kind of emotional connection and so make others around them do all the emotional work. Their unfortunate partners get nothing in return. (See Chapter 19 for more on this subject.)

Each person's degree of emotional unavailability helps determine the pattern of the relationships in which he or she engages. In the case of the chains, cha-chas, tracks, and tangos, both partners will usually be in the same range of availability/unavailability. Thus each has two things to overcome: working through his or her own issues of availability and working on changing the relationship to be healthier.

All these relationship styles have high levels of wariness and low levels of trust in the other person. The partners are attuned to one another for the wrong reason. Instead of being connected to build and link the relationship, they are wary of one another, so they always keep the precise emotional comfort distance. They don't achieve a balance in the relationship, however, because each has a different emotional safety zone. Thus, the dance continues and the dancers are always in motion.

To break the cycle, both partners need to reengage in the emotional parts of themselves and develop some trust for a restructured, more intimate relationship. This reengagement takes a leap of faith on the part of each partner, a determination to live in what may initially be an uncomfortable spot, and a desire for a more emotionally complete relationship and life.

## DANCERS CHECKLIST

☐ Ebb-and-flow pattern to relationship

☐ Both partners are emotionally unavailable

☐ Both partners fear intimacy

☐ Communication is activity-related

☐ Partners do not trust each other

# Chapter Five

# ROMEO . . .
# AND JULIETS
## Man, Women, and Trouble

*H*e sends flowers and candy and cards. He makes silly, sweet phone calls at odd moments that leave your heart doing the flamenco on your rib cage. When you are together, he is a hand-kissing, champagne-pouring, look-deep-into-your-eyes-and-get-mushy kind of guy, and you are swept off your feet and into his embrace.

The strains of "Some Enchanted Evening" flow through your thoughts and you find yourself daydreaming about that perfect wedding/honeymoon/happily-ever-after thing. You find yourself being nice to panhandlers and telemarketers, and you know this is it. You're in full-blown, dream-state *luuuuuuuuuuuuvvvvvvvvvvv*!

Then you enter the anxiety phase: "Does he love me? I wanna know." The old Motown song's advice is that the true test of love is "in his kiss." That may be one test since kisses are a good measure of intimacy and connection. But you might also want to consider such things as consistency, connection, growth of the relationship, respect, and honesty. Or you can ask.

Of course, that's taking a big risk. Most of us aren't willing to take that sort of plunge when we're blinded by the stars Romeo is flinging around the heavens . . . and the apartment. So we end up anxious, living from phone call to date, and hoping that one of these days he'll just *say it*! And he might. And you might even make the big trek down the aisle complete with rice, roses, and that fantasy honeymoon in Hawaii. You go on with your life thinking everything is fine.

Then one day there's a receipt for roses you didn't get. Or a hotel room you didn't stay in. Or an unfamiliar phone number that makes a series of appearances on your caller ID. So you ask Romeo about it and he gives you a plausible explanation having to do with some complex assistance to a friend you've never met who's in pursuit of a girl you don't know.

You love and trust Romeo, so you accept the explanation. But then he suddenly takes an interest in Sunday night football over at the house of one of the guys on his work crew—a guy you don't know—and he doesn't get home until the wee hours of the morning with some lame story about having to drive another guy home and running out of gas or falling asleep at Bill's house.

You love and trust Romeo, so you accept the explanation, but when you run it past your girlfriends they kind of shake their heads and make that noise that says, "Maybe so, but you may want to check it out."

Then one day comes that most awful moment. In my practice I've heard many stories of how the awful moment arrives including a phone call from someone who identifies herself as Romeo's girlfriend, finding two tickets to Jamaica with his name and that of a strange woman, or the appearance of a strange woman at the door. The world as you know it falls apart.

So what is this about? Why would someone be so romantic and dashing and then betray your love? Because it's not about *you*! Romeo is the problem. He's hooked on romance, but when he has to maintain a long-term relationship, with all its complex emotional tides, he loses the excitement of the romance and, as a result, has trouble feeling his way through the relationship. Instead, he chooses the quick jazz of a clandestine relationship in which he can get his romance needs met and feel something again.

Please don't misunderstand. I'm not saying that all affairs arise due to a Romeo syndrome. People have affairs for myriad reasons. Some, however, are because the Romeo can't sustain love and wants to feel the excitement of the early blushes of *luuuuuuuuuuvvvvvvvvv* rather than the deeper and more subtle shades of the kind of love that sustains relationships throughout life.

The pain of such a betrayal, whether you're married or dating a Romeo, is horrendous and it certainly feels personal, but I say again: it really has nothing to do with you. It's all about Romeo's relationship with himself or herself.

Let me set a couple of things straight. There are far more male Romeos than female. However, it would be inaccurate to claim that women don't ever behave this way (and for the very same reasons).

Romeos learn how to be the way they are because they are unable to feel more subtle emotions. Instead, they see emotions on a grand scale—the broad canvas—and expect all feelings to match those huge feelings. When love arrives, it's huge. But as time goes by, Romeo feels as though love is getting smaller and smaller.

The obvious thinking error is that *different* is *smaller*. Love certainly has its moments of grand scale, but it also has those subtle exchanges between two caring people who recognize each other's emotions and honor them. Luuuuuuuuvvvvvvvvv, on the other hand, is all peaks with no valleys or flat surfaces. It's all excitement and drama and very little is mundane. If luuuuuuuuvvvvvvvvv grows and becomes love it somehow appears less important, less intense to Romeo. As a result, his or her eye begins to seek out the more exciting peaks.

So why betray a love for luuuuuuuuuuuuvvvvvvvvv? Romeo probably doesn't see it as betrayal. Let me tell you about Luke. I first saw Luke and his wife Melissa sitting in the waiting room of my office. She was crying and he was totally attentive to her—focused on her completely. He kissed her hands, touched her shoulders, smoothed her hair, caressed her cheek, and dabbed at her tears.

I collected their intake forms from the receptionist, expecting to read that their purpose in coming was some terrible loss suffered by Melissa. To my amazement, Melissa had written "Husband's affairs," and Luke had written "My dirty little secret."

In my office, they sat together on the couch. Melissa told me, through her tears and Luke's constant attention, that she had recently discovered a series of clues that led her to a phone conversation with Julia, a woman with whom Luke had been having a torrid affair for more than six months. Luke sat silently, his eyes focused completely on his wife as she spoke.

Finally I gently interrupted Melissa to ask Luke for his input. He said, "I have been a complete jerk to my wonderful wife. I want her to forgive me. I adore her and I have no idea why I did this." I asked him if he had given Melissa a sincere apology for his behavior—always a good place to start the forgiveness process—and he assured me that he had.

Melissa began shaking her head as he spoke. I held my hand up to stop Luke's stream of confession and she said, "He's told me he feels like a rat and that he's been a jerk and that he knows he hurt me, but he hasn't really said he's sorry. I just need to hear him say he's sorry he's done this."

Luke tried again. "I've been terrible to Melissa. I have no idea why I did this. Melissa has been so good to me."

"Luke, Melissa said she needs to hear you say you are sorry you have had an affair."

He couldn't make the words come out of his mouth. We worked for several sessions on saying "I'm sorry." At the end of one of the early sessions he could say, "I'm sorry I've hurt you," but never "I'm sorry I had an affair."

Luke and I ended up meeting individually. During that session, Luke admitted that Julia was only one of many affairs he had had during his seven-year marriage to Melissa. He also admitted that he didn't see how it was something he had to apologize for since the indiscretions had nothing to do with his marriage. He told me that he adored his wife.

I asked him to help me understand that perspective. Luke explained that he was "European" in his views of the world and that many European men had affairs, which their wives understood completely. He went on to explain that he believed he deserved to have both love and romance in his life and that he loved his wife, but romance required the thrill of the chase and conquest—things that were impossible with his spouse.

I asked Luke where he was born. I hadn't been aware that Milwaukee was such a cosmopolitan spot! Luke had never been to Europe, much less had the opportunity to absorb the culture, but his understanding of the mistress tradition in some European countries fit his behavioral choices so well that he had decided it was his style.

Romeos like Luke really believe they have the right to dual relationships, though Luke stated it more clearly than most can. He is not troubled by the conflicts of interest inherent in having one relationship for love and another for romance. In his mind, they are two separate and unconnected things and he can't see how one relates to the other except that "it makes me more intense with Melissa because it gets my juices flowing."

Luke is emotionally unavailable to both his wife and his girlfriends. The connection he has is with the intensity of romance, which he is able to feel. Even his remorse is intense and that allowed him to appear to reconnect with Melissa. He could see her pain and could see himself emotionally when he was comforting her in the style of the Gray Zone person that he is, because she had emerged out of the fog and up onto his peaks. Once again he had momentarily found the thrill of the chase and conquest within the context of his marriage. It was almost as though he was pleased at being discovered because it allowed him to reengage with Melissa in a way in which he felt comfortable.

What Luke couldn't see was that his lack of an apology undermined everything valuable about true love: loyalty, trust, honesty, and truthfulness didn't exist for him. His view of the value of the relationship was to feed his own need for the rush of romance.

It took Luke six sessions before he could apologize for having the affair and then it was so insincere that Melissa walked out of the session and, eventually, out of the marriage. Luke was completely mystified because he felt they had become so much closer. He had misinterpreted Melissa's intense anger as connection. It brought him up out of his Gray Zone fog, so he thought it was a valid and appropriate emotional experience.

I suspect Luke, like most Romeos, has trouble identifying any emotion that doesn't fall into the romance category. The rest of the emotional horizon is cloudy for Romeos, broken occasionally by the thunderheads of anger or sadness.

Because they don't have access to their entire emotional range, Romeos try to push the whole world into the romance/chase/conquest scenario. Most of the Romeos I've met are in some sales profession, which has that same feel of chase and conquest. But don't count on them for follow-up customer service. That takes too much work.

Another truth about Romeos: they do not usually limit themselves to one affair, no matter what they may promise in the heat of being caught. That's because for Romeo, as Luke was open enough to acknowledge, romance and love are not the same thing. Therefore Romeo's feeling is that it should be OK for him or her to have both, even if that requires more than one relationship.

There's little or nothing you can do to change a Romeo's mind unless he or she becomes more connected with other emotions and can get the romance in some other way. Romeos are drawn to the chase and once you are familiar and ensconced as the primary love, you are no longer eligible for the sport.

You need to keep reminding yourself that the affairs have nothing to do with you or your worth as a person and that they are only representative of Romeo's inability to make a heart connection, no matter how romantic he might be. Remember, romance is a set of behaviors. Love is a set of emotions. Love is what you really want. Romance should enhance it, not replace it.

---

### ROMEOS CHECKLIST

☐ Intense interest in you in the early stages

☐ Unexplained absences, expenses, lateness

☐ Romantic but poor at intimacy

☐ Secretive

☐ Strong in a crisis, but unable to sustain a relationship

☐ Superficial and insincere

☐ Unconnected with his or her own emotions

☐ Unable to own his or her behavior

☐ No boundaries

# Chapter Six

# HEAD OVER HEART
## The Intellectual
## Ivory Tower

*P*eter is a doctor with a thriving practice in gerontology—the cutting-edge science of medicine for the elderly. He is much beloved by his patients and their families who believe he hung the moon. Sylvia, his wife, is an attorney. She's a warm, open woman who approaches people and problems in a centered, grounded way.

When they appeared in my office, Sylvia was tearful and Peter was mystified.

"Peter gives all of his emotional energy to his patients and there is nothing left for me," she said.

Peter shook his head. "That's not true. I'm here, aren't I? You know you're important to me. I try to tell you that all the time. I try to give you every indication of your spot in my life. You know you're important to me."

Sylvia shook her head. "I don't *know* anything because I don't *feel* anything from you. All I know is what I see— you give all your emotional energy to your clients and have nothing left for me."

Sylvia and Peter are talking about two completely different realms. She is talking about the realm of emotional connections—the heart hook between two people. He is talking about his mind and his thinking.

Sylvia is connected with her feelings. She knows at any given time what she is experiencing emotionally and would be able to talk about her emotional state in clear terms. Peter has somehow gotten the idea that emotions are an intellectual function that occurs not in the feeling self but in the thinking self.

A great many very bright people—male and female—have found a way to make emotions safe by chopping them up into bits and bytes of intellectual action and activity. Peter is able to show his patients and their families what appear to be emotions because he has, in the past, engaged in the intellectual exercise of looking connected and has found that people will buy into it. Peter believes the ability to verbalize emotions is the way to experience them. What he is not able to do is actually engage in the emotional process and the feelings that arise from doing that. Engaging with his emotions would scare him too much so he avoids it.

Peter's system works well in short-term, nonintimate relationships. When he has to make it last, his intellectualizing of his emotions falls apart because there is nothing emotionally stable underneath the intellectual process. Thus, the emotions aren't connected with the thoughts. It's a bit odd to think that emotions and thinking don't go together very well since both are functions of the brain and seem to be linked. That's the trap. The more you think about an emotion, the less likely you are to experience it and the more likely you are to continue substituting thought for feeling.

Thinking requires distance from the subject. If you're going over Niagara Falls in a barrel, you are in the teeth of the experience and not likely thinking about the physics at play or the geology that formed the Falls or the history of other idiots who have preceded you. In a sense, you are the experience. Once you've been rescued and are recovering in the hospital, you will have the time to think about the experience from all possible angles and appreciate it from a distance.

Emotional life is sort of like that. When you're in the middle of an emotional moment, you are lost in the emotion itself and don't have the ability to step back from it to break it down into crunchable little bits that can be analyzed and categorized.

People who intellectualize, on the other hand, keep everything and everyone at a distance all the time. They manage the emotional impact of feeling by discussing it from the safe, distant perch on which they sit.

Peter's a good example. He chose medicine, he told me, because everyone knows you have to be really smart to be a doctor. He said, "I knew that I was pretty good at figuring people out and really good at science, so it seemed a natural career choice. My father was a doctor and seemed to like his work and I know he made a very good living at it. I applied both to law school and to medical school. When I got into medical school first, it seemed the way for me to go." There is no passion for his work, no love of people, no emotional connection between who he is and what he does. He's all practicality, reason, and intellectual process.

Peter doesn't see this as a problem. Instead he sees himself as a rational, controlled, thoughtful person who doesn't do things impulsively and doesn't make decisions based only on feelings. Sylvia has been unable over their years together to encourage him to break out of this pattern of distance because he doesn't see that his style is emotionally damaging to her. The only way she's able now to talk about his distance is to be resentful of the attention his patients get because, from her emotional point of view, his energies toward the patients are the emotional connections she craves. She can't see that the superficial connections he makes with the patients are just that—superficial and temporary. Culturally, we respect intelligent people. We assume if someone is smart, he or she is also a whole evolved person. After all, he or she *sounds* whole and evolved. Until you crack the surface. One of the scariest clients I ever saw was also one of the smartest.

George is happy to tell anyone who will listen that his IQ cannot be measured by standard tests and that he is a member of Mensa. My own view is that intelligence is much more than just IQ; however, George doesn't share that belief with me. His job is to manage an extremely complex computer program and the associated hardware for a defense contractor. He is well known in the industry for the breadth of his knowledge in his field.

What people don't know about him is how cruel he is. George has a history of astonishing interpersonal violence both toward strangers and toward members of his family. He appeared in my office under court order because he had beaten his wife severely and she had decided to press charges in the hope that it would force him into therapy.

He was forced into therapy, but simply being present in a therapist's office doesn't guarantee there will be any change in behavior. In this case, George was physically present in my office but had not one iota of interest in changing. Instead, he wanted to engage me in a debate about his own view that therapy is just a scam.

Every time I tried to talk about how George might have felt about making a fist and striking his wife, he would talk about how therapists were all con artists taking money from the weak and mindless. We weren't getting anywhere, so I asked him to tell me about his relationship with his brother. He thought about it for a minute, trying to figure out where I was going with my question, but then he started talking about the things he and his brother used to do for fun when they were kids. Notice that I asked about emotion but the answer came in terms of action, which is typical of someone who is an intellectualizer.

George described a childhood in Chicago in which he and his brother, now a physician, used to make brass knuckles out of tin cans and then go out and find "bums to beat up." George laughed as he described how much fun they had watching "blood and teeth flying everywhere," and knowing that no one was going to press charges because no one would believe two boys who were in honors classes in high school would go out and do something like that. As he talked, George painted himself and his brother almost as avenging angels who were doing the community a service by beating up homeless people. He also let it slip that when he's tense or stressed now, he sometimes goes out and finds someone to beat up just to relieve the tension.

I asked him how beating up his wife fit into that picture and he frowned. "She didn't understand the rules, I guess. She didn't know she was supposed to just let that go. I can't imagine why she filed charges. She knew I wasn't going to kill her. I'm much too smart to do that and she knows it."

He was completely unable to acknowledge, intellectually or emotionally, the fact that he was causing pain to another person, either to his wife or to the strangers he believed he had the right to assault. I was chilled to my soul at this man's distance from any emotional life at all. He was unable to see the emotional part of himself or anyone else and was offended that people didn't agree with his intellectual viewpoint that he knew what he was doing and, beyond that, that he had the right to do the horrendous things he did.

George is an extreme example of an intellectualizer and he is also living proof that people can have a mixture of different types of emotional unavailability. In George's case, his bundle of types makes him a toxic person to be avoided at all costs.

Unfortunately, his wife wanted me to fix him (I didn't break him . . . I can't fix him) because she believed with his huge intellect he would have the ability to make the emotional connection. This was faulty reasoning. He didn't have the ability or the interest in emotional connection. He came for the ten sessions the judge had mandated, exhausting me every week as I tried to find the soft spot that would let me help him experience himself as an emotional person.

I knew the risk if he made any emotional connection with himself was that he would be overwhelmed by the feelings about what he had done to people over the years, but I was prepared to help him manage that if I could just get him to try it. It was the only way I believed his wife would ever be safe from another attack by him because as long as he could intellectualize away the pain he caused, he was a very unsafe individual. In a sense, George victimized everyone he met: family, friends, coworkers, judges, and this therapist. He held firmly to his intellectual stance, unable to release his emotions from the prison of his head.

George's wife came for our final meeting. I told them that I was going to inform the judge that George was not amenable to treatment and was unwilling to change. George then wanted to engage in a debate about what it would mean to be "amenable to treatment," but I told him we weren't going to do that. I then expressed my concern for his wife's safety if she allowed him back into their home.

At that George leapt to his feet and came at me menacingly. I looked into his eyes and found very little that was human, and I was scared! His wife was cowering in her chair whimpering. I had no idea what to do, so I just let my emotions guide me. I stood up and stepped toward George, my eyes on his. I said, "You don't need to complicate your life any more than you already have with your behavior. If you touch me, you will go to jail." To my relief, he hesitated, so I added, "Now sit down."

You could have danced to the sounds of my knees knocking together, but he did comply. Notice, however, that it wasn't an emotional breakthrough. All I did was access the intellectual process—hit me, go to jail. He didn't want to go to jail, so he didn't hit me.

If you're in a relationship with an intellectualizer, you will never lack reasons, explanations, ideas, and concepts to explain everything. What you will lack is feelings, emotions, and connections. Breaking that tightly defended system takes a commitment on the part of both partners and time to practice feeling rather than thinking.

Good emotional experiences, like good anything else, take practice. The language, intimacy, and communication of feelings all improve with use, but you and your partner both have to be willing to take the risk and do the work.

If one person is in his or her head and the other is in his or her heart, you are communicating from different places. In order to be physically or emotionally intimate, you must start by getting into the same place, make a commitment to work on it, and practice, practice, practice.

## INTELLECTUALIZERS CHECKLIST

☐ Distant, unable to be emotionally intimate

☐ Overanalyzes situations, ignores emotional content

☐ Unconnected with his or her emotions

☐ Proud of intellectual achievements, dismisses emotional connections

☐ Unable to identify emotions in self or others

☐ Highly defended

# Chapter Seven

# WHATEVER YOU SAY, DEAR
## Power Imbalances

hrough the local community college, I once taught a course that instructed couples how to resolve conflict. When I think of power imbalances in a relationship, I recall a couple who attended one session. There was an age difference between the two of them, but age differences don't necessarily imply power imbalances. More important to their relationship was the fact that he had been her boss in a company noted locally for its paternalistic and misogynistic policies and practices.

The man sat, his arms crossed over his chest, and smirked as I talked about the importance of good communication in a relationship. The woman was visibly nervous. Each time she spoke, her eyes would flash to his face and she would back away from some points if she sensed even the tiniest bit of disapproval from him.

At the end of the first session when the other couples in the room were working on a communication exercise designed to help them open up to one another, this couple sat side by side in silence. I went over to encourage them to try the exercise, and the husband shook his head. "No, we won't do it. You know why? Because she gets all the communication she needs. I tell her what I want and she does it. It was that way when she was my office girl and it's that way now." They then got up and left. To this day, I wonder if she's still putting up with that behavior. I also wonder how it was she chose to marry this man and how she managed to get him to even that one session. Incidentally, I declined their request for a refund of the tuition!

Power struggles are a constant in every relationship—not just for life partners but in friendships; school, work, business, and church relationships; and all other areas of the human arena. The battle for dominance is eternal and instinctive. It's the foundation for Darwin's theory of survival of the fittest, and it's the reason we as a species have survived.

The problem with the fight for control and power is that it inherently puts people in the position of being winners or losers in a relationship. That paves the way for uncomfortable relationships and more power struggles.

A philosophical digression for a moment, since this is a good spot to talk about the difference between surrender and submission. It is this principle that is at the core of power struggles in a relationship. It is important to remember that problems are most effectively resolved if people are able to keep their power base operating.

Surrender is the position of keeping your personal power while allowing the other person to win. In essence, you say, "I choose for you to get what you want in this negotiation between us. By choosing for you to win, I don't lose." In contrast, the position of submission is one in which the other person takes your personal power away without your cooperation or consent. The usurper's subtext would sound more like, "I want what I want and I don't give a hoot about you." Those are obviously very different positions. You can see how one is empowering and respectful and the other is the direct road to a bad relationship.

I often suggest to couples who engage in power struggles that they take the "I want *you* to win" position when they are negotiating with each other. If you want your partner to prevail, you will each seek a solution that enhances the other's situation. When each of you takes the stance of assuring your partner's happiness, both of you will emerge feeling good. When both parties in a negotiation feel good, you have a win-win outcome.

Power struggles that are win-lose are a hallmark of relationships with power imbalances. Think about the couple in my course. The wife was trying to find a way to at least get some power in the relationship, but the husband had always had the power and wasn't about to give up one iota of it. The wife had two choices: live by his rules or get out.

If you feel you are constantly giving in to keep your relationship, you have a power problem. Other signs of grave power imbalances include the feeling that you don't have a voice in a relationship or that you are always the one who is not important. If you find yourself doing things you don't like, eating food you don't like in restaurants you don't care for, being with friends you don't find interesting, or going places you don't want to go at times that are inconvenient, you may want to take a look at the power base in your relationship. You may also want to ask yourself how much of the power you've simply offered up because it's the path of least resistance.

In many cases people tell me it doesn't matter who chooses the movie or the restaurant in their relationship as long as they are together. Horsefeathers! If you frequently give up your power to another person, you are inviting terrible trouble—not because you might never get to eat at your favorite restaurant but much more because you are conditioning yourself to be in the position of being one-down.

Being in the disempowered position can have all sorts of negative consequences. First, your self-esteem takes a battering over time as you struggle to retain your personal worth in the face of evidence that you aren't worthy.

Second, you begin to extend this powerlessness into other relationships, almost as though you are justifying the surrender of power in the primary relationship. You begin handing off power to your boss, your job peers, the guy down the block. It's as if you're trying to make everything OK by spreading your power around. All that does is lower your self-esteem.

Third, not all power imbalance relationships are violent, but most violent relationships have power imbalances. In these relationships, each partner feels the other has all the power. The partner who becomes violent is trying to equalize the imbalance by using physical force. The victimized partner, on the other hand, believes the violent partner has all the power because he or she is stronger, more violent, and less predictable. In truth, neither had any power or any self-esteem because neither claimed any.

The process of losing personal power is usually slow and subtle. You might have to take an inward journey to think about whether or not you're giving up your power in exchange for your relationship. It might be that the power imbalance in your relationship is a benign one that is mostly a matter of habit, or it may be that your partner is aggressively taking your power away. In either case, it is not to your benefit to allow that to continue.

It also goes hand in hand with emotional unavailability, as the need to maintain, monitor, and control power flows between the couple takes all the emotional energy that might have been spent on building and connecting.

So how do you interrupt the power flow and balance it?

1. Work on your own self-esteem. The belief that you are a person of value who deserves to be treated well in all circumstances and deserves to keep your power is central to restoring self-esteem. No one will take better care of you than you do!
2. Keep your choices open. If you hold onto your freedom of choice, you hold onto your power.
3. Confront the power snatcher when you feel him or her trying to keep you in the one-down position. You do that by building good boundaries and by being assertive.

**Assertive Language** recognizes and respects the personal power of others while still asking for what the speaker wants and/or needs.

- "Mr. Clark, I'd like to take Tuesday off, but I'll make certain my work will be covered."
- "Harry, I'd appreciate your help getting ready for the party."
- "Julie, I'm not comfortable loaning money. I'd be happy to help you figure out your budget, though."

**Aggressive Language** disregards the personal power of another and seeks only to get the speaker what he or she wants, no matter the cost.

- "I'm taking Tuesday off" or "I took Tuesday off. So what?"
- "Harry, you better be here to work on the party or you're cooked."
- "Don't even ask."

Assertiveness is asking for what you need or want but not at the expense of another. Aggressiveness is demanding, threatening, disregarding, or disrespecting.

Learning how to be assertive takes practice and some basic tools. It also requires a level of self-esteem, a belief that you *deserve* to get what you ask for. Of course, your request must be possible, achievable, and reasonable. No matter how assertively you ask, it's unlikely you'll get younger, taller, or thinner. What you can get, however, is more cooperation, more respect, and better communication.

There is no rationalization for physical abuse of any kind under any circumstances. Period. If you feel your partner is out of control, call the police or leave. Do not try to reason with someone who has abandoned reason. Protect yourself from the assault at all costs.

Short of violence, however, power imbalances are still unhealthy in relationships! It is vital that you do not ever allow *anyone* to abuse you—verbally, emotionally, sexually, financially, religiously, morally, or physically. You deserve to be heard. You deserve to be honored and you absolutely deserve to keep your power. You also deserve to have a connected, balanced, emotionally available relationship. When you get a balance of power, you are opening the door that gives your emotional connections room to grow.

## POWER IMBALANCE CHECKLIST

☐ Conflict resolutions are win-lose.

☐ One partner wants to control the relationship.

☐ One partner seems to give in all the time.

☐ Low-power partner has low self-esteem.

☐ High-power partner has low self-esteem.

☐ Aggressive behavior is present.

☐ There is no emotional connection between partners.

# Chapter Eight

# THE ADVENTURERS
# Relationships on the Edge

*T*here was a couple I saw for a while who represent the very worst kind of on-the-edge behavior, and I'll tell you briefly about them before we talk about people who take a route closer to the middle of the road.

Mickey and Josie had met in high school and married the day after graduation. She was from a wealthy, crazy family and he was from a wealthy, crazy, criminal family. They divorced the first time after two tumultuous years and both quickly made revenge marriages, which ended when they ran into each other in a shopping mall and spent two weeks in a motel room before bothering to call their respective spouses.

They married again. This time it took less than a year for them to part but not before she had torched his Corvette and he had given all her clothes to the Salvation Army. This time the revenge marriages both produced children (unfortunately for the children who continue to be the innocent bystanders to this emotional train wreck). I wasn't surprised to learn there had been jail time for Mickey during this time as well.

They came to me three years and one joint child into their third marriage to one another. By this time, cocaine had become a partner in the marriage, as had the money Josie had inherited when her father died. They had several odd business ventures they were pursuing, fueled by the false energy of cocaine and the desperation to pay for it, but their marriage had again deteriorated. Each session sounded like dueling attorneys as the partners struggled to justify the rude, petty, inappropriate, and mean-spirited things they did to get each other's attention—sort of a Marquis de Sade version of "Can you top this?"

He had six restraining orders against her and she had seven against him, complete with multiple court dates. Both had charges of other kinds pending as well, reflecting their rather outlaw approach to the business world. There was also an episode of an exchange of gunfire in the parking lot of a restaurant where Mickey had discovered Josie with another man.

Clearly this was a relationship on the edge. It was also a highly toxic and badly enmeshed pairing, which was obsessive on his part and connected to some long-term problems on hers. But this case provides a very powerful example of how wrong a relationship can be and still survive, and it is a perfect example of life on the edge.

Relationships on the edge are characterized by extremes of behavior by the partners toward one another or in the world in general. The partners seem to connect only through the wild actions. One example would be violent or damaging fighting over the least little thing. We've all heard the old myth, "It's terrible when we fight, but it's so great when we make up." That is the theme of the relationship on the edge!

People who are drawn to relationships on the edge are attracted by the danger of it all. The danger can come from either the physical or emotional realm, but the effect is the same as the couples attempt to destroy in vicious ways those things they say they love.

A more middle-of-the-road example would be Gary and Linda, who had married after a four-month courtship, motivated by Linda's unanticipated pregnancy. Unfortunately, she had been engaged to another man when she and Gary met and that relationship was unresolved before she moved forward with Gary.

The excitement of their whirlwind wedding (with a little family-of-origin turmoil thrown in for good measure), the pregnancy, and the birth carried them through the first year of their marriage. As they settled into being spouses and parents—as well as successful businesspeople—the thrill wore off and they began to see the undeveloped parts of the relationship as flaws and cracks.

Because of their inexperience with one another, they had no foundation to work out the problems, so they retreated behind threats of abandonment. When they first appeared in my office, they had each played the let's-just-get-a-divorce card on each other more than once, and neither felt they could trust the other anymore. Still, they had their child and their comfortable life together, and they didn't want to give all that up.

They also had a lot of love for each other but didn't have a way to recognize it because it had grown in the shadow of the excitement of their marriage, baby, careers, and chaos. The edge-living, not the love, was the focus of their relationship.

Gary and Linda, like many other couples, had to approach the edge of the end-the-relationship chasm to bring themselves to awareness that what they had been doing wasn't working. The divorce chasm is a dangerous one, but it's one that gets more and more familiar to people who have relationships on the edge. Sometimes a look down that chasm can be healing in itself as the couple gets a glimpse into the loneliness and sadness of parting and ending. They may step back, filled with determination to work things through. This is most often what happens with longer-term, more mature relationships that have a strong foundation.

Other couples approach the chasm, look at the possibilities, and decide "what the heck," as they throw themselves over the edge. These relationships are probably hopeless to start with, filled with flaws the couple doesn't give themselves time to work on before the flaws become fatal.

Gary and Linda approached the chasm and retreated many times, but each approach was painful and chipped away at the small foundation that they had been able to build in their time together. They didn't seem to know how to stop before getting to the edge—there was no middle ground for either of them. By taking it to the edge each time, they were almost certainly going to end up in the chasm unless something changed in the way they communicated with one another.

Communication is key to understanding why the relationship on the edge doesn't work. Part of the problem when there is fighting or constant threat of abandonment stems from the fact that the members of the pairing may not be able to communicate the emotions they have; or it may be that they are not in touch with their emotions at all.

In the case of Mickey and Josie, neither had any clue what he or she was feeling. Everything was a reaction to an external stimulus and all the reactions were enormous—far out of proportion to the situations at hand. In one session they fought bitterly over who had last changed their toddler's diaper. The fight escalated to threats of reports to child protection and restraining orders before I was able to help them back away from their positions. Mickey later told me that they were so excited after they left my office that they went directly to a motel room. For them the excitement of being on the edge obviously also had a sexual component. Sex is often a part of the magnet that draws edge-living couples together again and again.

With Gary and Linda, the emotions were there but the inexperience with how to read and interpret each other meant they each had to resort to the most extreme threats to even feel that the other person was paying attention.

Mostly because of this poor communication, both Gary and Linda and Mickey and Josie were emotionally unavailable to one another.

Both Mickey and Josie came from chaotic families where

no one was safe or predictable. It's pretty easy to see how they later re-created the chaos in their own relationship. If you're not from a chaotic family, it sounds horrific to live in a world of restraining orders, police calls, and the occasional exchange of gunfire, but to Mickey and Josie it felt normal.

Now you can understand why therapists cringe when clients tell us, "I just want to be normal," as though that's something that is (a) definable and (b) desirable.

With high-functioning people like Gary and Linda, however, it's harder to see the isolation brought on by their emotional unavailability because they are so adept at keeping it hidden. Both Gary and Linda are very much aware that people have expectations of connectedness and they have each found ways, through their social skills and business abilities, to appear connected. The systems fall apart, however, when they have to sustain the connections for any length of time. False connections require a great deal of psychic energy to maintain, and such an expenditure takes its toll. Eventually, the system crumbles and they resort to a trip to the edge of the chasm to make a point with one another.

Gary and Linda also come from chaotic families and they also reflect the kind of chaos they saw at home. Gary's biological father's name and unexplained absence are the big family secret. All he knows is that he was adopted by his stepfather who, with his mother, had four other children. Gary never felt he was a full partner in the sibling relationship, so he had to shield himself from that hurt in addition to the pain of his biological father's abandonment.

The emotional unavailability that comes from living in a chaotic family is a protective device. The chaos-family member recognizes that he may be victimized if he is too open, so he builds a wall that makes it very hard for anyone to approach him emotionally—including himself. When he brings this into an adult relationship, the wall stays intact, which helps to re-create the family chaos all over again.

Linda's family was chaotic, too, but in its own, unique way. She referred to her biological father as Satan. In fact, that may be the nicest thing I ever heard her say about him. Her family dynamic in childhood was controlled by the need to protect the family from the crazy father, who would appear without warning, make a huge emotional mess, and then disappear, leaving Linda's mom to clean up after him. Since the mom was also emotionally damaged, her cleanup efforts were primarily defensive and were not very effective. She would frequently run away from home when she became overwhelmed, mad, or stressed. She would be gone for days or weeks and Linda's grandmother would appear to care for the children with no explanation. When Linda's mother would return, the grandmother would disappear without a word of good-bye or explanation to the kids. Linda quickly learned to seal herself off from her family to protect herself emotionally. She used high activity to shield herself and was always busy with work, after-school activities, or sports. In that way she did not have to engage with her family nor experience them emotionally.

So what about people with happy childhoods who don't come into relationships damaged but then find themselves running to the edge of the chasm? There have been some studies of just this sort of thing, looking at women who have come from reasonably "normal" families only to become involved in emotionally or physically abusive relationships as adults. I don't mean to suggest that such women enter relationships they know to be abusive. Abusive or controlling (verbally abusive) relationships emerge over time as the two people in the couple try to adjust their personal history to the relationship. If a person comes to a relationship burdened with a family history of violence, power imbalance, verbal abuse, jealousy, or controlling behavior as the tool to solve problems, the relationship can become abusive when normal problems arise.

One study stated that after only six months in an abusive relationship, a woman who had no childhood damage will act in many ways just like an adult survivor of child abuse.

The sad message here is that we can be profoundly

changed by negative experiences no matter when they arrive in our lives. This message makes it a mandate to make good choices in relationships!

Relationships on the edge can incorporate physical risk as well as emotional. I know a couple who constantly try to top each other with risky behavior. He takes up skydiving, so she takes up snowboarding. She wants a cat, so he buys an ocelot. They plan a vacation—an Arctic trek in the winter.

With these folks, the excitement of the physical risks they take masks a lot of discontent in the relationship. When they spend too much time at home, they begin to discover they have little or nothing in common outside the chances they take. This discovery leads them to the emotional brink many times, but their way of fixing it is to find another physically risky adventure to unite them.

If your relationship is constantly on the edge, you can turn the pattern around with better communication techniques and better emotional connections.

Excitement and danger are fun once in a while but they are not a plan for living day-to-day if you expect your relationship to grow and mature. Having the ability to be comfortable without getting to the edge comes with awareness and communication and from practicing keeping your balance in the middle of the road.

## ADVENTURERS CHECKLIST

☐ Action in place of emotion

☐ Challenges, both physical and emotional

☐ Frequent conflicts

☐ Threats of abandonment

☐ Extremes of behavior by both partners

☐ Poor communication

☐ Detachment from "smaller" emotions

# Chapter Nine

# I'VE GOT A SECRET
## Lies, Half-Truths, and Hidden Traps

What's the difference between truth and honesty? Truth is about demonstrable fact. You can stick it to the wall and look at it. You can prove it. And you will be able to prove it in six weeks or six months or six years. It is, essentially, a constant. Water boils at 212°F. The law of gravity doesn't change. Either you were at Woodstock or you weren't. Truth is demonstrable fact supported by concrete evidence.

Honesty, on the other hand, is about emotions and feelings. It can change. Today you might honestly love your boyfriend. Tomorrow you might find out the truth that he is married with seven children and your feelings might, justifiably, change. Today you can honestly say you love him, but you can't predict what you will be feeling tomorrow. You can only guess. There are no absolutes when you are talking about emotions because emotions are part of the human condition.

Thus when someone says, "let me be honest with you," you would be able (if you agreed with my definitions of truth and honesty) to assume he or she is talking about emotions. By the same token, if a person says, "let me be truthful with you," you could assume he or she is talking about fact. Wouldn't those be nice, convenient cues to figure out where someone stands?

Unfortunately we have muddied the meanings of truth and honesty and tend to use them interchangeably, which leads to a lot of confusion. If you are in a relationship with someone who is emotionally unavailable and he offers to be honest with you, it may be a cue that the message is going to be neither truthful nor honest!

Sometimes emotionally unavailable people will use "let me be honest with you" as a way to keep you at a distance emotionally so they can stay in control of the situation and not have to engage the emotional part of themselves in the relationship. In these cases, the person may be guarding something more than just his or her emotional self. Let me give you an example.

William and Sarah had been married for almost twenty years. They were the quintessential urban couple. They both lived and worked in the city, had no kids, had plenty of investments and 401-Ks firmly in place for their future. When they came into my office, they had each played the divorce card several times. They indicated that they wanted to decide whether or not it was time to end the relationship.

Sarah's issues with William were that he'd had an affair, which he believed was not an issue since he'd told her about it while it was going on; that he had forced her to have an abortion, then changed his mind after the procedure and was now sending her on guilt trips about it; and that he was verbally abusive. I asked her what form his verbal abuse took and she said, "William says, 'let me be honest with you,' then says terrible things to me such as that I'm not tall enough or pretty enough to be good enough for him."

William became very agitated when she said this. "I am being honest. It hurts me that Sarah isn't pretty. I feel sad that she has short hair and needs to lose twenty pounds because she doesn't look right when she's with me. I could just cry that she's over forty. But I am not verbally abusive and I believe she's being abusive when she says things like that."

When I asked him why he didn't just divorce her if she wasn't the woman for him, William said, "My family would be very upset if we got a divorce. Only my sisters have gotten divorces."

William was from a family of fourteen children, equally divided between boys and girls. His parents had been rural Midwesterners—stoic, emotionally distant, traditional in their roles, closed and secretive about their feelings, and rigidly religious.

William painted his siblings into the Grant Wood portrait with a mixture of condescension and admiration. He related that he and his brothers had all been very success-ful while his sisters were "weak" because they had all been in therapy and four of the seven had been divorced.

When I asked him if he knew what their issues were, he sneered slightly and said, "They all want people to believe our childhood was miserable, which is a complete lie. We had a wonderful childhood." He didn't say anything about the issues that ended the marriages.

I had noticed on his intake sheet that he responded "yes" to the question "Have you ever been sexually victim-ized?" I asked him about it. He shrugged and waved his hand dismissively. "It was two times but it really means nothing."

I told him I was glad to hear he'd worked through the issues and he shook his head. "I don't know what you mean by 'worked through.' I told myself it meant nothing, so it meant nothing."

*Victimization never, ever means nothing!* The experi-ence of being treated like an object permanently changes the way a person views the world. A person can never again feel safe if someone has invaded his or her most intimate space and self and taken his or her power away. I made this observation to William. His response was, "Let me be honest with you. The first time was when I was about twelve and my church baseball coach took our team on an overnight road trip. I found myself in bed with him and just laid there while he did what he wanted, but it didn't mean anything. The second time was the youth pastor of our church. I was about eighteen and I found myself in a sleeping bag with him on a church camp trip. He did what he wanted, but I didn't participate. That's why it meant nothing. See, I can talk about it and it doesn't matter." I again made the observation that being victimized and stripped of your power by someone is a terrible experience and that it would be worse if the perpetrator of the abuse were a trusted person. He dismissed it again.

Later when we were talking about his affair, he said, "It wasn't my fault. Lily was the one who pushed it. I was just there and she did everything." Suddenly it was all clear to me. William believed if he didn't actively initiate something, it didn't happen. When I noted this to the couple, Sarah immediately agreed. She characterized him as "Bambi in the high beams," when it came to any kind of confrontation or need to set limits with anyone. She was tearful when she added that she had been the one who pushed them into marriage and she could now see that if she had not been pushing, they would never have made that step.

William became angry. "And now you want to push me into a divorce just because someone else pushed me into an affair. It's not fair. What will my family think?"

William has a slippery relationship with both truth and honesty. He has built such an intricate web of reconstituted reality that if he engaged any part of the emotional content of his marriage, his affair(s), or his victimizations, he'd have to look at the emotional content of everything, and that would overwhelm him.

Instead, he looks at the superficial (appearance, weight, image) and tries to make that an emotional setting. In addition, he casts himself as the victim of everyone else's whims and failings, then behaves in a victimizing way from that position. When William attacks Sarah for her looks, hair length, age, and weight, he couches it in terms that he is personally hurt by her shortcomings.

William is trying to get his power back by victimizing

someone else. He is unable to be either truthful or honest about any of his real feelings. To feel safe, he needs to be in the victim role because in that position he doesn't have to acknowledge his own responsibility for not resisting what happened to him, either at the time or later in processing. But he also needs to be in the perpetrator role to keep at a distance anyone who might get close to him.

He is completely emotionally unavailable from any direction, trapped in the limbo of keeping the honesty of his emotions as far away from his reality as possible and keeping the truth of the terrible things that occurred in his life pushed back and hidden. William lives in a manufactured reality, neither truthful nor honest.

*The presence of a pernicious secret in a relationship precludes an open, honest connection. Period.*

The other side of this picture is the lie of the spy. In this case, instead of keeping a secret about himself or herself, the emotionally unavailable person tries to uncover *everything* about you while revealing very little. By doing so, he or she takes your power away and victimizes you.

It may start with a lot of questions. Everyone likes to be asked about themselves: what do you do, what do you think, what do you like? Questions make us feel important and interesting, so we try to give thorough, complete answers that will present a detailed picture of who we are. This give-and-take is a natural part of the getting-to-know-you process.

What isn't natural is what happens next. You may find her checking your pager or listening to your answering machine. He might go through your address book or your mail. She might pay a little too much attention to what's written in your checkbook or on your day planner. The extreme of this is, of course, the person who becomes so intrusive that he is virtually stalking you. He may hire a detective, not to check you out to be sure you are who you say you are but to uncover information about your private life that's just none of his business. He does this to feel in control of you. What he is seeking is information that makes you vulnerable and puts him in a position of knowing more about you than you do about him.

I once knew a woman who wired her boyfriend's apartment with enough bugs to make the KGB jealous, then was mad when she found out he was planning to break up with her because she was so intrusive!

I can't resist the comment here that when you snoop and find something, you are then stuck with the decision about what to do with the information you have and how to explain how you got it. There simply is no respectful or appropriate way to do this, so you are trapped in a lie or locked in mortal combat with the information you weren't supposed to have in the first place.

There's a better way to do it! A couple who is being both honest and truthful with one another can talk about even the most painful information in a way that allows respect and healing.

"Clark, I feel very sad when I think about the affair you had. I know it was a while ago, but I still feel sad sometimes."

"Lois, I was wrong to make that choice and I regret it every day. I also feel bad that you were so hurt by something that was selfish and meaningless. I'm really sorry. Is there something I can do to help you feel less sad?"

Both Lois and Clark are being *truthful* in talking about the event of the affair, and they're being *honest* in relating their feelings. Their verbal exchange gives them a foundation of openness on which to build.

If you are in a relationship, make sure it is both honest and truthful. If it isn't, you don't really have a relationship.

## SECRET KEEPERS CHECKLIST

- ☐ Has difficulty being truthful or honest

- ☐ Blames others for his or her behavior

- ☐ Keeps secrets, bends the truth to match the situation

- ☐ May snoop or pry into partner's personal life

❖

# Chapter Ten

# TALKING TURKEY
# The Emotion Stuffers

When a person has an intense emotional experience that he or she doesn't process, the result is that the emotions get stuffed—pushed down and cleverly hidden away.

I'm a very visual thinker—when I imagine something I tend to put it in visual terms first, then verbal. When I think about the memory part of the brain, I imagine it as a huge room filled with filing cabinets. Some are used frequently, so the drawers and files are open. Others are closed and dusty and contain memories that rarely are called up into conscious thought. Then there's a special section surrounded by a heavy chain-link fence that's locked with giant padlocks and has all sorts of warning signs: "Keep Out." "Contents Are Toxic." "Do Not Enter." These file cabinets are painted red with huge locks and hasps holding the drawers closed. Some of the cabinets have an evil glow around them that makes them scary even to look at. This red file room is where the dangerous memories are stored.

When a person is young, these cabinets have lots of room and they can easily contain the icky memories that we stuff in before fleeing the area. But as a person accumulates more experiences and more emotions, the cabinets can begin to strain to contain the memories and keep them hidden. Some even spring a leak and the toxic memory begins to contaminate the benign memories.

That's the danger of stuffing emotions. Sooner or later, ready or not, they will break out and it's usually at the least opportune time. Still, I have found it very hard to persuade someone who has spent his or her whole life stuffing emotions to voluntarily open those red cabinets, even though I assure the client we can do it a little at a time. Remember the example I gave earlier of the toxic balloon? It's what we're talking about here.

Minnesota, where I practice, is the national capital of stoicism, which is another name for emotion stuffing. Stoicism is honored here as the way traditional Minnesotans approach emotional situations. Emotions are seen as something to be hidden or, if they emerge, as an embarrassment. (I used to tease my great Aunt Valborg about her "Minnesota hugs and kisses," which were hugs delivered with only the lightest touch of her forearms—no hands!—and kisses no closer than a foot from the recipient's cheek.) A quietly spoken "oh my" suffices for really big surprises—positive or negative. The wildness and cheering in the Dome during the two times the Twins have won the World Series was so unusual for Minnesota that the behavior made the local news.

Considering the stoic nature of so many (not all, mind you) people in Minnesota, you can see that stuffing emotions is a very common problem in relationships.

Sally is from a rural Minnesota family whose ancestors came from the Scandinavian countries. She and Nick had been married for five years and had two kids when they appeared in my office. Nick said, "She never reacts to anything. When one of our kids almost died, she told me about the accident in a flat voice that sounded like she didn't care. If you look at our wedding pictures, she's smiling but she doesn't look very happy. It's the same expression you see in the pictures with the new babies. And she never cries. I have no idea what she's feeling. I'm Italian. Everything I feel is always right out there. I need to know what she's feeling."

Sally had listened to Nick's speech with an impassive expression. "It's just how I am. My family is like that too. We just don't make a big deal out of things. If you get too excited, you will then have to get very sad. If you stay in the middle you don't get hurt and nobody thinks badly of you."

I asked her what the saddest thing was she'd ever experienced. "My mom's death last year," she answered. I asked her to tell me about it. With the same flat expression, she gave a report of the details of her mother's illness and death. As she spoke she was completely devoid of emotion. Her expression never changed.

I then asked her how she felt about her mom's passing.

"It's sad," was her response.

"I agree that it's sad, but how do you *feel* about it?" I persisted.

"It's hard on my father."

Sally and I went on for several more repetitions of the question, but she never got to talking about her *feelings* about a heartbreaking event in her life. She talked about events and ideas but not about feelings. As we worked together, it was clear that she couldn't identify her feelings on any subject.

What Sally wanted most to do was to stay "in the middle," as she described it. To Sally this meant not feeling anything; she had been stuffing all her emotions throughout her life.

Sally worked hard in therapy. She was lucky to have Nick, a man with full access to his emotions, to support her change. As she began to feel her emotions, their marriage became much closer.

If you are in a relationship with someone who has been stuffing his emotions for a long time, he will be unlikely to open up to you, not because he doesn't trust you so much as he doesn't have the know-how to open the emotional door inside. Someone who has a toxic file cabinet full of unprocessed memories and emotions unfortunately has both the good and bad memories locked in there, linked with the happy and the sad and the scared and the mad experiences they generated. These people fear that the sad and scared and mad, once opened, will be uncontainable and lead to continued stuffing. The problem with their reaction is that the cabinets eventually become overloaded and the memories jump out anyway. Consequently, the person is constantly having to work to manage the unprocessed emotions and his or her attached memories. This process takes up all the person's emotional energies.

William, our "let me be honest with you" guy from the last chapter, is a good example of a person who has stuffed his feelings. Unlike William, however, people who stuff their emotions don't usually make up lies and stories to cover their emotional unavailability. They simply deny that any feelings exist at all.

If you ask, "How do you feel about that?" the most common answer from a stuffer is a shrug and the comment "I don't know." This isn't a lie. Stuffers genuinely don't know how they feel about what you've asked or about anything else, for that matter. Feelings simply don't exist. People who have developed the habit of stuffing their emotions believe they're just fine and that it's the rest of the world that's nuts.

If you are in a relationship with someone who stuffs his or her emotions, you will hear a lot of denial of feelings. You'll also observe a lot of behavior designed to avoid making any emotional contact with others. This behavior might take the form of joking or teasing so that nothing ever gets too serious. It might mean lots of startling subject changes—one minute you're talking about love and commitment and then bang! you're on to the score of the Yankees game. Emotion stuffing might also show up as angry outbursts every time you try to talk about emotions or feelings. There may be many stormy departures followed by absolute sealed-up calm as though nothing happened.

For the stuffer, nothing did happen. He or she had one

brief flash of emotion, which sealed up instantly before it was processed either internally or externally.

What you will not get is any sense of connection. It's like looking into a black mirror—nothing comes back to you. No matter how hard you work to make the connection, you will continue to get nothing in return because you don't have the keys to the file room where it's all being carefully held. Your partner is spending all his or her emotional energy to keep those files sealed up tight—even while everything might be leaking out anyway.

For a stuffer, the process of healing means venturing into the file room, opening those drawers, and looking at what's in the files. This journey will be less threatening if accompanied by a therapist who can help the stuffer become acquainted with himself or herself as an emotional person. This kind of exploration is difficult without therapeutic support. It would be like someone who has never been to the Amazon leading a tour there—if you don't know what you're looking for, the journey takes much longer, is much scarier, and isn't as thorough or as interesting.

The memories a person finds hidden in the toxic files require processing. The joy-filled memories will need less work; negative memories might require some management and here a therapist's help is invaluable as well.

If a stuffer doesn't explore those toxic files and process the contents and you're around for the explosion when it finally all comes apart, you will see a great deal of raw emotion, much of it fear. None of it will make much sense.

# STUFFERS CHECKLIST

☐ Limited or nonexistent emotional presence

☐ Few memories of emotions

☐ Unresponsive to emotion in others

☐ Distant or cold

☐ Extremely tight boundaries

☐ Poor communication skills

# Chapter Eleven

# YES, BUT . . .

## You, Me, and All the Other Bad Stuff in the World

Your office friend comes to you looking for help to work out her relationship with her boyfriend, the apparent poster boy of problems. But because you are a solution-focused, caring, and helpful person, you listen carefully, do some thinking, and offer a suggestion.

"It sounds as though he's really insecure about your commitment. Maybe if you reassure him that you're not planning to leave, he'll feel better," you say.

"Yes, but if I do that, he'll think I'm pressuring him." She gives you that wounded puppy look, so you try again.

"Well, maybe you could tell him you care about him and have noticed that he seems to be worried about something. That would encourage him to talk to you."

"Yes, but if I do that, he'll think I'm watching him too closely." She smiles bravely and fixes you with an expectant gaze.

Now you're starting to get a little frustrated. "Well, how about asking him if he's upset about something?" you ask tersely.

"Yes, but if I do that . . ."

You have entered the "yes, but" zone, a place in which you have been put in charge of someone else's problems but have no power to solve them and are locked forever in offering solutions that are rejected. This is a wonderful example of a no-win situation.

The first thing to understand is that you are not responsible to fix this! You didn't break it, you can't fix it!

The second thing to understand is that this is a setup. The person asking for your advice doesn't really want to find a solution. What she does want is to ventilate, complain, get sympathy, feel sorry for herself, and affirm that someone cares for her. This is the relationship she is seeking and you are the partner of the moment.

Over time you will discover that this friend has a circle of partners of the moment among whom she circulates, always seeking advice and never taking it. Your job in the relationship is to come up with new answers and suggestions that will affirm her by demonstrating that she has your attention and caring.

The requests for advice will come on different topics— boyfriend/girlfriend, aging parents, adolescent children, money (a real time bomb), health. It doesn't matter what the topic. The fact that there is a topic makes these affirmation seekers once again feel connected with someone. But remember, no matter how good your suggestions and advice are and no matter how hard you work to come up with the perfect solution, you will always be met with "yes, but. . . ."

The need to "yes, but" arises in people who have extremely low self-esteem and don't believe they deserve to have a relationship based on their own merits. Instead, they believe they must have an excuse to make a connection with someone they value. The person with low self-esteem, however, is not interested in change because that's too threatening. He may actually not have the problem he presents. Therefore, he has to give you a reason why your solutions won't work because he doesn't have the courage to tell you there really isn't a problem (or that he really doesn't want to solve it). To make matters worse, he probably doesn't realize consciously that he is doing this.

I'm not talking about mutual venting between friends,

in which each of you tries out solutions by bouncing them off one another to see how they sound, then picks them apart to see how they hold up. The "yes, but" person is seeking solutions to problems she doesn't want to solve simply to keep you interested. At the core of this is the fact that she doesn't believe she's interesting enough to warrant your friendship without an excuse.

What hooks you into this relationship is your own ego. Most people like to be asked for advice. It makes us feel valuable and smart and worthwhile. When someone responds with a "yes, but," at first it seems like shorthand for "that's a really great idea and I would do it in a minute, but you don't understand my idiot boyfriend who is the problem here," and not shorthand for "I don't really have a significant problem that I couldn't solve myself, but what I really want is a relationship with you and I don't think you would like me if I were just myself." Therefore, when we hear the first "yes, but," it works to hook us more rather than send us backing politely away as we redouble our efforts to find the "right" solution.

A branch of the "yes, but" personality is the person who catastrophizes. Helen is the mother of two active, challenging adolescent girls who are about eighteen months apart in age. She first began coming to see me when the girls were twelve and almost fourteen, and every session she would talk about what a challenge these two kids were. They were *always* in trouble at school. They *never* followed the rules. They *always* caused her immense emotional pain with *every single terrible* choice they made. Each week there was a new problem with the girls, and I began to wonder if perhaps Helen had Rosemary's Babies. She began to ask about residential treatment programs for the girls, so I suggested that she send them to one of my colleagues for a neutral assessment.

My colleague is a wizard with kids. He is able to get inside their heads quickly and creates a mutually respectful environment in which they can talk openly to him. He had four sessions with the girls, then we consulted with Helen present. My colleague asked a lot of questions of her, then finally said, "I'm mystified here and wonder if I saw the same girls you're describing. What I saw was a pair of smart, pretty, active teenagers who are doing what smart, active adolescents do: trying to figure out how the world works on their own terms."

He then asked Helen about specific instances that she had complained bitterly about to me when we had met privately and which he'd heard about from the girls. One particular episode sticks out in my memory. He asked, "On the day the girls missed the school bus, how did they get home?"

I remembered Helen taking a whole session to talk about the girls hitchhiking and being picked up by a truck driver who could have been a murderer-rapist-child molester-kidnapper. She had been agitated and tearful. When my colleague asked about the incident, she replied, "Well, I think you're talking about the day they got a ride home with our neighbor in his big truck. They should have called me from school and I grounded them for that."

I was staring at her. "You knew the driver?" I finally managed to ask.

"Yes, didn't I tell you that?"

My colleague pointed out that the girls had told him that Helen had been "hysterical" and had called the police because they'd arrived home fifteen minutes late. They had reported that Helen had insisted she had to go to the emergency room for some "nerve medicine," and that the ER doctor had refused to give her drugs and told her she needed therapy. When Helen had told me the story, she'd left out the part about the emergency room too.

I was angry with Helen because I felt betrayed. She had used our trust relationship to hook me with stories that didn't match reality and asked for my support for something that wasn't a truthful account. I told Helen I felt our relationship had been compromised by her choice to exaggerate and she reacted immediately by bursting into tears and sobbing, appealing tearfully to my colleague to convince me not to dump her.

Helen is a catastrophizer. She creates catastrophes where they don't exist in order to solidify connections with significant people. As with anyone who exaggerates or lies, Helen would often get confused and not remember the details of what emergency she had reported at what time and to whom. This style also comes from low self-esteem and creates the same kind of confusion as the "yes, but" style does for the listener. I offered to continue to work with Helen, but my condition was that she had to report things precisely as they had happened so we could work on real issues—first among them her self-esteem. I should note that at the time she left therapy because she was moving, I still didn't really trust her reports. I was never able to be 100 percent sure she was giving me an accurate picture, though she did manage to get to what I figured was a 90 percent confidence level with me. Ninety percent, however, isn't a good foundation for a trusting, growing relationship.

Helen's need to make a connection by creating a bigger problem than actually existed gave her a complicated parenting style. Her kids were constantly having to assess reality versus their mom's version of reality and then figure out which was the more real. Reality is the casualty in a relationship with a person who is either a "yes, but" or a catastrophizer.

Healing from a betrayed relationship requires a rebuilding of trust in the relationship as well as working on self-esteem issues. If you are in one of these relationships, it's very important to keep your boundaries tight and to confront things that do not match with your observations or that seem evasive. Be clear that the relationship *can* exist without an excuse or exaggeration.

## "YES, BUT" CHECKLIST

☐ Has low self-esteem

☐ Seeks advice constantly

☐ Devalues or ignores advice

☐ Connects through problems

☐ Catastrophizes

☐ Maintains poor boundaries

❖

# Chapter Twelve

# THE ONE-WAY MIRROR
## Narcissists

*P*arker, a client of mine, provides a good example of the self-focused, misplaced, and misinterpreted emotions narcissists experience. If you were to meet him—tall, late thirties, jock type, handsome face, expensive suits and silk ties, oozing executive confidence—you might be instantly charmed. He looks you directly in the eye, seems to be listening intently, smiles at the right time, nods where you would expect.

He came into therapy originally because his wife, to whom he had been married for more than ten years, had recently told him that she was tired of waiting for him to learn how to connect with her and had decided she wanted a divorce. Parker was completely mystified and very tearful.

Parker was the king of mixed messages. His eyes would fill with tears as he talked about being repeatedly abandoned by his successful father, yet he was unable to see how he similarly abandoned his own four sons and wife to go off to spend extensive time alone on his houseboat on the Mississippi River.

Parker would also become tearful when he talked about how desperately he wanted to preserve his marriage. Never mind the fact that he was going out to local bars to meet women. He was genuinely surprised when I told him, *firmly*, that marriage and dating are mutually exclusive and that if he wanted to try to get his wife back, he needed to stop picking up other women.

Parker knew he should be feeling something—probably because that's all we'd worked on for our first three sessions—but he had no idea *what* he should be feeling or toward whom. It was as though his emotions were wired with all the wrong things connected. I had a sense he was trying to align with me by coming up with the "right answer."

Parker was completely unable to connect his body emotion—the experience—with the heart emotion—the feeling. He couldn't do this for his own emotions so he certainly couldn't do it when observing the emotions of others. It never crossed his mind that the other people who were involved in these complicated and self-focused relationships of his had emotional lives, expectations, hopes, and dreams.

Parker couldn't connect with his wife's isolation and pain because he couldn't connect with his own. He was able to recognize the mad and argumentative parts of their relationship, not from an emotional perspective but because they were loud, vivid, and uncomfortable for him. What he couldn't do was complete the picture to see the pain he'd caused her.

When I told him what I thought she might be feeling, given the circumstances, he was first puzzled, then angry, and finally the tears flowed again. When I asked him why he was crying his response was, "She must think I'm an asshole!" We spent the rest of the session trying to connect *his* self-focused assessment with *her* emotions.

Parker's motivation was self-gratification. Parker wanted to feel good all the time, and that's what got him into trouble. Parker's focus on himself combined with his funky wiring between conduct and emotions and his inability to recognize his own or others' emotions made him seem malicious to people who were connected with their emotions. If one is connected with his emotions, he doesn't make the damaging choices Parker-types make.

Once more: this is an explanation, not an excuse. Parker's lack of recognition of his impact on other people didn't mean the other people weren't damaged and shouldn't feel pain. You can imagine what his wife and the other women he met in his bar forays must have been feeling while he floundered around in his emotional dark.

Having a relationship with someone who's totally immersed in a relationship with himself or herself is frustrating and painful. It's also important to recognize that the person trying to make the relationship work probably didn't come to this point without baggage! So what's in it for that person? What needs is he or she getting met by engaging in this sort of frustration? To change and grow, people must look at how they got where they are, and they must *want* to change. Otherwise they will continue to get hurt.

How could Parker do all those terrible things and not have a clue what his wife and others were really feeling? *Narcissistic people process what they see in you in the mirror of themselves.*

Let me explain that statement. Narcissists lack an internal feedback system. They have to rely on strictly external signals to determine the impact of their behavior and to develop a sense of an emotional life. The external signals come from the people around them, but, remember, each of us filters our experiences through our own particular bias and perception. Therefore, the narcissist is using external signals to establish a guide to interpret the emotions he or she sees in others, but first he has to run them through a self-focused, childish set of filters. Thus the connections made are a distorted mirror of the world.

Let me add that this is not a conscious process but the way in which the narcissist has learned to adapt. It's rather like an old friend of mine, a martial arts expert who won many titles in competitions of his specialty, which involved fighting with sticks. In the competition, points were acquired for a hitting gesture that stopped just short of contact. The closer the stop, the higher the points. My friend always scored very high. What almost no one knew was that he had lost an eye in childhood. He had been so clever in his adaptation to depth perception with one eye—a very difficult task—that no one could perceive his disability.

Emotional adaptation is a double-edged sword. It allows the person to function in the world, which is good. But the way in which he or she functions is damaged, so it becomes damaging to the self and to others. The narcissist becomes so able to mirror the emotions of others and to create the illusion of emotional presence that he or she is rarely forced to connect. This illusion keeps the narcissist in damaging patterns and behaviors and keeps spreading the frustration to those around him or her.

The narcissist is a highly skilled observer of others. That observation intensity alone creates a problem of deception for the potential partner because the observation feels like an intense connection. The nonnarcissist then begins to build on what he or she believes is a heightened level of interest on the part of the narcissist, creating goals and plans around that misinterpretation.

Let me give you an example. Caroline had fallen in love with August in college. He was the prototypical handsome football star and she was the fabled small-town girl with stars in her eyes. When they married, she believed her dreams had come true.

Caroline reported to me that she had some concerns when she was pregnant with their first child. August booked a four-week trip to Canada to go fishing during the time the baby would be born. Caroline had many more concerns during her troubled second pregnancy with twins. During that time August dropped her off at the hospital when she went into early labor. He went to play golf while she had a late-term miscarriage. Then, after the births of two more children, August told Caroline he wanted nothing to do with their second and third children, didn't believe they were his, and wasn't sure whether he'd support them.

As their nineteen-year marriage went along, August was

verbally and emotionally abusive—demeaning and debasing Caroline no matter what she did. He also became physically aggressive and sexually abusive. Caroline told me in her sessions, through many tears, that August had told her that all wives exchanged sex for household money and if she wouldn't give him oral sex, he wouldn't give her money for groceries.

Still she believed she loved him deeply because he always seemed to know what she wanted. As we worked together, she began to see that it wasn't August recognizing what she wanted and working to provide it for her but August reflecting through Caroline what he wanted and convincing her it was her idea. He had a perfect mirror of Caroline and used it to manipulate her to get what he wanted.

This skill of projecting their own desires into the behavior patterns of their partners is another adaptive skill of narcissists. Because they lack the ability to connect with other people, they can't see that they could simply ask for what they need and be granted it.

If you think about it, from childhood most people learn, with varying degrees of success, that if they ask for something reasonable they will get it. Narcissists don't grow up with that belief. They are raised to believe that in order to get what they want, they must manipulate both the situation and the people in it. To do that, they must be able to read others accurately and recognize their soft spots. Those soft spots then become the focus of the pressure narcissists apply.

This need to manipulate is a reaction to mixed messages the narcissist got from parents and other family members when he or she was a little kid. An example of this type of message would be when a parent tells a child, "You're the most wonderful kid in the world," and then proceeds to ignore all the child's wants and needs.

Let's go back to August for a minute. His father was a well-known, successful businessman. He would take his two sons to business meetings and civic organization events and present them as leaders of the future. August revealed this one day when talking about his father. He said, "My dad treated us like he treated his expensive car. We were his proudest possessions and we had to live up to that." When I asked him how he accomplished that, August replied, "It was different every day. I never knew what he expected except that I'd better be perfect most of the time. I got really good at being perfect, but I was never perfect enough. My dad would always find something to criticize."

August and his brother both got the clear message from their dad that their only value was what they could do to make him look good. Their focus became pleasing the dad, and since the dad didn't come with clear instructions, they had to watch him carefully to try to figure out what he would want even before he knew he wanted it. They would then, of course, be wrong. This cycle is typical of the mixed messages and unspoken demands that lead to the narcissistic personality later in life.

First, the child becomes very externally focused on interpreting the signals and messages of the parents and fails to develop an internal feedback loop in which she can reliably assess the world on her own terms. Second, the only reality she comes to trust is her own, which often doesn't match the reality anyone else sees.

This response is partly because this reality is that of the child. Children are very self-focused—how does the world affect me, not how do I affect the world. Instead of making the usual transition from the childish how the world affects me to how I affect the world, which usually happens in adolescence, the narcissist remains locked in the childish view. Freud called this arrested development.

When that childish self-reference enters the world of adult relationships, nonnarcissistic adults get caught up in the close inspection and misinterpret it as interest. Meanwhile, the narcissist remains externally focused, locked off from his or her true feelings, and only interested in the childish goal of total self-gratification. This difference of goals re-creates the mixed messages and misinterpretations from the narcissist's relationship with his or her parents and extends them to significant others.

The ultimate goal for narcissists is to feel something. Often the assumption they make is that if they are gratified, they are feeling something. That's why their focus on self-gratification is so complete. It's the way to provide them with a connection they can recognize.

Sometimes the narcissist will be able to reach a point where he or she begins to connect with feelings, and often the first feeling is one of emotional emptiness. If you think about it, this is a pretty uncomfortable first feeling to engage, and it often sends the client flying out the door— sometimes never to return. I try hard to help a client work through this initial feeling and stay with the experience long enough to let it grow into more of a range of emotions.

The emptiness, although scary for the person feeling it, is a good sign that healing of the childhood chaos is beginning to happen. We work from the spot of feeling the emptiness and then begin to put emotions into that emptiness. This way the narcissistic person can begin to experience an emotional life and develop an internal feedback loop.

If you are in a relationship with someone who has a narcissistic style and you decide that there's the seed of possibility of change and you are willing to take your chances on being hurt or abandoned, you will need to be consistent, predictable, and clear about your feelings and needs. It can be hard work and has a low probability of success. Unfortunately, the majority of narcissists have little interest in changing their style and will most often choose to abandon you if you seem to be demanding something they are unwilling to give.

Recognize that you deserve to have a full and connected relationship. You do not deserve to be in the role of provider of gratification for someone who will not even appreciate the sacrifice you're making. If you decide to give the narcissist a chance to change, keep your eyes wide open and make the window of opportunity a limited one so you won't be destroyed in the process.

Remember: you are not the problem and you're not in charge of fixing something you didn't create!

# NARCISSISTS CHECKLIST

☐ Gratification-focused

☐ Unable to make emotional connection with others

☐ Unable to recognize emotions of others

☐ Charming, confident, manipulative

☐ Self-focused

☐ Sees others only in the mirror of themselves

☐ Observant of others

☐ Highly defended: extremely tight boundaries for self, none for others

*Chapter Thirteen*

⊸◈⊷

# LET ME FIX IT FOR YOU
# The Codependency Cage

"*D*on't worry about a thing. I'll take care of everything."

Those words should strike terror in your heart. That's because such a statement is not usually an offer of help. It's the announcement of an invasion. The helper seems to want to be supportive and provide assistance but the real motivation is to be able to control you.

Please note: not all offers of help are attempts to control. That's why the helper's offer works. It starts insidiously. "You have to clean your apartment rather than go somewhere with me? I'll be happy to come help you and that way we can do both." Is there any person who wouldn't jump at help with tidying up the pit? So you open the door a crack. The crack widens with, "I'm doing my laundry anyway, so why don't I just take care of yours?" Then, "Why don't you just let me take care of that formal dinner for your boss?" and pretty soon, your life is no longer your own.

Remember the old saying, "There is no free lunch"? Well, there is also no free cleaning, laundry, or dinner for the boss. With each bit of assistance, you are surrendering more of your power and the "helper" is gathering more steam. By the time you start to feel uncomfortable with the

- 155 -

level of invasion and attempt to set limits, the willing helper suddenly is the wounded, abused victim who has been taken advantage of by the mean old opportunist—you. In order to salvage your self-esteem and personal feelings of worth, you apologize profusely for trying to be so foolish as to take your power back and then you're really in the soup. Welcome to the codependency cage.

This behavior of creating a trap for another person by being more present in their lives than is reasonable is a form of codependency—with a bit of a twist. Usually when people talk about codependency, they are addressing the behavior of the codependent, not the effect it has on the target of their attention. Codependents could be characterized as persons who believe they can make an emotional connection with another by reading the other person's mind and anticipating his or her every need. It's a behavior designed to make the codependent feel safe.

"I know exactly what you need," they begin right before they come thundering through your life, fixing things that aren't broken, and intruding on your space and privacy with a vengeance. "Don't worry about a thing. I'll take care of everything for you." By taking care of everything, the codependent person is able to create a world in which the experiences of the target person are limited to those that the codependent can control. From this control, false as it may be, codependents are able to tell themselves they are safe in the world, that they can never be abandoned or hurt.

Safety issues pervade a lot of dysfunctional behaviors. *Safety is the knowledge that you have the power of choice in all circumstances.* You can see from this definition that people who feel unsafe are those who have learned from life experiences that their choices can be stripped away.

Remember, choice is power and lack of choice is powerlessness. Therefore, people who have in the past had their choices stripped away often become people who have a very strong interest in keeping their power. There are healthy ways to do that, but generally people who have experienced power outages and haven't dealt with the effects of those outages don't choose the healthy ways of setting boundaries and being assertive. Instead they put their emotional energy into trying to control another person, believing that if they have control over that person, he or she will not be able to abandon, abuse, hurt, or in some way take advantage of them. The fallacy in this thinking is that no one can control another person completely. I spend a lot of time working with the parents of my adolescent clients on just this subject!

Kitty was raised by a narcissistic father. Her training as his daughter made her vulnerable to the two narcissistic men she later married. She came to therapy after her second divorce wanting to heal as well as to learn how to prevent herself from choosing another damaging relationship.

Kitty is a bright, funny woman who has been extremely successful in her own business. Two of her three sons were athletic and academic standouts and were in prestigious colleges on scholarships. Her third son, Scott, lived with her and had other interests that kept Kitty busy meeting with probation officers and the disciplinary dean at the high school Scott attended sporadically.

Kitty paged me frequently with complaints about Scott, agonizing about his exploits and asking for my approval of her elaborate plans to "teach him a lesson this time." She took away his car, his bike, his skateboard, his telephone, his shoes, and his computer. She bolted the windows shut in his room and put a lock on the outside of his bedroom door. When he left home to go to school, however, Scott invariably found trouble. Even when Kitty changed her hours at work so she could take him to school and pick him up, he found ways to break the rules.

Each time Scott got into trouble, Kitty would drop into her fix-it mode. She'd hire a lawyer, call the probation officer, talk to the judge, or negotiate with the cops.

Each time she paged me to run her solution by me, I would tell her the same thing: "Scott will only learn his lessons when you stop trying to control him and fix the world. You must let him face the music and work it out for himself."

She couldn't bring herself to let Scott learn from his bad choices. Scott knew Kitty would bail him out, so he never tried to make better choices. Instead, his choices became worse and worse and the legal tangles more intricate.

The day after his eighteenth birthday, Scott made another bad choice and was arrested. This time, however, he went into the adult criminal system rather than the juvenile courts. Kitty was beside herself when Scott's bail was set far above what she could afford. Feeling that she was out of options, she called Scott's father.

"Tom not only wouldn't help me," she reported tearfully, "but he told me to let Scott take the consequences of his behavior. I can't do that!"

I told her I agreed with Tom. Kitty was furious but she was forced to let him suffer the consequences because there was no place to get the money.

When Scott got out of jail, Kitty was surprised to find him packing. In a panic, she asked him where he was going.

"I'm going to live with Dad," he replied. "He lets me be a man."

Kitty never learned to let go—a really hard lesson. Instead, she tried to exercise control over Scott by fixing. That's manipulation. The sad truth is that although manipulation may work initially, as the targeted person feels more and more trapped, he or she pulls away and takes back his or her power. Scott kept trying to feel powerful by choosing to act up and be in trouble. It was his way of declaring his independence from his mother's intrusions.

Scott's attempts to be independent made Kitty feel all the more unsafe and her response was to increase efforts to keep him on the string. "I'll take care of it. I can be the perfect mom by fixing everything."

In any relationship, if one person seems to be doing all the giving, it creates a sense of obligation even if the helping behavior was unsolicited. The helper gives and gives and gives while closing in tighter and tighter. Meanwhile, the person whose life is being fixed begins to feel like a jerk because this nice person has done so much for him or her.

The helpee owes the helper so much and keeps asking himself or herself, "Gee whiz, why am I kicking this person who's obviously just trying to do what's right for me?"

The helpee is not a jerk. The helpee did not take advantage of some helpless victim. The helpee didn't start this. The mistake the helpee made was to be too nice by accepting what seemed to be graciously offered gifts.

Remembering this will help: the gifts the codependent offers are gaily and brightly wrapped and tied up with a bazillion strings. The objective of those strings is to tie you into a relationship in which you will get lots of strings but probably no real emotional connection of any kind.

Codependents' need for safety dictates that they will never make themselves emotionally available in any relationship. It's too vulnerable a position. Their safety alarms tell them that emotional availability leads to vulnerability, which leads to unsafe relationships, so they armor themselves behind a flurry of activity and outwardly directed behavior.

People who have been victimized feel unsafe when they feel vulnerable. Many people who behave in a codependent way have been emotionally victimized or abandoned in the past. Emotional abuse occurs when someone you love and trust betrays you by physically or emotionally harming you. Your brain neatly stores all the experiences of your life, complete with emotions attached. Thus, the abuse gets connected to feelings, and emotions suddenly become bad or dangerous or unsafe. Emotions are emotions. They are neither bad nor good, they simply are. The healing for the emotionally abused person comes from learning how to make healthy connections that do not require manipulation.

Before you get caught in the I'll-fix-it-for-you trap yourself and try to repair the codependent, remember that he or she is carefully armored against anyone getting too close. Defense mechanisms will quickly kick in. You'll find yourself right back in the codependent cage in quick order. Keep reminding yourself: I didn't break you, I don't have to fix you!

Relationships work best when both partners contribute roughly equally and each partner takes responsibility for his or her own mistakes and takes action to correct them.

---

## CODEPENDENTS CHECKLIST

☐ Controls by helping

☐ Connects by controlling

☐ Fears abandonment

☐ Offers assistance that turns into intrusion

☐ Has no boundaries

☐ Fears vulnerability

# Chapter Fourteen

# 'HOLICS

*J*f you are in a relationship with someone who has a relationship with a substance or a negative behavior, you have a rival with whom you cannot compete. You need to give some long, hard thought to the relationship and to your expectations about the relationship; you need to make a careful assessment of what really exists versus what you would like to have exist.

I am not a twelve step–style practitioner. I believe people become addicted to addictive substances (crack, cocaine, heroin, amphetamines, and, in some cases, alcohol), but I don't believe people become addicted to behaviors (sex, gambling, shopping, etc.). Those are choices, not diseases. I believe some twelve-step programs work for some people, but I don't believe any one program style fits everyone.

When I work with someone who is making repetitive behavioral choices such as binge drinking, marijuana smoking, overworking, overeating, gambling, or shopping compulsively, I don't use an addiction-model approach. I try to find what problem people are trying to solve with the behavior, and then we try to find other ways to solve the problem.

When you are in a relationship with someone making repetitive bad choices, however, it's not your job to be a therapist; it's your job to be a partner, and that's where things get fuzzy. As you try to get your needs met in the relationship, your partner focuses his or her attention on the relationship with the bad behavior. Because this behavior is a choice, the probability for change of behavior and focus certainly exists if your partner is willing to make that commitment.

If, on the other hand, you're in a relationship with someone who's flat-out addicted—to heroin, cocaine, crack, methamphetamine, alcohol, etc.—you are in a far more difficult situation with a far higher probability that the relationship will fail.

Partners who indulge in repetitive behavior are difficult because you not only must deal with the usual relationship challenges, but you also have to compete with the repetitive behavior for your partner's attention. If you challenge this competition, you are seen as trying to interfere with your partner's ability to make his or her own choices. Your partner may see you as the problem. This view can lead to some major battles as you try to hold onto your own turf and your partner tries to keep things balanced and still get everything he or she wants. In the process of the addicted partner getting everything he or she wants, however, the probability is high that *you* will be the one who makes the sacrifices.

If you are making sacrifices so that your partner can continue making repetitive, negative choices, you are part of the problem. Sacrifices might seem like the only way to save the relationship, but in the long run you will play second fiddle to the negative choices and get nothing positive in return. That doesn't sound like much of a relationship to me!

If you are in a relationship with someone who is addicted, you will never be first choice. Period. The primary relationship, the relationship the partner will choose and seek again and again at any expense, will be the relationship with the addictive substance. You are not strong enough to overcome the power of the substance. You cannot compete successfully. You will end up hurt and probably broke. These relationships need to be put on hold until the partner is clean and sober, and you cannot force your partner to make that choice.

I can't stress this strongly enough. Be very clear about the difference between *behavioral choices*, which can be managed and negotiated, and *true addictions*, which can't. If your partner is addicted, you can't fix him until he's ready to fix himself. You can't make her get ready to fix herself. Your partner is the only person with the power to make these changes. You will not be able to make anything happen unless your partner is ready to make it happen. It's not your fault. You didn't break them, you can't fix them.

If, however, your partner is clean and sober or is willing to stop making negative choices, you can work through restructuring your relationship in a healthy way and find a better balance for the two of you. If your partner is not willing to give up the substances, you don't really have a relationship. You're simply an accessory. I know that's painful news but it's less painful than living a lie where you pretend you have a relationship while your partner is focused only on his or her substance of choice.

---

## 'HOLICS CHECKLIST

☐ Primary relationship is with the substance

☐ You make the sacrifices

☐ No realistic emotional connection

☐ Poor boundaries

☐ You will always be in second place to the substance

☐ Many promises of change with no action

*Chapter Fifteen*

# THE ROCK
# AND THE ROCKET

*H*e likes to lie on the couch, a bowl of popcorn balanced carefully on his tummy, watching his favorite sports team. He's content, at peace, at home. She likes to be on the go, every minute filled with some sort of activity. She's on the phone while she's doing the laundry and baking a six-layer cake for her kid as she's planning the opening of her new business. When the two of them talk, he's slow and deliberate with a low level of excitement. She's jumping from subject to subject, filling the space between them with chatter and conversation, which may or may not be related to the subject at hand. She prefers spending money and being on the go. He's a saver who likes to stay home. She fills her emotional world with activity; he fills his with quiet but neither fills the world with the other.

She's a rocket, lighting up the sky with her brilliant sparkle and surprising booms and pops. He's a rock, anchored deeply in the earth with no interest in flying.

How did these two end up together? If we look at the obvious, each person contributes something the other lacks: she gets stability from him and he gets excitement from her. In both cases, the stability and the excitement are lacking but so is the internal emotional connectedness to create them.

I sometimes tell clients that the process of therapy is a bit like peeling an onion: first you work your way through that crackly, papery outer layer. That's the issue that gets you into therapy in the first place—the motivator that shoves you through the door of the office. The next layers are increasingly thick and filled with juice. The thickness is the complexity—and the juices make you cry!

Peeling the onion a bit here, the deeper reason the rock and the rocket end up with one another is a bit more complex. My theory is that this is a case where people are used as medication by one another.

The rocket can be either male or female as can the rock. Don't be misled by the genders in my example. The point is that the rocket is often someone who has pretty wild mood swings. The rocket might even have bipolar disorder (what used to be called manic depression) or what's called cyclothymia (literally, "cycling moods" in Greek), which clinicians sometimes call baby bipolar. These disorders are characterized by mood swings between deep depressions and bursts of wild energy that usually don't have much direction but have lots of drive.

The rocket needs to find a way to anchor itself and to feel normal, and that's sometimes accomplished by being in a relationship with someone who is slow and solid. In essence, the rock's very *rock*ness is what the rocket needs to feel safe.

The rock, on the other hand, is often someone who is depressed. The rocket brings that buzz of excitement into the rock's life, enabling the rock to rise up out of the depression. I've also seen cases of rocks who had been using stimulants (cocaine, amphetamines) and then had quit. The rocket came into their lives and filled the excitement and stimulation void left by the departure of the drugs.

The twist here is that the rocket resents the limitation the rock imposes on high flying, and the rock resents the rocket's impulsiveness and energy. In other words, the very thing that draws them together is the thing they resent the most and against which they rebel the hardest.

This conflict of objectives is also at the root of the emotional unavailability between these two partners. They both hold back from one another to protect themselves. Holding back produces more strenuous rock and rocket behaviors. It's a vicious circle.

Jeff came into therapy to "try to understand his wife." When I read that on his intake information sheet, I sighed, thinking that here was another guy who wanted his wife to be the problem. As it turned out, he had a point.

Jeff and his wife Marla had been high school sweethearts. He was a rough, quiet guy who'd gone into the family's heavy equipment business. He liked talking to people about machines and liked being around machines, so he enjoyed his job a lot. He also made a lot of money doing it.

Marla had never been able to settle down into a job. She'd gone to beauty school, dental assistant school, bartender's school, medical assistant school, and business college. She'd worked as a waitress, bartender, telephone operator, flight attendant, nurse's aid, dental assistant, medical secretary, store cashier, and commissioned salesperson for a variety of firms. When Jeff first came in, Marla was selling cars. During the year Jeff was in therapy, his wife changed jobs about twenty times more.

Marla also had problems settling into her role as mother to their four-year-old daughter, Melissa. Marla loved to dress Melissa up in a junior version of her own outfit and then take the child to bars or other adult spots.

Money was another problem between the couple. Jeff made an excellent salary and had quite a large family fortune to draw on. The couple lived in a 5,000-square-foot house on a lake, and they both drove new vehicles. Marla loved to shop and did so often. It was not unusual for her monthly credit card purchases to approach $10,000. When Jeff attempted to set limits, Marla acquired cards he didn't know about. One month her cellular phone bill was $3,000.

Although she did things that infuriated him, Jeff and Marla also had good times together. Jeff said he loved Marla's spontaneity. He also admitted he felt "most alive" when he was with her. The problem was, however, that Marla's behavior was escalating as time went along. She was spending more, working less, drinking more, seeing less of Melissa, and being mad more often. Jeff had tried pleasing her, fighting with her, cutting off her credit cards, and demanding that Marla be in control, all with no effect.

Marla came in with Jeff. She was a tall, slim, beautiful woman whose internal engine ran very fast. As she sat, her foot jiggled, her hands were never still, and she blinked frequently. She seemed to have trouble keeping her focus on the topic at hand, changing subjects frequently. She felt the problem rested with Jeff whom she described as "a stick-in-the-mud who never wants to do anything but fall asleep sitting in his chair with the television on."

Anything Jeff brought up was his fault. Her spending was his fault because he was boring. Her drinking was his fault because he was boring. Her lack of connection with her daughter was his fault because he never let her be the parent.

Marla described a terrible childhood with an alcoholic father and a mentally ill mother. She described sexual, emotional, physical, and mental abuse. She talked about being abandoned alone in the house for days at a very early age while her mother was hospitalized and her father was drinking and staying with various women he knew. Her father had been killed in a car accident and her mother had committed suicide before Marla was out of high school, so she had raised herself. She said Jeff was the only sane spot in her crazy world at that time, but now he was boring.

Jeff agonized for months, trying to make a decision about what to do and trying to find the magic words or actions that would fix Marla. Marla continued to launch herself through life, acquiring new jobs and more debt and more trouble.

Finally one night Jeff paged me. He sounded very frightened and agitated as he described what Marla was doing. He said she was talking extremely rapidly and couldn't sit still. Jeff put her on the phone and Marla told me she was leaving immediately for Hollywood because she had been listening to a rock-and-roll song on the radio and heard the hidden message in the song that she would become a movie star if she could just get herself to Hollywood. She also said she knew the secret words to say to the head of the studio, which would let that person know she was the chosen one. She informed me that she was being held prisoner by Jeff and had no idea who he was.

I told Jeff to call the police and take her to the psych unit at the local hospital. There Marla was diagnosed with bipolar disorder. She had been in the midst of a manic phase when Jeff called me. (Sometimes people in a severe manic phase lose track of reality completely.) Marla was put on medication and released. The medication had no effect on her condition. She had another severe manic episode a short time later and was hospitalized again. By the time Jeff decided to end the marriage, Marla had been committed to the state hospital. Even then, he was torn between loving the excitement of Marla and hating her extremes of behavior.

This push-pull quality is enhanced by the inability of either partner to connect on an effective emotional level. The conflict and excitement of the rocket and the inertia of the rock take the place of true emotional connections between them. They can't let go of one another or take control of themselves.

These relationships are hard to change because they represent an intricate blend of behavior and chemical imbalances. Rockets are frequently bipolar; rocks are frequently clinically depressed. Both conditions can be helped by medication, but some bipolar people don't like the sense of flatness the medication produces and frequently resist taking it.

Each party in this type of couple has individual issues to work on before the relationship issues can be addressed. Often medication in combination with therapy can enhance individual work. Both partners must be willing to commit to change individually as well as in the relationship. It can be done, but it takes time and therapy and, most of all, a long-term commitment to the process.

If you're a rock, recognize that another person can't make you feel less depressed or give you more energy. If you're a rocket, understand that repetitive patterns of flying and crashing are no way to live. It is possible to live in the middle and still have fun!

## ROCK AND ROCKET CHECKLIST

☐ One partner is volatile, the other is quiet

☐ Partners "medicate" using one another

☐ Relationship is marked by conflict and chaos, which replace emotional connection

☐ Poor boundaries

☐ Much emotion, no connection

*Chapter Sixteen*

# EMOTIONALLY UNAVAILABLE PARENTS

*W*ithout question, the relationship with our parents is the most complicated of all our life relationships. It's what sets our feet on the emotional and psychological path we travel throughout our lives. It's the relationship that defines, in one way or another, all our other relationships, and it has profound pull on how we connect with our children.

Parents who are emotionally unavailable raise children who are emotionally unavailable. Remember Parker, the narcissist in Chapter 12? Parker's parents were very socially active when Parker and his siblings were young. He told me that he remembered his mother saying to him, "We spend more time with our friends because you kids will go away but our friends will be with us for life." Parker got the clear message that parents must choose between their friends and their kids. Not surprisingly, that was how Parker later approached his relationship with his own children, often choosing to spend time with his fishing buddies rather than his kids, even though his buddies often brought their kids along.

Many Baby Boomers are the children of people who were raised by people who were raised by Victorians. During the Victorian era, the rule was that children should be seen and not heard. Those Victorian grandparents were bound by strict cultural rules. Interpersonal warmth and connection with other people were seen as improper. People kept their distance, physically and emotionally.

Our parents, born as the rules were changing during the boom times of the twenties and raised in the thirties when economic hard times isolated people, came to their own parenthood with no clear style and no real rules about connections. As luck would have it, at just about that moment, along came B. F. Skinner and his most famous disciple, Dr. Benjamin Spock.

Skinner and Spock were behaviorists. Briefly, these theorists believe all behavior is created externally with no internal emotional input. Thus Dr. Spock recommended parenting that involved shaping a child's behavior by rewarding those behaviors that were deemed good and punishing those that were deemed bad. Because Spock and Skinner didn't recognize the internal process—the *emotional* process—no attention was given to making emotional connections with children. This behavioral perspective fit fine with a generation who had minimal emotional connection with its own Victorian parents. The unfortunate result has been that a large percentage of Baby Boomers have emotionally distant relationships with their parents.

A colleague of mine, Andrea Mullenbach, has much expertise working with elder clients. We have often talked about the emotional distance among so many people in our generation and their parents and how it seems to become more complicated as we all get older. Andrea suggests that this distance comes from two places: emotional unavailability in earlier life and a later-in-life gelling of that distance into personality styles that are angry and distant. She calls this "crystallized personality disorder," in which our parents become people we don't know and don't always like. Since we had a somewhat tenuous emotional connection to start with, these changes drive us further apart and make us more isolated emotionally from one another.

The people who comprise Generation X are happy to

point out that the Baby Boomers are not perfectly open and connected parents either. Many of my Generation X clients talk about feeling overparented by parents who were involved in everything they did, video cameras at the ready, but who didn't connect emotionally enough to understand their children's need for space and individuation. The parenting style of connection between Baby Boomers and their Generation X kids, then, continues to reflect the behaviorist perspective—the focus is on action and behavior, not on being and emotions.

Generation X is now entering the world of parenthood. Their experience has, in many cases, taught them emotional distance. It will be interesting to see, given our new focus on emotional connections in our culture, if they can be connected with their kids in a more appropriate and emotional way.

The parents about whom I'm most concerned, however, are the adolescent single moms who are having babies long before they are ready to be parents. I see many adolescents in my practice and I am very familiar with the angst of that time period. To add the incessant needs of a baby to the other pressures of that time of life creates terrible problems not only for the mother but also for the baby.

Often I see these young moms in the stores with their toddlers and I'm struck by how unhappy they look. The toddler is doing toddler things—screaming, demanding, whining—but the adolescent mom is still a kid too and doesn't know how to accept the child's need to do this; instead she feels threatened. She may lash out at the toddler verbally, and sometimes physically, creating an emotional distance from the child that I fear will last long into both their lives.

No parenting is going to be perfect. Perfection is not the human condition. But let me repeat: this is an explanation, not an excuse. I'm not suggesting that parents should be blamed for the emotional distances between themselves and their children. What I am suggesting is that we learn our style of emotional connection from our families of origin. The hope is that we don't perpetuate negative behavior.

Remember we have choice in all things in our lives. Just

because we have learned a particular style doesn't mean that has to be all we can learn. Understanding where we have come from is important, but it's not grounds for an indictment of our parents or grandparents. Neither is it grounds for an indictment of our children as they become parents or of the adolescent single moms who are struggling to learn how to be parents before they have learned how to be adults.

What understanding of our style of origin does is give us a foundation to look at our own choices and styles and make the necessary changes to form better emotional connections with everyone in our lives.

Kitty, whom we met in Chapter 13 when we looked at her codependent relationship with her son Scott, was the daughter of a highly successful father who built a multi-million-dollar manufacturing company from the ground up. Although he indulged his three daughters' every whim and gave them everything they wanted, he was rarely home. On the occasional evening when he would arrive at the house in time for dinner with the family, he would spend the mealtime interrogating the girls about their grades, dates, achievements, and goals. He showed no interest in them as emotional beings, but instead dismissed their needs for love as weakness.

Kitty has married a replica of her father twice. The first marriage lasted twenty years. Her three sons were born during that relationship.

Her first husband, Tom, was a highly successful businessman who was rarely home. She attempted to confront his approach to the relationship by insisting that they go to couples therapy and work on their issues. Tom found it impossible to see why she was upset. He pointed out that he gave her everything she wanted and provided money for all the things she and the kids wanted to do.

When their oldest son showed a talent for hockey, Tom suddenly became interested, traveling with the son's teams and taking Kitty and the other two boys along. He became obsessed with his son's hockey playing. When Kitty confronted him about this extreme focus, he told her he thought that was what she wanted.

After becoming completely fed up with Tom's emotional distance and narcissistic style, she divorced him. About a year after her divorce, she was working at a convention for her employer when she met Dave. He'd been a career military man, he told her, much decorated from his multiple tours in Vietnam. After leaving the military, he'd opened his own construction business, which he told her was very successful. His marriage of twenty years had ended at about the same time as Kitty's had.

Dave pursued her and for the first time, Kitty said, she felt as though she were important to the man in her life. She wanted to take it more slowly, but Dave was anxious to get married. Kitty felt she had found the right guy. Her sons liked Dave, though Scott and he had butted heads a few times. She felt Dave handled Scott's testing pretty well. Kitty was encouraged.

Within a month of marrying Dave, Kitty found out that his construction company wasn't at all as successful as he'd led her to believe. In one of her fix-it frenzies, she liquidated Scott's college fund and invested in Dave's business. Dave immersed himself in the business, abandoning Kitty and the boys. When she confronted him about his distance, he yelled and threatened. Dave refused to go to therapy to work on the distance in the relationship and wouldn't allow her to go to work on her issues.

After four years of increasing threats and financial losses, Kitty gave up on the relationship and came to therapy. After we worked on her issues with her son, we began to look at why letting go felt so unsafe to her. Kitty began to realize she feared letting go of her sons because she had never connected with her father or her husbands. She felt that if she let go of her children, she would be completely alone in the world.

Kitty worked hard on her anger at her father, finally dealing with the issue of his abandonment of her. She hadn't spoken to him in many years but decided to try to build a relationship as part of her healing. At first he was angry with Kitty because he believed she had abandoned him. I encouraged her to continue to make the connection and over time they began to have a relationship. It wasn't perfect, but it allowed them to connect.

The connection released Kitty's need to resolve this dilemma by working it out with a surrogate and opened the door for her to start an unencumbered relationship. She is presently dating a professor at one of the local universities. He has a balanced life with Kitty, friends, work, and hobbies. He has a good relationship with his own parents and with his kids. Kitty reports that he even has a good relationship with his former wife. Kitty is experiencing being a partner in a relationship for the first time and she reports that it feels good. She's also continuing to develop her connection with her father and to make appropriate connections with her sons.

Kitty chose her first two husbands on the basis of what she learned in her family of origin, but when that method didn't work, she was able to learn a new style.

## New Tools

Having new tools helps people change. You can think of your people skills as tools in your human tool kit. The more varied skills you have, the better your tools are.

The remainder of this book will help you add some new tools to your collection and give you ways to use them effectively. The good news is that if you have tools to help you get what you want in relationships, you will be better able to recognize the relationships that won't work (Kitty didn't find the professor when she first began to look for a fulfilling, healthy relationship) and know which relationships are worth working on and which people are able to change.

The tools will also help you tune up your skills and change those behaviors and beliefs that are getting in your way of finding a relationship that's not emotionally unavailable!

# Check Yourself Out First

What if you suspect you might be emotionally unavailable yourself? How would you know? That has a philosophical sound to it, sort of like the old "If a tree falls in the forest" question. Your question might be, "If I'm not connected to my emotions, how would I know I'm not connected to my emotions?"

Try the following quiz and see where you are on the scale of emotional unavailability.

---

## EMOTIONAL UNAVAILABILITY QUIZ

Rate yourself from 1 to 4 on each of the following questions.

1 = Never     2 = Sometimes     3 = Often     4 = Always

| | |
|---|---|
| 1. When I watch a movie, I really connect with the emotions of the characters. | 1  2  3  4 |
| 2. When people tell me they feel sad, I can share their emotion. | 1  2  3  4 |
| 3. When I look at my partner, I feel many things at different times. | 1  2  3  4 |
| 4. I get over being mad right away. | 1  2  3  4 |
| 5. I look forward to a long relationship with my partner. | 1  2  3  4 |
| 6. When I hear a happy song, I feel happy. | 1  2  3  4 |
| 7. I like to laugh and to cry. | 1  2  3  4 |
| 8. I can figure out everything my partner is feeling from his or her behavior. | 1  2  3  4 |

| | |
|---|---|
| 9. I tell people what my emotions are. | 1  2  3  4 |
| 10. When I feel scared, I am able to work through it. | 1  2  3  4 |
| 11. No matter who I'm with, I'm clear about who I am. | 1  2  3  4 |
| 12. I know my values and beliefs and I stick to them. | 1  2  3  4 |
| 13. I'm clear about my personal and relationship goals. | 1  2  3  4 |
| 14. I am able to talk to my partner about my feelings. | 1  2  3  4 |
| 15. I like to see emotions in others. | 1  2  3  4 |

Now add up your total score. If your score is:

1–15: Emotions are just a mysterious rumor to you and you need to work hard to find your emotional self.

16–30: You have some connection with your emotional life but spend a lot of time in the Gray Zone.

31–45: You're connected emotionally in several areas of your life, but there are things that make you run and hide.

46–60: You're plugged in. You know yourself emotionally and are able to recognize emotions in others.

Now that you know where you stand, the next step is to begin making some positive changes in the way you connect with other people. Remember, change can be uncomfortable no matter how positive the outcome, so don't rush yourself. Take time to let change become habit—and safe. That way you'll be more likely to incorporate the change into your life.

# Chapter Seventeen

# A FRAMEWORK FOR CHANGE AND GROWTH

*N*ow that we've looked at emotionally unavailable people and relationships and you've figured out where you stand emotionally, we can tackle gathering tools. Good tools help our partners and us to become emotionally available to one another and help us manage people who don't choose to change.

Change is a matter of choice and it's a choice only the person in need of change can make. No matter how much you'd like your partner to behave differently, the fact of the matter is that he or she may choose to stay that way. You can't make him or her move one micron unless he or she is ready. You are left with the obligation to make a choice for yourself: stick around and hope for the best or decide that the best may never be any better than it is and leave the relationship.

Recognize, too, that although it may be appealing to stick around and hope for the best, people will only choose to change when they get uncomfortable enough where they are. People who are emotionally cut off from themselves have developed so many coping techniques that they often take a very long time to get uncomfortable. You might find yourself waiting in vain for change that the emotionally unavailable person finds far too threatening.

However, if the emotionally unavailable person is willing to change or if it's a relationship that you cannot easily abandon—your parents, for example, or your kids—the key to opening up the emotional world is opening the lines of communication.

We don't learn much about communication skills and listening techniques in school or in our culture in general. The only way we learn how to communicate as adults is by what we see in our homes as we are growing up. If you grew up in a family where you had to yell to be heard, while your partner grew up in a family where emotional outbursts were rare to nonexistent, your divergent communication styles are going to get in the way of your communication. You'll struggle with what each of you believes is the correct way to do things. You may spend a lot of time wondering why your partner looks like a deer in headlights when you begin to air things in your way. Your partner may spend a lot of time misinterpreting your high-volume debate for angry yelling. Seems like there's a lot happening, right? What doesn't happen is communication.

There is a dimension that you may find helpful to consider every time you have an exchange, verbal or nonverbal, with anyone else: Emotional Location.

Emotional Location is the feelings perspective from which a person is operating at any given moment. The person or persons with whom you are communicating are also operating in their particular emotional position. Think of Emotional Location as a hopscotch layout with five primary boxes anyone might occupy emotionally at any time. The way in which communication develops has to do with the box the person with whom you are communicating occupies at that moment as well as the box you occupy yourself. People often shift boxes midcommunication without warning. But don't panic. When we finish, you'll be an expert in Emotional Location!

First let me define the communication unit that I call an

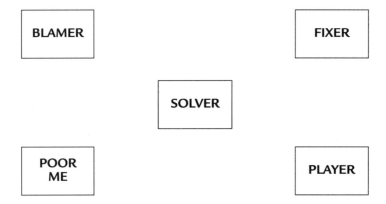

exchange. An exchange is any verbal or nonverbal communication between two or more persons. It can be as brief as a second or as long as hours or years; it can take place in person, by letter, on the phone, or via any other means of transmitting ideas. It can involve two people or millions or any number in between. An exchange can be one-sided (someone waving as they pass you, a teacher giving a lecture, or a television newscast, for example), two-sided (a conversation, an argument, a joke), or multisided (fans at a game, group discussions, congressional debates). It might be obvious that within the many-sided exchange, there could be a number of one- or two-sided exchanges. An exchange can be completely devoid of emotion or overflowing with feelings. It can be important or trivial. Exchanges are the foundation of communication and thus the foundation of relationships of all kinds. Exchanges are also the tools of Emotional Location.

## The Five Boxes of Emotional Location

First the bad news: of the five boxes, four are dysfunctional. I really don't like the term *dysfunctional* because it has become vague and overused. Clients come into my office and confide, "I come from a dysfunctional family," as though that not only explains everything I might need to know about the family but also is a dirty family secret. I'm never certain how they expect me to react. Dysfunction means different things to different people. One person might mean he comes from a family where people don't always get along with one another. A second person might mean that her family of origin is alcoholic or abuses drugs. A third person might mean he was ritually tortured. This broad application makes the word practically meaningless.

It's also judgmental. Clients who use the word say it almost in a whisper as though they are somehow in charge of how poorly their family manages emotional issues. People who feel ashamed of themselves in the context of their families and who own their family's craziness have trouble seeing themselves in a positive light and that makes it hard for them to give themselves permission to change and heal. *Dysfunctional* is overused in the media in talking about family, school, social, and work relationships. I've even heard whole nations referred to as dysfunctional!

In an effort not to contribute to the vague, overused, and judgmental career of the word *dysfunctional*, I'll give you my own definition: dysfunctional behavior interferes with growth, clarity of communication, and equitable conflict resolution. This behavior can take place in a relationship, family, or culture. Anything else deserves another name.

## Emotional Location Basics

Emotional Location is a tool you can use to understand your communication partner in a different way, one that will facilitate the communication process.

Remember that people choose their Emotional Location—and their behavior—for a reason. Whether or not you think it's a good reason, it serves a purpose for that person. Also remember that the choice is often made at a non-conscious level. That's why if you confront someone about his motive for behavior he may deny it and the denial will appear to be very sincere because the choice was not made consciously.

People most often choose their Emotional Location because it is a position in which they feel safe. To most people, feeling safe usually represents being in control, and that's not illogical. The problem arises because what seems safe and in control to one person may seem very unsafe and out of control to the other party in the exchange.

Greg and Lola are clients who have different views of what represents financially responsible behavior. Both are professionals who make excellent incomes, but Lola constantly worries about money. Greg, on the other hand, spends heartily but not to excess. He records the checks he writes in their joint checkbook and they have never had money problems.

The issue that brought them into therapy was grief over three miscarriages. However, every time they came in for a session, the focus became money. Usually this issue was raised by Lola, who raged at Greg over his "irresponsible" spending. Each session she would go over every check he wrote, criticizing his decisions. Greg would respond with logical arguments that the checks were well within their budget and remind Lola that she knew about each expenditure when it happened.

Greg would offer each week to give responsibility for the checkbook to Lola if she wanted it, and each week she would angrily decline, accusing him of trying to control her by being passive and not confronting the real issue. The problem was she couldn't define the real issue beyond restating that Greg spent too much. Greg responded with his belief that she was trying to control him with her focus on meaningless details.

Greg and Lola were caught in an exchange pattern that stemmed from both of them feeling unsafe. As we worked, it became clear that each had unresolved fears and losses from childhood, which had crystallized with the emotional losses from the miscarriages. Money became the battleground of each of their old fears and old safety issues. Money is a strong symbol of safety and power to almost everyone. Lola saw Greg's free spending as a threat to her safety. Greg saw Lola's objections as an attempt to control him. Neither could see the deeper issues under the volatility of the money issue.

Control is a big motivator. It is both an internal and external function. Internally, control brings safety because the person feels in charge, able to make life decisions that will keep his or her world from flying off in a million directions. Externally, control is a need to take power from someone else in order to feel powerful.

Control is a gratification-focused position: I will take whatever I need from you so I can feel better and I don't care what it will cost you. Control becomes a battle of wills, a very unsafe position for both parties.

As with a mind-set, a person will tend to take the same primary Emotional Location time after time. It's familiar and has predictable results even if it might be unhealthy and even unsafe. If you recognize yourself as being emotionally at home in one of the less-than-healthy Locations, and you are uncomfortable with the results it has been producing for you, you can make the choice to move. By the same token, a partner can also make the choice to move. The framework of Emotional Location allows for change and growth together. It takes practice and a desire to change plus some knowledge of how to make the shift and feel safe with it. But before you can move, you need to know where you are, so now we'll go on to the framework of Emotional Location.

## The Solver

This position is the one that allows all concerned to grow, communicate clearly, and resolve conflicts equitably. The Solver is a position in which a person feels competent, able, and open. This position is respectful to all persons involved.

---

## SOLVER

☐ Focuses on the problem, not the person

☐ Is respectful

☐ Seeks a solution, not gratification

☐ Empowers both speaker and listener

☐ Is assertive, not aggressive

☐ Seeks win-win resolution

---

The Solver stays focused on the problem, not the person, and looks for solutions, not gratification.

The objective of these techniques is to remain solution focused. What that means specifically is the exchange stays focused on the problem and its solution. It does not wander into personalities, history, or other problems. Instead, the objective of the exchange is to find a solution in which both (or all) parties involved can win.

Gratification-focused exchanges, on the other hand, occur when people are trying to get their needs met even at the expense of the other person's feelings, needs, growth, communication, or life. Gratification-focused exchanges don't have much to do with solving problems. Instead their message is: I want what I want and I don't care if you get hurt in the process.

Solvers are solution focused, emotionally available, respectful, limit-setting, one-thing-at-a-time people who want to find answers or resolution. The Solver seeks to empower himself and others. He hopes to control only his behavior. The Solver is also assertive, not aggressive. People who are aggressive are generally gratification focused because they want to get their needs met without considering the needs of others. People who are assertive are able to ask for what they want but don't expect to get it at the expense of another. Instead they want to find a way for all concerned to be gratified.

## The Blamer

Everyone has had contact with a Blamer. This is the person who wants to accuse everyone else of being the source of the problem. Almost anything the Blamer says is accompanied by the admonishing finger of shame. Blamers are blaming and shaming in their relationships. Their objective is to make the other person feel unworthy, unable, inept, and, in short, abused. In this way, Blamers hope to make themselves feel better, more powerful, more in control, more able, and more adept.

The Blamer attempts to exert control over others by using fear and condemnation. Typical language of the Blamer includes the words *should*, *always*, *never*, *fault*, and *if only*, as in "if only you had done this right in the first place," or "if only you knew how to. . . ." It is a position in which solutions take a backseat to the gratification of the Blamer. The Blamer looks to find fault with others, to assess blame not only for behavior but for events, and to make certain none of that blame arrives on his or her doorstep.

A Blamer, looking at the back porch damaged by a fallen tree that has been struck by lightning might say, "You know, I told you three years ago that tree was too close to the house, but you didn't do anything about it. And when this porch was put here, I warned you that it was too close to the tree, but you wanted to leave the tree and build it here. If only you had listened to me and built this right in the first place, this would never have happened! Now it's all your fault that we're in this mess, and it's going to cost a lot of money to get it fixed. You never listen to me."

Blamers choose this aggressive style to accomplish a couple of things. First, it helps them feel better and more powerful to be able to push someone else into a submissive position. That spot, in this case, is the position of being at fault. Second, attempts at external control by Blamers come in the form of the fear they create or try to create. The fear can be physical—a fear of violence or assault—but it can also be emotional or psychological—fear of abandonment, fear of loss of love or connection, fear of psychological assault, fear of being shamed or blamed, or fear of not being good enough to keep the love and attention of the Blamer.

No one wants to feel as though she's made wrong decisions or been deliberately neglectful or caused problems in her relationship, but when making a wrong choice is connected to being a wrong person, the damage is much greater than feeling guilty because that damage is shame.

Guilt is something you feel about something you have done. It's connected to behavior or choices you have made. Shame is feeling bad about who you are as a person. It is not focused on the behavior but on the behaver. The message of shame is that you as a person are bad or wrong. That undermines a person's self-confidence. It is a power-down position and that lowering of power in the blamed person is what allows the Blamer to feel more powerful and stronger.

In this situation, the Blamer wants to make it clear not only that the blamed person was at fault for the problem of the damaged porch but also that the blamed person is a terrible human being. Indeed, the Blamer may have issued a clear warning (or many, for that matter) that the tree and the porch were headed for disaster. But once disaster has struck, little is achieved by taking an I-told-you-so stance except to distribute blame and shame.

The Blamer remains emotionally unavailable by slinging blame and shame around to keep the other person off balance and at a distance. Being in a relationship with a Blamer means not only having to defend yourself constantly against the attacks of blame and shame but also knowing that every exchange has the objective to put you into the one-down position.

Sadly, parents sometimes get into a Blamer mode with their kids, focusing on negative behavior and ignoring the

## BLAMER

☐ Shaming

☐ Self-gratifying

☐ Focuses on the person, not the problem

☐ Seeks to find fault and have someone to blame

☐ Attempts to avoid being blamed

☐ Is aggressive and attacking

☐ Attempts to gain control

☐ Attempts to create fear

positive things the children do and the positive choices they make. Often these parents believe the child will learn from the stream of negativity. They fear that the child will grow lazy or arrogant with praise. The constant blaming and put-downs, however, give the child the message that he or she is the problem, not his or her behavior. This can quickly translate to the child feeling that there is nothing good about him or her. Instead of correcting bad *behavior* the child interprets the criticism as a personal attack; with no offsetting affirmations, the child comes to believe that he or she is a bad person with no redeeming value.

## The Poor Me

As the Blamer seeks to cast blame, the Poor Me accepts it. "Yes," says the Poor Me, "it *is* my fault. You're right. I never do anything right. I am completely hopeless, bad, wrong, but it's really not my fault because I'm the victim of _____." You can fill in that blank with any number of excuses, all of which blame the Blamer. If the exchange is with a Blamer, the Blamer has no interest in accepting the responsibility and deflects it back to the Poor Me. Thus begins a cycle that can escalate quickly. The Blamer's position is that the Poor Me is a bad person. The Poor Me's position is that, although that might be true, it's not really his or her fault.

While the Blamer uses fear to take control, the Poor Me uses helplessness, waiting passively for others to read his or her mind, then looking hurt and sad when that reading is inaccurate. The helplessness is a chosen position designed to shift any possible responsibility to someone else. After all, if you believe you are helpless, wrong, and powerless, how could you ever be responsible? And if you are helpless, wrong, and powerless, you also are completely emotionally unavailable so you don't have to risk being vulnerable with all the rest of that one-down location.

The Blamer says it's the Poor Me's fault and that if the Poor Me had only listened, this terrible event would never have happened; because the Poor Me didn't listen, he is a bad person. The Poor Me agrees but, because he doesn't want to feel bad, tries to push the responsibility to another spot. That spot is either back to the Blamer or onto a third party or to uncontrollable events. What nobody seems to recognize is that in many cases, no one need be blamed at all. This recognition would be uncomfortable for the Blamer because you can't take power from a situation where there is clear ownership, and it would be uncomfortable for the Poor Me because there is nothing to deflect and therefore no connection.

The Poor Me has trouble recognizing herself emotionally without an external definition. In a situation where there is blame and shame, a clear definition is provided. The Blamer also has trouble recognizing himself as an emotional being, but the power surge feels like a connection.

The Poor Me's language typically sounds helpless: "I can't do anything right. I always mess up anything I do so I must have someone else do all my thinking and acting for me."

Underneath that rhetoric, however, is the deeper intent,

which is to avoid any situation in which the Poor Me might have to absorb any responsibility or make any decisions, and to provide the emotional connections the Poor Me so desperately needs to define herself in the world.

There is also an underlying belief on the part of the Poor Me that she deserves what happens to her. In the case of bad stuff, the belief distills to, "I deserve to be abused because I'm a bad person," something no one deserves. The belief can become one of entitlement, which translates to, "I deserve not to have to accept any blame for anything, even if I am responsible for it." Neither of these positions is emotionally available, solution focused, or healthy for anyone concerned.

Sometimes the Poor Me will initiate the exchanges in an attempt to engage the Blamer in some emotional communication, saying in effect, "I'm helpless. I need you to tell me how to do what I need to do." By engaging the Blamer, the Poor Me is seeking an emotional connection even though it's negative. The relationship between the Blamer and the Poor Me is intense and enmeshed. Furthermore, the roles can often flip back and forth with the Blamer taking the Poor Me role and the Poor Me taking the position of the Blamer.

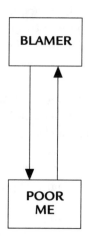

This Poor Me/Blamer pattern is found in many misconnected relationships. Often this pattern features rigid roles

---

## POOR ME

☐ Controls through helplessness

☐ Focuses on perceived victimization

☐ Seeks to blame someone else for behavior

---

for both participants, with a great deal at stake for each to stay in his or her prescribed role. The relationship is burdened with rules and expectations. Any variation from those roles, rules, and expectations produces chaos in the relationship and chaos fuels the blaming/shaming spiral. This is also the relationship in which you find physically or emotionally abusive partnerships. The attempt on the part of the Blamer to control the Poor Me's behavior through fear is only part of it. The other part is a desire by the Blamer to punish the Poor Me and for the Poor Me to *accept* the punishment. The Poor Me is not only getting the emotional connection she wants in a form she can understand, she is also getting reinforcement for her belief that she deserves to be abused.

The Blamer may get power by striking out physically but then is burdened with the load of shame and guilt about this behavior. The Blamer then must find a place to unload. Guess who the target becomes! This pattern perpetuates the cycle of victimization while still giving both partners what they need emotionally.

The Blamer/Poor Me relationship is a passionate one with lots of high emotion and drama. It is often accompanied by yelling and turmoil and has potential for violence.

## The Fixer

This is not the loving, caring person who exists within each of us, the person who loves and cares for self and others in an appropriate way. This emotional location is occupied by an emotionally unavailable person who says, in essence, "I know more about what you need than you do so I'm going to get it/do it/fix it for you no matter what you may say you want." This is caretaking with a whip and a chair!

---

***Taking care*** **is doing something for people they can't do for themselves.**

✦ ***Caretaking*** **is doing something for people they can and should do for themselves.** ✦

---

The Fixer tries to take control by smothering and enfolding the other person. Unlike the Blamer who tries to control by fear, or the Poor Me whose control attempt is through helplessness, the Fixer controls with kindness. His or her control is by aggressive caring liberally laced with guilt.

Using the earlier example of the tree and the porch, the Fixer would say, "I know you're upset about all this, but don't worry because I know just what we need to do. I'll go out and get a second job to pay for the repairs. I'll take care of having this tree removed, and I'll choose a new tree to be planted there and pay for it. You don't have to do anything at all." You might be asking yourself what's so wrong with all that. The porch gets repaired, the repair gets paid for, the tree problem is solved—why isn't this perfect?

It isn't perfect because only one person in the exchange has any power. True, you might think this sounds pretty good, but what happens when the porch of your ranch-style home is built to look like something out of a Civil War novel and painted lavender and the chosen tree is a red-leaf maple? You come back to the Fixer and say, "I'm not crazy about the design of the porch. I thought it would be like it was before." The Fixer's kindness fades and is replaced with pouting and anger. "You don't like my choices? I guess you must hate me. I worked extra sixteen-hour shifts to pay for this and you don't like it? I can't believe you'd say that to me when I work so hard to make you happy. . . ."

Where the Blamer relies on shame, Fixers use guilt to tip the power balance in their direction. The Fixer sounds like he's victimizing himself for the good of others, but that's only an illusion. The Fixer is attempting to sap power and independence, to take control by offering what looks like caring. The message is, "I care about you so now you owe me."

Fixers smother and their attempts at fixing extend far beyond assistance and problem solving. Instead, the solutions become chaotic and enmeshed because the Fixer is always at the center of the solution. "I'm the answer," is the essence of the message. The real need of the Fixer, at the core of everything, is the need to be loved. Fixers will do whatever it takes to get the love they so desperately want and have never felt to a satisfying level.

The language of the Fixer revolves around words like *your needs* and *help you* and *protect you*. None of these have the loving support of a Solver offering a hand; rather, if you look beyond what is said, you will find it involves submission to the Fixer's solution.

"OK, you spent all the rent money at the casino. I'll manage our money from now on and I'll get an extra job and you just don't have to worry at all because I can make it all right again."

That sounds like help, until you think about how much power is being siphoned away from one person and onto the Fixer. The Fixer is placing herself in the control position by seeming as if she is caring. But she's not caring. She's controlling. And if the fixee doesn't perform precisely the way the Fixer requires, the so-called caring will be wrapped in guilt. The Fixer's efforts to control are, once again, an attempt to feel safe, to feel loved. The fact that these attempts often result in chaos simply gives the Fixer more to try to control.

The Fixer can sometimes resort to physical violence but does not do so from a desire to create fear or connection

## FIXER

- ☐ Controls with "kindness"

- ☐ Becomes increasingly intrusive

- ☐ Attempts to produce guilt in the fixee

- ☐ Offers seemingly helpful ideas that are attempts at control

- ☐ "I'm the answer to the problem."

- ☐ Intends to create an obligation

like the Blamer does. Instead this violence comes from frustration. The Fixer's perspective is "If you don't let me take care of you and then love me for it, I'll hit you." This is especially clear in situations when the recipient of the Fixer's attention tries to resist or to change the relationship once it's been established.

In general, the Fixer's primary relationship in the grid will be with the Player.

## The Player

Players are very self-focused people, who are most concerned with getting their needs met and who are not much concerned at whose expense. The Player often is alcoholic or drug addicted. He's apt to gamble the rent money, have affairs, spend wildly—all the while using other people and not caring much about who gets hurt. The Player controls by carelessness and manipulation: "If you love me, you'll make this right." This attitude is coupled with an even more seductive element, withholding. "If you're perfect, I might love you," is the message of the Player.

One of the defining traits of the Player is emotional

unavailability. This position would be a natural challenge for the Fixer, who would like very much to control the Player and who may believe that if she can just become perfect, she will be able not only to win the love of the Player but also to control him. The Player on the other hand wants nothing to do with an emotional involvement. Players only want the illusion of a relationship—and the benefits.

Players are highly skilled emotional seducers. Early in any relationship, they appear to be loving and attentive, seeming to fill every need of the partner. Invariably there will be some event or disagreement and suddenly the balance of power will shift, with the Player demanding more and more and giving less and less in return. When this happens, the Fixer becomes frightened of losing the Player and increases fixing and caretaking activities in an effort to rehook the Player.

You can imagine how quickly this pattern can grab someone who's a Fixer. The Fixer wants to fix, make better, control with kindness, and manage the behavior of other people, ostensibly for their own good. The temptation to help someone unlock his or her hidden emotional self is a siren song for the Fixer.

What does the Player get out of this? Everything. The Fixer does all the work in the relationship while the Player sits back and waits for the Fixer to produce the magic. When the magic doesn't happen, the Player has someone to blame for her own problems. And it's someone who won't leave when he gets blamed. Instead, he'll try harder to be perfect, to take care, to make magic. Underlying Players' emotional unavailability is fear of abandonment and their firm belief they are unable to care for themselves. Under Fixers' guilt and control is a profound feeling of unworthiness that says they can only be accepted and loved for what they do, not who they are.

These are the hooks that set the relationship. The Fixer tries to earn the love of the Player by doing everything perfectly. The Player believes he needs someone to do things and produce feelings because he's unable to do this work for himself. But the Player cannot allow anyone to get too close because vulnerability is too dangerous.

The Player's language includes phrases like, "I didn't mean to use all the money, but . . . ," or "If the bartender/casino owner/drug dealer/prostitute hadn't ripped me off . . . ," or "I got such a good deal on . . . ," or "If so-and-so hadn't been such a flirt. . . ." The general theme is that the Player was the innocent victim of someone else's conniving. The biggest phrase of the Player, however, is "yes, but. . . ." This phrase deflects excuses and demands all at once. When you hear, "yes, but . . . ," begin to listen carefully for other Player clues. Many people say, "yes, but. . . ." When it is the answer to almost every question or suggestion, however, you're most likely dealing with a Player.

The Player wants someone else to take responsibility for his or her own behavior and actively deflects the focus to anyone and everyone else, meanwhile putting the Fixer in the position of making everything right again. The message is, "If you love me, you'll . . . ," and the Fixer wants love desperately so he or she does everything possible not only to take responsibility but also to repair the damages. Of course, it's never *quite* enough for the Player, but that's what keeps the relationship rolling.

## PLAYER

☐ Controls by uncar ing and manipulation

☐ Is evasive and irresponsible

☐ Can be emotionally seductive, but unavailable

☐ Uses "yes, but . . ."

☐ Seeks someone else to be responsible

The dance of the Fixer and the Player is as entrenched as the one of the Blamer and the Poor Me, but instead of the yelling power struggles, the Fixer/Player relationship is more often characterized by tears and abandonment. Unlike the Blamer and the Poor Me, however, the Fixer and the Player do not switch roles. These two are very fixed, each locked in their respective roles in the relationship.

Do you see any of these connections in your life? Did you cringe when you read any of the descriptions? Did you mutter to yourself, "Gee, that sounds just like what so-and-so and I do all the time"?

Remember, everyone jumps in and out of Emotional Locations all the time. If you find yourself and your partner jumping into particular locations or patterns, you have the option to choose to jump together into the Solver spot. That's a safe and healthy location, but be warned: going there and staying there takes practice.

## Other Connections in the Grid

The Blamer/Poor Me and Fixer/Player relationships are the primary connections in the diagram. Remember, these are not just for intimate partners but also for friendships, work relationships, parent-child relationships, and hundreds of other emotional connections. Remember, too, that people jump in and out of the various positions in the diagram, depending upon the situation of the moment. Each person, however, will have one spot he or she occupies most often. Have you found your usual spot?

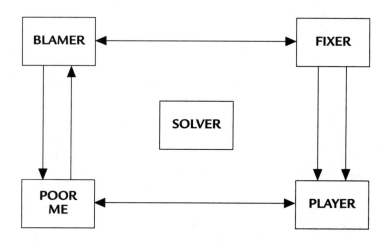

## Blamer/Player

What do you imagine a relationship between a Blamer and a Player would be like? Remember, Blamers want to control by using condemnation and/or fear. They like to find someone to blame and punish. The Player also wants to find someone who will take responsibility and then fix the situation. The Player wants to avoid being blamed. So the Blamer says, "It's your fault," and the Player says, "*Yes, but* it's really so-and-so's fault, not mine. And besides, who's going to fix this?"

Blamers do not tend to be Fixers and Players have no interest in being blamed, so either someone shifts in the grid—the Player shifts to the Poor Me role or the Blamer takes on the Fixer role—or the relationship falls apart.

## Blamer/Fixer

A Blamer/Fixer relationship is problematic because both positions want to be the one in control. There may be power shifts back and forth, but the Blamer's attempts to control by blame/shame/fear are met with the Fixer's attempts to fix the relationship with control by guilt-caring. Blamers will lash out at this smothering, which either increases the Fixer's efforts or discourages the Fixer enough that he or she slips into the Poor Me slot. This position might be familiar to a long-term Fixer because he or she may have learned the Fixer role in a family with a Blamer/Poor Me relationship between the parents.

Children of people who occupy the Blamer/Poor Me position get the message early that they must be in charge of fixing things for mom and/or dad. They become the Fixers of their adult family members. That role will continue into adulthood if they choose partners *for* whom, not *about* whom, they can care.

## Fixer/Poor Me

What about the relationship between the Fixer and the Poor Me? It sounds almost as though it would be a primary connection, but it isn't because it really doesn't work. The Poor Me may seem to be asking for someone to fix things, but that isn't the true message.

The Poor Me is accustomed to being blamed and shamed for who he is and what he does. His basic belief is that he doesn't deserve to be fixed or that he can't possibly be fixed. Anyone who tries to help or fix is viewed as intrusive, crazy, or untrustworthy.

The Poor Me doesn't want things fixed because then she might have to take some responsibility for how her life goes. Instead she wants to continue being helpless and hopeless and have the Blamer reinforce her own negative beliefs about her power and her value as a person.

The message of the Fixer is that everyone can be fixed

if only they will surrender the power to the Fixer. The Poor Me doesn't believe he has any power to surrender nor anything of value to fix, so the smothering of the Fixer is either frightening or surreal. In neither case is there a real connection. The Poor Me backs away even further and may eventually shift into a Blamer role to scare the Fixer away.

## Player/Poor Me

The other possible secondary connection would be between the Player and the Poor Me. This connection might seem like a natural: the Player is looking for someone to blame and the Poor Me is accustomed to being blamed. However, the Player wants more than just someone to blame. He wants someone to pick up the pieces and that's where this connection falls apart. The Player says, "It's your fault," and the Poor Me agrees. Then nothing happens, so the Player does something else outrageous and says, "It's your fault." Again, the Poor Me agrees and nothing else happens. The Player, in an attempt to make some recognizable emotional connection, keeps escalating his behavior and the Poor Me, waiting for the other shoe to drop, becomes more and more inert. Eventually one or the other will become frustrated enough to shift roles. Most often, the Poor Me will either become a Blamer to drive the Player away or will take on the role of Fixer. In some instances, the Player will shift to the Blamer role and may use physical violence to express frustration with the passive behavior of the Poor Me.

Two people trying to occupy the same position will also produce some interesting emotional exchanges.

## Blamer/Blamer

Two Blamers will engage in major power struggles. First they will check each other out, size up the competition. Next they might challenge each other a bit to see how strong the competition is. There will be jockeying for turf and maybe a few confrontations. Eventually, inevitably, there will be a battle royal. This kind of behavior is common in big corporations and major universities where there is high pressure to rise through the ranks, and limited space at the top. These institutions have almost formalized rules of combat for their survival-of-the-fittest wars.

Two Blamers sometimes develop an emotionally intimate relationship, but the struggle for dominance, control, and power soon drains the energy of the relationship and the participants.

## Poor Me/Poor Me

A relationship between two Poor Me types would almost certainly be a whiny one. Each of them would try to out-"poor me" the other, and consequently no one would take any action to fix the problems.

What would finally happen is that one would change to the role of Blamer or Fixer. This relationship often occurs in a family where there is one dominant Blamer and several persons taking the Poor Me role. It could also occur in an organization or relationship where there is a large power imbalance maintained by the dominant Blamer.

## Player/Player

Two Players can be buddies who go out to play—drinking, gambling, getting into minor or even serious trouble. These relationships occur between intimate partners where neither takes responsibility and both like to play, or within organizational relationships. But Player/Player relationships are fraught with financial and legal problems and burn out fairly quickly.

You might see this in a business partnership of two people who see themselves as high rollers and entrepreneurs. At first the competitive quality of increasingly risky investments reinforces the two Player egos involved. The problems begin because neither Player considers where the money to follow up on these investments or the management prowess to keep them going will come from. Handling such details themselves would prove far too boring for the two Players.

Instead, both stay busy playing the game until the IRS or INS or bankers show up demanding accountability. Both Players then seek someone to blame for the problem and someone to fix it.

## Fixer/Fixer

Two Fixers might battle in much the same way as two Blamers, each one trying to outcare the other while grabbing for power.

There can also be three-way connections, four-way connections, and so on. When you are confronted with a multiple exchange, stop and look at the participants and see if you can figure out where they stand within the exchange. Once you understand the chosen position of each person, you'll have all the information you need.

You'll notice that in many connections there is often role shifting during exchanges. The choice of which new role to take will depend upon how important the relationship is to the participants, how emotionally available each partner might be, and/or how unresolved the situation is. It will make multiple exchanges confusing but not impossible. As long as you know where you are standing, you don't have to get caught in the turmoil.

## *Dr. Collins's Magic Words*

None of the connections we just looked at are solution focused. In every case, people are trying to get their needs met without considering the needs of the other person in the exchange.

## A SPECIAL THREE-WAY CONNECTION

In many relationships a special three-way connection will evolve. It starts with a Blamer/Poor Me connection, but the Poor Me reaches out to someone else, usually a Fixer, to come "rescue" him or her. It looks like this:

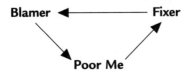

The Fixer, responding to what looks like a legitimate request for help, rushes in and chooses to help the Poor Me by attacking the Blamer.

This shifts the relationship. Now the former Fixer becomes the new Blamer. The former Blamer, under attack, becomes the new Poor Me. This leaves the former Poor Me to take the role of the new Fixer who now can rush in to rescue the new Poor Me by attacking the new Blamer for what he or she had requested in the first place.

You can see what a vicious circle this could become! It's a common pattern among parents and kids, among siblings, and among peers in an office or social setting. It is the foundation of every mother-in-law joke or sitcom.

If you find yourself in one of these whirlpools, step into the role of Solver and stop playing. It's the only way out!

As long as you stay in the Solver spot, you will be able to work through almost any exchange without getting caught in a negative position.

---

If you find yourself in one of these patterns and are ready to change, there is a way to stop the dysfunctional connections and at the same time build healthier relationships. And all it takes is a little magic!

Imagine this: Your boss is a notorious Blamer. Every word that comes out of his mouth is blame/shame/condemnation. If you ask him a question, the answer is often intertwined with something abusive.

"You know, Phil, you must be the stupidest fool who ever lived. Any idiot could figure this out. If I've told you once, I've told you a thousand times. You must just be an incompetent, useless fool."

What did you just feel like saying in response? The temptation might be either to shrink into a teeny little ball of Poor Me and agree with your boss that, indeed, you are the stupidest fool who ever lived, or to get into a Blamer contest and lash back. You might even drop into the Player spot and tell the boss to buzz off. Any of those choices will keep you standing firmly in a dysfunctional spot, getting nothing but more frustrated and angry—or fired. You will never be able to say anything to the boss to change his mind because he's getting what he thinks he wants. He's feeling good by making you feel bad.

What if you could be in the Solver mode instead?

Try this. Read the boss's lines above with as much venom as you can muster, then, in your own voice, respond with:

## Dr. Collins's Six Magic Words:

◆ *"I'm sorry you feel that way."* ◆

Now try to imagine how the boss would respond. The standard escalation won't work because you've just announced that you are unwilling to play. And you haven't been disrespectful. You are, indeed, sorry he feels that way. You have, however, respectfully disagreed and declined to continue an abusive conversation.

The power of Dr. Collins's Six Magic Words is amazing. If you add Dr. Collins's Magic Question, you'll set the whole communication in a completely different direction.

---

## Dr. Collins's Magic Question:

### *"What do we need to do to solve this problem?"*

---

To see what I mean, read the boss's lines again—venom and all—and then use the Magic Words followed by the Magic Question. Doesn't that sound amazing? Suddenly, you're changing the texture of the whole exchange. You have acknowledged your boss's communication—unhealthy as it is—and still invited him to join you in looking for solutions and in being emotionally available.

Because life isn't always as orderly as we'd like, the boss may give you some abusive retort such as, "The way we solve this problem, Phil, is for you to get less stupid. You're just an idiot." Try again. This time you might want to vary the Six Magic Words. (Please feel free to be creative once you have the feel for the solution-focused phrase. Take the system and make it your own.) Here are a few examples:

"Thanks for your input."

"Thank you for sharing that."

"I appreciate your interest."

"I see you feel strongly about this."

"I'd like to find a way for us to work together to solve the problem, not attack each other."

"Let's see what we can work out together to solve this problem."

The essence of the message is that you acknowledge the other person without getting enmeshed in his dysfunctional position. You are focused on solving the problem. You are staying in an emotionally available position and inviting the other person to join you there. Keep repeating the Magic Words and the Magic Question until the other party hears you and begins to join the process.

The magic in the Magic Question comes from an opportunity for transformation. It asks a person who wants to take an adversarial position to step to the other side and become a partner in problem solving. Further, it puts aside all the old business to focus on the present problem. And it reinforces the invitation to be emotionally present and to eschew the hiding and distance.

Being in the Solver mode lets you stay out of unhealthy connections. It also costs a lot less emotionally because you don't have to constantly defend yourself. You can spend your energy on making healthy connections and enjoying life. Staying in the Solver mode also helps you teach other people how to join you there. Most interesting of all, the Solver spot is the only one in the grid that can comfortably be occupied by *everyone* in an exchange! Once you can stay in the Solver spot, you will find the number of destructive conflicts and the amount of chaos in your life drops quickly. There may still be conflicts, but they are apt to be healthy learning and growing experiences between people who are emotionally available. You'll see how good it feels to be in the Solver spot and to see problems solved and people being respectful and cooperative with one another.

Good communication skills are at the heart of emotional connections. After all, good communication is what lets others in on what we're thinking and how we're feeling. I find in my practice that a lot of people's communication problems begin in childhood with parents who aren't open and available. The children of these parents grow up believing their partners should be able to read their minds. As we all know, that doesn't work very well.

The good news is that communication skills are easy to learn and, once learned, are easy to practice. What that means is that once a couple begins to use good communication skills, the habit of being open will continue and other emotional doors will start to open.

## Practical Applications

So now that you understand the theory, how do you put this knowledge into effect? First, an observation: Practice is mandatory for good communication. Nobody is going to be perfect at communication on the first try—or on the tenth, for that matter! But the more you use good communication techniques, the better your communication becomes and the more able you are to overcome problems with an emotionally unavailable partner. It's not the sole management tool, but it is the foundation of many of the tools we'll consider as we try to help an emotionally unavailable partner connect.

It's important to remember that change is not something you can inflict on another person. The person who is emotionally unavailable must be willing to change. Without that commitment, you will be using your excellent communication techniques in vain.

Remember that you want to stay in the Solver spot as much as possible, not only in dealing with your emotionally unavailable partner but in your contact with the world in general. Staying in the Solver spot will lower your level of general aggravation and raise your level of effectiveness in your business and personal life. Staying in the Solver spot keeps you out of those no-win conflicts that arise with kids in general and adolescents in particular. You will avoid those circular arguments that seem to whirl around adolescent-parent communications and only serve to get both parties anxious and mad. Being in the Solver spot also works with difficult people in other areas of your life—bosses, parents, neighbors, and even angry strangers. So how do you go about staying in the Solver spot? You begin by using feelings language.

## Use Feelings Language

We looked at the difference between "I think" and "I feel" in Chapter 2. When you are attempting to stay in the Solver spot, begin by letting others know how you feel.

It's a good idea to say your partner's name. Most people enjoy hearing the sound of their names. And using the other person's name accomplishes two other things as well. First, it gets the person's attention. Second, it personalizes the conversation, which reinforces the feelings position of effective communication. Staying in the feelings position is important. It shows the other person that you're not out to objectify him or her. Objectifying is used by abusive people to depersonalize and deemotionalize others. When you use a person's name, you are attracting his or her attention and taking steps to prevent abusive communication or behavior.

Begin with the person's name, then "I feel," followed by the name of the feeling. Remember, this is not the "I feel" substitute for "I think," but the name of a true emotion.

"Jim, I feel mad when . . . "

Next you add the name of the offending behavior.

"Jim, I feel mad when you don't listen to me when I talk to you and the TV is on."

In an ideal situation, Jim's response is, "Rhonda, I hear you say you feel mad when I don't listen to you when you talk to me and the TV is on."

You would respond, "Yes, that's right. I feel ignored by you. Is that your intention?"

Jim might then say, "Of course not. How about if we set aside some time every day so we can talk with each other without any distractions?"

You would respond, "Thank you. That sounds like a perfect solution."

Believe it or not, when you and your partner are emotionally connected with one another and have been practicing, that's how the conversation goes. And not just for dull people with no issues! The key is that both parties have to be willing to use solution-focused language, have to be focused on the problem, have to be committed to finding a solution for the problem, have to be available to listen to one another, and have to remain in the Solver spot.

## Focus on the Problem

Finding a solution for the problem requires good communication in itself because often people are fighting about two different problems. Because neither is committed to listening to his or her partner, they don't realize they're talking about two different things. Here's an example:

"Jim, I feel mad when you don't listen to me when the TV is on."

"What?"

"I said, I feel mad when you don't listen to me when the TV is on."

"Well, what about when the kids are screaming? You let those kids get away with anything they want and you never tell your mother to stop interfering with them either."

Well, now we've got a merry mess! You and Jim have three subjects on the table within thirty seconds. That's impressive. These three subjects don't allow you to accomplish anything constructive because you're not aimed at solving the same problem. All is not lost, however, because you are listening to Jim even though he's not listening to you.

"Jim, I hear you say you have some issues about the way I manage the kids and with my mother. I think it's important that we talk about all three issues, but not all at the same time. Which would you like to talk about first?"

You have acknowledged the importance of Jim's issues, reminded him that you had brought up an issue as well, and offered him the opportunity to discuss all three issues. You have also made an important step—you've identified the problem. Or in this case, the problems.

## Use Open-Ended Questions

In the exchange with Jim your final question was open ended. What that means is that it can't be answered with a simple yes or no. Using an open-ended question makes it more difficult for your partner to stonewall you. You not only have asked Jim to commit to talking about the problems but have also kept yourself and Jim in the Solver spot. You have kept your power and allowed Jim to keep his power of choice.

But Jim is in high-blame mode: "I don't want to talk about any of it. You need to get control of the kids and your mother. If you were anything but a professional shopper, these problems would never happen. You don't spend enough time being a mother and you spend too much time being a shopper."

Jim has now further muddied the waters by introducing at least one more issue he has obviously been brooding about. Don't get distracted. Don't get discouraged. Jim's tough, but you still have the Solver spot firmly in your grasp and you are determined to get some solutions. At this moment Jim is in the Blamer box—*you* are the problem in his view, but that doesn't mean you have to agree with him or jump into the Poor Me position to play the abuse-excuse game.

"I'm sorry you feel that way, Jim. I want to hear your point of view and see if we can find a way to solve these problems. Do you want to set a time when we could talk about the problems you raise?" That's how Dr. Collins's Six Magic Words and Dr. Collins's Magic Question work. The objective is to stop the Blamer's abusive language and to redirect the Blamer into the Solver spot. You are again asking for solutions and setting limits. But here comes Jim again.

"Oh no, you don't get to make this a big deal. I told you I don't want to talk about any of this. You just need to get control of the kids, tell your mother to mind her own business, and stop spending my money. That's how we'll solve these problems."

Jim is really tough. He's not willing to hear your side of things, he's anxious to assign blame and accuse, and he sounds pretty mad. You can try again.

"Jim, you sound mad to me. I'm sorry you feel that way. I hope we can talk about the issues you raise as well as my feelings, but I will not allow you to blame me for things that aren't my fault and then not talk about our problems. Which issue would you like to discuss first?"

## Set Clear Boundaries

It is extremely important to set boundaries with people who use abusive language or blame or who will not participate in a reasonable dialogue. By setting limits for Jim in a clear and respectful way and then again asking for him to participate with you to find a solution, you are taking care of yourself.

You have also reached the point of no return. If Jim continues to be circular and refuses to participate in a reasonable and appropriate way, you have evidence that he may be unwilling or unable to change. That will be important for you to know in the future. Jim may be trying to protect himself, or he may be feeling accused or attacked, but if he won't or can't communicate with you about what he is feeling, you are not responsible for reading his mind. If Jim continues to respond in a dismissive or abusive way and refuses to seek solutions, you have a problem beyond communication. That doesn't mean good communication is unnecessary or unhelpful. You have the right to be heard and to have your feelings treated in a respectful way. If you do not get that in your relationship and your partner is not willing to work on communication and issues, you may have to reconsider the relationship.

Jim has another choice and that is to discuss at least one of the problems the two of you have brought to the table. If you think about it, Jim's issues are pretty large. He questions your child rearing, the intrusiveness of your mother, and your ability to handle money. You have raised the issue of communication by stating that you feel left out. All four of these issues deserve to be discussed and resolved in a respectful and healthy way.

Identifying the problem is a first step toward having those kinds of discussions. Making sure you're both talking about the same problem is also part of the first step in good solution-focused problem solving. Both parties must be committed to finding a solution to the problem and to listening carefully to one another. In that way, good communication joins with emotional availability to make everyone involved feel empowered. Empowered people are good at solving problems because they don't feel threatened by someone else's feelings and they want to find ways for everyone to win. That's one of the reasons using feelings language when talking about emotion-charged issues is so important. It's very hard to argue with someone who is speaking from feelings.

## Don't Tolerate Abusive or Attacking Language

"I feel dismissed when you don't seem to hear me when I talk."

An attacking answer to this statement wouldn't make any sense. A person could hardly say, "You don't feel dismissed," without sounding illogical and childish.

There are people who try to deny us our feelings, to be sure, but that's a move that doesn't make much sense. "That's not what you feel," they say, directly or indirectly. When someone responds to a feelings statement with a denial of what you have just said, that person wants to dictate the way you should feel. This is controlling behavior. It is abusive. It is not solution focused and it accomplishes nothing except to create bad feelings.

If you get this response, you can redirect it using another form of Dr. Collins's Six Magic Words: "I appreciate your input (interpretation, thoughts, etc.), but I spoke accurately when I said I feel dismissed." That remark reaffirms your feelings, sets limits for the person who is trying to define your reality for you, and refocuses the conversation on the issue at hand.

## Practice, Practice, Practice

It's not easy to remember all these details. When you first begin to use the technique it feels very awkward. But you will improve with practice, as it becomes second nature to use this sort of language. If both you and your partner practice, or if only one of you practices and is careful to use the techniques, it will become habit. This habit simplifies the process, makes for a much higher comfort level for all concerned, and produces solutions. It also lowers the volume and intensity of confrontations because it's not the two of you against each other, it's the two of you joined as partners against the problems.

## PROBLEM-SOLVING COMMUNICATION RULES

1. Partner 1: Use feelings language. State the feeling and the behavior that produces the feeling. Do not use accusations or blame.

2. Partner 2: Beginning with the phrase, "I hear you say," repeat verbatim what Partner 1 has just told you.

3. Partner 1: Affirm or correct Partner 2's repetition of the issue. At this time add any further information to clarify what you have said.

4. Partner 2: Listen to all information given by Partner 1. Don't deny his or her feelings, but respond with supportive language and your proposal for how the problem might be solved.

5. Partner 1: Repeat Partner 2's suggestions for a solution, then add your own. This is the time for brainstorming. Make notes. Consider each suggestion individually for its possible usefulness.

6. Together: Decide on the solution that works best for both of you. When you have agreed, say, "Then the solution we've come to is ____. Is that what you believe?"

7. The other partner then affirms or corrects until there
   is agreement on the solution. Then decide when and
   how the solution will be implemented and who will be
   responsible for which part of the implementation.
   (Both partners should be involved in implementation
   to some extent.)

8. After the solution has been implemented, agree on a
   time to evaluate the solution and tinker with anything
   that isn't working.

It's going to feel awkward when you first begin using
this technique, but it will get easier with practice and you
will be pleased at how quickly matters get solved. Eventually you and your partner will work out some shortcuts as
you develop your own style. Do remember, however, that
the success of this tool demands that both parties stay in
the Solver spot.

There are other techniques to use with a partner who is
emotionally unavailable, techniques that will help both of
you improve your communication and your relationship.

## Confrontation

I can almost hear you say, "I *hate* confrontation! I'll do anything to avoid it." That might be just what has gotten you
into a relationship with an emotionally unavailable person.
People who are emotionally unavailable often do everything
they can to avoid confrontation because it demands an emotional presence. People often confuse confrontation with
aggression, feeling that confrontation has to be loud, pushy,
and angry. Confrontation doesn't have to be any of those
things. It is far more effective for confrontation to be quiet,
focused, and assertive without anger.

Keeping Emotional Location in mind can help you be confrontational without ever raising your voice or your blood pressure. You want to stay in the Solver spot and you invite the person you are confronting to join you there. Once again, you can begin with "I feel" language, but there are other approaches as well.

"Susan, I feel taken advantage of when you borrow money from me, then don't make much effort to pay it back. I would appreciate it if you would return the twenty dollars I loaned you. When would that be convenient?"

"Excuse me, sir. I have been standing here waiting for the next available teller. The next position in the line is behind the woman in the purple coat."

"Mother, I appreciate your love for Gregory, but we have asked you several times not to give him candy because he gets pretty wild when he eats sugar. I know you want him to be comfortable and feel in control, so will you please not do that again?"

"I know it's hard to find a parking place in this area, but I have been waiting here for fifteen minutes and I intend to take this spot when this woman pulls out of it."

In each case, the feelings of the other person are acknowledged but you are able to be clear in identifying the issue and stating your position.

## Confrontation vs. Problem Solving

So when do you use confrontation as opposed to problem-solving language? The situation that demands confrontation is one in which your rights or boundaries are being violated by the actions or decisions of another person. Susan has borrowed money without returning it; someone has cut in front of you in line at the bank; your mom has been giving your child candy in direct violation of your requests; someone is pushing to take a parking place you've been staking out. All of these are violations of your turf. These situations *do* contain problems, but your objective is not to solve a mutual, negotiable problem. Instead you are trying to set the limits of what you will tolerate.

If the other person's response to your quiet, nonaggressive confrontation is aggressive, you can again set limits by saying something like, "I'm sorry if you feel mad about this, but I will not tolerate aggressive [or abusive] language [or behavior] or yelling." You remain calm, keep your voice low, and behave in a nonaggressive way in response. Usually the other person will calm down. If not, you have the option to walk away from the situation without having escalated it and without increasing your own level of frustration.

## Assertiveness

Assertiveness is the objective. Remember, assertive people ask for what they want, don't allow themselves to be victimized by others, and stay in the Solver spot.

When you are assertive rather than aggressive, you create a safe environment for your partner. This is very important because, as you recall, one of the core issues for many emotionally unavailable persons is safety. If you are being clear, assertive, and in control of your own emotions, your partner can feel safe enough to be more vulnerable and hear what you have to say.

Remember, when you are confronting someone, your objective is still to find a solution to a problem, not to attack the other person and force your views on him or her.

## Reframing

The technique of *reframing* comes from family therapy and is very effective in breaking communication logjams as well as helping the other person feel supported rather than attacked. Reframing helps a person open up emotionally and promotes emotional availability.

Here's how it works. Think of the position taken by a person as being a picture of his or her perspective. That picture is enclosed in a frame, which changes from situation to situation. The objective of reframing is to change the frame to something that will improve communication.

For example, have you ever called something that seemed bad a "challenge"? Do you have one of those magnets on your fridge that says, "Ewe's not fat, ewe's just fluffy"? Have you ever tactfully called your nephew's violin recital "interesting"? Then you already know something about reframing.

Peggy and Laura have been friends for years. When Peggy got involved with a man, Laura felt she was one of the casualties of his apparent intention to eliminate all Peggy's friends. Laura was grieving over this exclusion and enraged because whenever she tried to contact Peggy, she had trouble getting past the censoring boyfriend, who listened to Peggy's portion of the phone call and commented. Whenever she managed to see Peggy alone, Laura would try to talk about it. Then Peggy would accuse Laura of being jealous of her relationship. Peggy was unable to hear Laura's fear and pain.

Laura came to therapy to resolve her own feelings, but couldn't let go of the pain of Peggy's abandonment. I encouraged Laura to invite Peggy to come into a session so we could work on communication between the two of them. In that session, Laura said, "Peggy, I feel abandoned when you let Mike censor all your phone calls and when we don't do anything together anymore."

"I think you're jealous of my relationship with Mike," Peggy responded.

Obviously, they had two very different views of the problem.

"Peggy, do you understand what Laura is feeling?"

Peggy replied, "I think she's wrong. She's still my best friend. She's just jealous because I'm in a relationship and she's not."

"Laura, if Peggy were in danger, what would you do?" I asked.

"I'd do everything I could to protect her," Laura responded instantly.

"And how would you know she was in danger? I mean, other than if she told you."

Laura thought about it for a minute, then said, "She might be doing something I know is dangerous, like using drugs, or drinking and driving, or skydiving. Or she might be hanging around places that I know are dangerous. Or she might be associating with people who are dangerous."

"In each of those cases, however, it's not Peggy's definition that she's in danger, but yours. Right?" Laura nodded. "But you would still do what you needed to do to protect her?"

"Of course."

"So if you didn't know her very well, how would you know what's dangerous and who's dangerous for her?"

"It might be harder. I guess I'd have to be more cautious."

"Is it possible that Mike is just trying to protect Peggy in a relationship he doesn't know very well?"

Peggy nodded. "That's exactly what Mike does. He's very protective because his first wife was murdered. He's suspicious of everyone."

So now we had a better picture of common ground. "Laura, if you could think of Mike as protecting Peggy, would that be more comfortable for you?" That was the reframe. Mike was now cast as a protector of a dear friend rather than a dragon at the gate keeping Laura out. Laura had already acknowledged that she could understand and support protecting a friend. The reframe of Mike as a protector helped Laura and Peggy find some common ground. Peggy was then more willing to set limits for Mike, and Laura was more willing to see Mike as an ally rather than an enemy.

Reframing, then, is finding a different way to look at the problem in order to gain some common ground. It is not sugarcoating something unacceptable. If, for example, Mike were beating Peggy up, I would never have used a reframe that cast him as a good guy. But, in a situation where two people have very different views, reframing can provide another way to solve the differences.

With emotionally unavailable persons, reframing can be a way to provide a new, safe perspective for them to open up. You don't need a therapist or a mediator to help with reframing once you practice this tool. The key is to think of another way to look at an issue. You can practice reframing when you watch TV or movies. Listen to the dialogue between characters and try to find a different way to interpret the situation. Consider, for example, how important Peggy's involvement with Mike was to Peggy. She would not be open to hearing Laura criticize him. Laura's objective was to maintain the friendship and hope that Mike would either change or disappear. The reframing of Mike as a protector allowed Peggy and Laura to continue their friendship, gave Laura a different way to see Mike's behavior, and respected Peggy's choice. The reframe allowed everyone to win and feel respected.

## Boundaries

Emotionally unavailable persons, in general, do not have healthy boundaries. What they have, instead, is armor that prevents them from opening up at all. When you are in a relationship with someone who has poor boundaries, you need to have very good boundaries to keep yourself from getting hurt or damaged.

Good boundaries come from staying in a Solver spot and being appropriately assertive. Good boundaries allow you to limit another person's access to your life and emotions without cutting him or her off. Good boundaries give you measurable borders, which are then easy to reinforce.

So what constitutes good boundaries? The following list of behaviors of persons with healthy boundaries should help you not only define good boundaries but also check out your own boundaries to see where you fit.

## PEOPLE WITH GOOD BOUNDARIES

☐ Are assertive

☐ Stay in a Solver post

☐ Use "I feel" language

☐ Are in touch with their feelings

☐ Keep private information private

☐ Neither give nor receive inappropriate gifts, sex, contact

☐ Are clear in their various roles in life

☐ Don't use sex as a substitute for love

☐ Don't give gifts to get favors or advantages

☐ Are respectful of others' bodies, turf, thoughts, and feelings

☐ Don't tell everything

☐ Don't gossip

☐ Have clear, readable emotions

☐ Are able to identify bad boundaries in others

☐ Don't expect others to fill their needs automatically

☐ Don't believe others can or should be able to read their minds

☐ Don't allow self-abuse, sexual abuse, physical abuse, verbal abuse, or emotional abuse by another for any reason

☐ Don't allow others to define them or their reality

☐ Don't allow others to take without limits or give without limits

Good boundaries make good relationships. Having good boundaries keeps you safe in the context of a relationship whether or not your partner has good boundaries. If you keep your boundaries clear, you will help a partner whose boundaries are unclear to be more connected because you will be more readable and safer emotionally.

## The Forbidden "Why"

When I work with couples in my practice, one thing we do early on is forbid either partner from asking the question, "Why?" We do that because "why" is a gateway for blame. The question itself is often abusive as it contains an invisible addendum, as in "why the heck would you _____."

Most important, though, is that people use "why" as though an explanation is a solution to a problem or a magic palliative for emotional pain. It's as though knowing *why* someone made the choice they did will somehow make the pain go away and thereby solve the problem. Remember, an explanation is not an excuse. Nothing will change simply because the motive for the action has been explained.

When one partner asks the other why, it changes the direction of the communication between them. Instead of being solution focused, it becomes gratification focused for the asking partner. Even when the explanation is negative, the asking partner acquires power because she is attempting to put her partner in a one-down position. It also shifts the focus away from positive emotional connection as one partner struggles to explain what is oftentimes unexplainable. Usually the explanation makes the situation all the more complicated since motivations for decisions people make are rarely linear and simple.

Among many couples I have seen in my practice, a common issue is an extramarital affair by one of the partners. Invariably we reach a point where the partner who did not have an affair will turn to the one who did and ask, often tearfully, "Why?"

The reasons for outside relationships are very complex. They are also very personal and often very hard to put into words, particularly if the offending partner is emotionally unavailable.

Someone who is emotionally unavailable will have trouble recognizing his or her own emotional state and may also be blind to the emotional reactions of both the primary partner and the secondary partner (the affair). Thus an explanation is apt to be much more mechanical than emotional, which will be all the more painful for the partner.

"Why" allows an emotionally unavailable person to stay inside his or her head as opposed to connecting with his or her emotions. Asking "why" allows for the very intellectualizing and mental tricks and turns that have kept the emotionally unavailable person emotionally unavailable.

"Why" is a morass that can do a lot more harm than good. When you are communicating with an emotionally unavailable person, resist the temptation to ask "why." Instead, stay in the Solver spot and be assertive.

"Help me understand" is a phrase that works. "Help me understand your feelings when you decided to look outside our relationship." You're not asking why your partner chose to seek another person. Instead, you're asking about feelings and you're asking for understanding. On that basis you can then build some common ground for problem solving because you have asked about your partner's emotional state of mind at the time the affair began. By exploring that, you can begin to see where the problem began and maybe even identify solutions. This is a building tool rather than a tool of destruction.

Another helpful way to ask questions is to use "I wonder," as in "I wonder if you know how painful it is for me that you had an affair." "I wonder if you thought of the emotional consequences to our relationship before you started your outside relationship."

Both "help me understand" and "I wonder" allow you to ask difficult questions in open-ended ways, which will facilitate open discussion of the issues. When you're dealing with difficult subjects, you want to keep the discussions as open as possible to allow everyone to feel heard.

"Help me understand" and "I wonder" are also very useful in less emotion-charged situations. "Help me understand your decision to skip school" is a way of asking your adolescent to take responsibility without closing communication doors. Often when you ask for understanding, an adolescent will stop shrugging and mumbling "I dunno," because the question is asked in a way that allows his or her answer to be heard.

With both phrases, you are opening the possibilities of the broadest communication channels and thus helping everyone, emotionally available or not, to speak their feelings in a safe, nonaccusatory, solution-focused environment.

## Goals and Structure

Emotionally unavailable people have a tendency to drift through relationships. They go with the flow created by the more emotionally available partner until the situation gets uncomfortable, then suddenly depart. This drifting is very frustrating to the partner who wants the relationship to move forward and grow. Drifting arises from the emotionally unavailable partner's lack of clear goals and/or lack of structure to achieve them.

In some relationships, the lack of goals and structure exists in both partners. These relationships have had some time-limited driving force initially—a common seasonal interest, mutual involvement in a political campaign, a common project at work. When the driving force disappears, it takes away the glue of the relationship. The relationship is carried forward by habit for a time. In some unfortunate situations, that habit leads to an unhappy marriage.

Emotionally unavailable people are frequently very skilled at starting relationships, in part because they do it so often. The problems arise when they have to move from the safe, known opening phase into a more intimate, connected, ongoing relationship. Because the emotionally unavailable person hasn't been successful in this position before, he or she will have no idea how to proceed. This partner will feel unsafe and so will leave the relationship. A person who is more experienced with the various stages of relationships may expect her partner to know how to make these transitions, so she'll be surprised to find that he can't.

If you want to help yourself and your partner to move forward, set goals together. Goal setting requires communication in a solution-focused mode and the ability to be assertive without being aggressive.

"Vanessa, I feel really happy when we're together and I really enjoy working out together. I'd like to spend more time with you. Can we work out twice a week?" Here you are setting a goal with structure since you and Vanessa will need to plan around your schedules. The plan will require an ongoing commitment from Vanessa. You have also talked about your feelings, and this will help Vanessa understand that you have an emotional involvement as well. In addition, you are being very clear about what you're asking for, which will help Vanessa identify your feelings and begin to connect with her own.

When dealing with kids and adolescents, goals and structure are helpful because they help to keep everything clear and predictable. Goals and structure help kids know where their boundaries are. They can exercise freedom of choice within the structure and feel safe.

Goals and structure also provide a framework on which to build a relationship. Both partners know what to expect and where they are going. If people are clear about expectations and targets, it allows for freedom within that context and fosters healthy relationships and emotional connections.

Setting goals involves having a clear objective in mind. That objective must be respectful to both sides. An inappropriate goal would involve personal gratification for the goal setter at the expense of the other person in the relationship. Appropriate goals have an eye to growth or positive change.

The first step in goal setting is to discuss common objectives. When you asked Vanessa to work out twice a week and spoke about your feelings of enjoying the time you spend together, you were proposing a goal. It was then up to Vanessa to agree with that proposition, to reject it, or to propose her own goal. Although it might not feel like it as you are doing it, you are each giving the other parameters—boundaries—and information that can lead to a better relationship.

Goals can be short term, medium term, or long term. Short-term goals are achievable within hours or days. "This week I'd like to get everything in the garage put away." "Today we must call your mom to wish her a happy birthday." "Tomorrow night would you be willing to sit down and talk about our vacation plans?" These are all examples of short-term goals.

Medium-term goals extend from about a week to about a year. "By the end of this year, I hope we can be in our new house." "In July, I think we should decide on a wedding date." "Next winter, let's be sure we plan to have that party we've talked about." Medium-term goals often include complex tasks, so they may involve setting some short-term goals within the larger goal. For example, being in a new house involves house hunting, getting a mortgage, packing, and moving, all of which are short-term goals that must be set in order to meet the medium-term goals.

Long-term goals involve objectives that are to begin about a year or more in the future; some can even take most of a lifetime. "When we retire, we hope to live in Arizona." "Ultimately, in my job I'd like to be the president of the company." "Our relationship is growing and building toward a lifetime commitment to each other." Notice how broad the goals are in the longer term. The specifics and details will come in the medium- and short-term goals you set to accomplish the longer-term goals.

Healthy relationships have goals of all three types. The

short-term goals are positive for daily living and keep things moving forward. Medium-term goals provide objectives that help set long-term goals and give purpose to daily activities. Long-term goals set a path for life.

People who don't have goals live in a very reactive way, jumping from one event or person to another without consideration for the future. This lack of focus makes it hard for a person to connect, for he or she isn't able to say what he or she wants from life. On the other hand, this individual may be very clear about what he or she needs in the moment. This type of reactivity is frustrating to someone who has good goals and clear objectives.

As with communication skills, goal setting is learned in childhood. People who are able to set goals for themselves as adults either have grown up with adults who were good at that and have modeled it, or have made the effort to learn goal setting and to practice it. A strong internal feedback loop and good boundaries are essential to the process of setting good goals. In short, goal setting is a skill that uses all the other skills we've been exploring.

## Emotional Responsibility

Each of us is responsible for our own feelings and emotions and for the behavior we demonstrate in response to those emotions and feelings. People who are emotionally unavailable don't take responsibility for what they can't see in themselves and can't identify in others. When confronted, they will often deny or deflect ownership of the problem to the person who is emotionally present.

This deflection not only creates frustration, it also creates a potentially abusive emotional environment in which the emotionally available partner feels abandoned or manipulated and finds himself or herself doing all the emotional work, without response from the emotionally unavailable partner.

Teresa and Jerry had been married for about fifteen years when they came to see me. Teresa was feeling abandoned because of Jerry's focus on his job. Jerry said he thought everything was fine in their marriage and attributed the problem to Teresa's hormones.

"It's her PMS. She's fairly OK two weeks a month but the other two weeks she's crying all the time or she's just out of control," Jerry told me. "If you can just get her on some medicine, she'd be fine."

Teresa, on the other hand, reported, "Jerry treats the company he works for as though it's his own. When things go smoothly, he's able to proportion his time and give some attention to me and some to his job. When things are not going smoothly at work, which is most of the time, he's obsessed with making everything right and can't think of anything else, so our marriage goes onto the rocks. Incidentally, I've been to my gynecologist and I do have some PMS but it's more like a couple of days of crankiness than two weeks of hell. Jerry just needs an excuse to be mad at me for two weeks a month so he can feel OK about going to work and staying there for three or four days at a time. And my doctor said he doesn't think medicine will help because my PMS isn't out of control."

Jerry admitted he was concerned about the company at times but said it was part of his job to be worried. He had a high-level management position in the computer group of a multinational company. He told me there were two other people in the computer group who had the same title and admitted that they rarely came in for extra hours but didn't seem to suffer at evaluation time. He also admitted that his plan was to leave the company eventually to start his own business so he was not worried about promotion potential.

When I asked him if he could see Teresa's pain, he shrugged. "She overreacts to everything. I suppose if I start my own business, she'll be upset about that too. She's just jealous. And she has PMS."

You can see that Jerry isn't able to take responsibility for the emotional debris he's creating with his focus on work.

When I asked him if he were thinking about ending the marriage, he was surprised and offended. "Of course not. Why would I want to divorce Teresa? I love her."

Jerry's position puts Teresa in a very uncomfortable spot. In order to ask for what she needs, she ends up being blamed for feeling something legitimate. Her realistic feelings of abandonment are translated by Jerry into something negative, which he expects her to correct. His own role is glorified: he paints himself as the loving husband who sacrifices his time and energy to keep his job and potentially build a business. He is unwilling to see that he is responsible for creating the environment in which Teresa feels abandoned, frustrated, and blamed.

If your relationship is similar, you must set your boundaries firmly. Make your expectations known assertively, set clear goals, and stay in the Solver spot using Dr. Collins's Six Magic Words and Dr. Collins's Magic Question to help your partner take emotional responsibility.

Teresa was finally able to do just that. She set her boundaries, proposed a goal, and told Jerry she would not allow him to blame her for mutual problems or to blame her hormones. She was also clear about the issues she felt needed to be addressed. Finally, she asked him to take ownership of his portion of the problem—to take emotional responsibility.

Jerry was now the one who was unsettled. He had been in the position of being the aggrieved spouse for so long that having to take responsibility for his part of the problem was uncomfortable.

At first Jerry tried to create several new problems that might keep him in the Blamer spot. He attacked Teresa's housekeeping skills, her money management, the way she drove, and her taste in music.

Teresa stayed firm, using Dr. Collins's Six Magic Words and Dr. Collins's Magic Question whenever they were appropriate. She didn't get into a Blamer/Poor Me swirl and clung firmly to her Solver stance. She also kept restating her goals and expectations of Jerry and of the relationship.

Finally Jerry realized he was not getting anywhere and joined Teresa in the Solver mode. Over time the issues were resolved as they began to work as partners rather than adversaries.

## Using the Tools

If you can use these tools—confrontation, reframing, clear communication, good boundaries, goal setting, and emotional responsibility—in your relationship with an emotionally unavailable person, you will help yourself feel less frustrated, and you will help the emotionally unavailable person feel safer and more empowered to be vulnerable and connected.

By staying in a Solver mode when you are using these tools, you will keep the level of conflict low and the level of solution high, which is both respectful to all concerned and effective for growth and change.

Another benefit of allowing someone who is emotionally unavailable to experience emotional connections is that he or she may discover emotions are safe and decide it's worth the work to try to become more emotionally available. If he or she wants to change, Chapter 18 has tools that can help.

# Chapter Eighteen

# TOOLS FOR CHANGING AND GROWING

We have looked at the tools for changing your relationships and helping them grow. Now we will learn some tools for individual change and growth.

As with partner-focused tools, these individual tools require commitment and practice before they can become part of your life. Remember that people find change unsettling and uncomfortable, so don't be surprised if you have a bit of emotional discomfort. Reframe it for yourself as evidence of growth!

## An Internal Feedback System

Earlier in this book we looked at internal locus of control as a factor of emotional unavailability. Just for a brief review, *locus of control* is psychobabble for determining where people look to help them identify their feelings and the ways in which they react to the world.

An *external locus of control* means the person looks outside herself to establish how she reacts and to figure out what she feels. External locus is typical of adolescents, for example, who are very concerned with what other people think of them and act according to the reactions of people around them so they will be deemed acceptable by their peers. An extreme example of this behavior would be gang membership. Kids in gangs are completely externally focused as they make behavioral choices and block off any connections to what they believe in favor of the groupthink attitude of the gang.

*Internal locus of control*, on the other hand, means the person has an internal feedback system that helps him decide what to do and how to feel in any particular situation. You can think of it as having an internal emotional measuring device. It develops during late adolescence and sets the course for a person's belief systems and emotional reactions throughout life. That's why a person who has not developed an internal feedback system seems so self-focused and immature. Though he may be forty or fifty years old, the emotional process he exhibits is more one of early adolescence.

Think about Tom Hanks in the film *Big*. He was a thirteen-year-old who was suddenly zapped into physical adulthood without the appropriate emotional growth. In the film, he's a charming man who acts irrepressibly and spontaneously but without much consideration for the feelings and rights of others. It's because he is a kid in the body of an adult. Emotionally unavailable persons are similar—they are kids in the form of adults. They can be charming, but they have so little connection with their own emotions—a stunted internal feedback loop—that they are unable to see the emotional consequences of their behavioral choices. In other words, though they may be fun and charming, they are usually unable to give a partner any sort of emotional connection or depth of feeling.

Emotionally unavailable people often have not developed their internal feedback system. Therefore, they get stuck in the adolescent pattern of looking to others to define their emotional reality and to establish reactions to the way the world works.

This pattern might work fine for an adolescent but

adults who look outside themselves to determine how they feel and how to react are cut off emotionally from themselves and others. One result of this distance is that the emotionally unavailable person lacks empathy—the ability to realize how others feel—and a blueprint for emotional responses of any kind.

The development of an internal feedback system provides that blueprint. To develop an internal feedback system, essentially, we need to go back to adolescence and start again—this time without the angst and the acne!

## Identify Your Feelings

The good news is that developing this system is not as difficult as you may think. Remember, this is a developmental issue. The first step in this process is to learn to identify your feelings and understand how you experience them. In Chapter 2, we talked about the basic four emotions and how they connect with mind-sets. Just as a reminder, the basic four emotions are *mad*, *glad*, *sad*, and *scared*.

All other emotions can be seen as either subdivisions or combinations of these four. For example, if you are feeling *confused*, the emotion might be a combination of mad and scared or sad and scared. *Irritated* can be all mad or it might be a combination of mad and scared. There's nothing arbitrary about this system because it is as personal and individual as emotions themselves. What is universal is the need to connect with one's emotions as a step to connecting with other people.

Emotions reside not only in the brain but also in the body. Here's an example. Imagine you are walking through a dark, unfamiliar house on a stormy night. Lightning is crackling and thunder is booming. Your flashlight is dead and you have to feel your way along. Suddenly a hand grabs you from behind.

What do you feel in your body, and where? If you're like most people, your heart will pound and your stomach will feel very quivery. Perhaps your knees will knock and your hands will shake. Certainly your breathing rate will have increased and you will have a lot of instant energy.

This reaction is called the flight-or-fight response. It's produced in your body by a hormone called adrenaline. The physical feelings of accelerated heart rate, rapid breathing, shaking, and a surge of energy are products of the physical response to an emotional situation.

There is a parallel and connected emotional response— scared. Your body and your mind are connected, so when you have the *physical* experience of scared your mind links that with the *emotional* experience of scared. The next time you experience something that fits into the scared category, your body's response and your emotional memory of the last time you were scared will both be present. In other words, your mind reads the physical response and adds the appropriate emotional information to complete the experience.

When your brain has linked the body feeling and the emotion, it stores the total experience. The next time you encounter a similar situation, your brain accesses the old experience and joins it with the new one.

This linkage was really useful in the time of the cave dweller when it was important to be able to remember the mind and body responses of encountering that saber-toothed tiger. With the mind-body memories, the cave dweller didn't have to reexperience the fear each time and could immediately start running for dear life.

This heightened response can be beneficial to us now as well because it helps us create an internal feedback loop.

## State-Dependent Learning

The mind-body state you are in when you learn something is stored along with the learned information. Then when that state is reexperienced, you also may reexperience the learning—the memories of the emotional and physical feelings experienced at the time of the original learning. This link is called state-dependent learning.

Let me give you an example. A team of experimenters took a group of college senior psych majors and got them drunk (a state, to be sure), then taught them a math problem with a trick embedded in it. You couldn't solve the problem unless you used the trick. They practiced with the intoxicated students until everyone could do the problem perfectly, then sent them home with instructions to come back in three days.

When the students returned, sober, they were given the problem to solve. None could solve it. The experimenters then got the students drunk again and—surprise!—every one of them could solve the problem perfectly. This is a vivid example of state-dependent learning. The state of intoxication was stored along with the trick to solve the problem and was only retrievable when the state was duplicated.

## Traumatic Memory

State-dependent learning helps to explain traumatic memory. When a person has been exposed to a traumatic event, the event is stored differently than everyday memory: it's stored with many cross-references to both physical and emotional memory. The smells, sounds, feelings, physical experience, and emotional experience all connect the traumatic memory to the rest of the person's memory trails.

When the trauma victim is later exposed to one of those elements, it can suddenly bring up the traumatic memory. If that person has the misfortune to be exposed to another trauma, it can open the door to *all* the traumatic memories the person has stored.

That's one component of posttraumatic stress disorder (PTSD), and one of the reasons it's so hard to treat. Everything that feels similar throws open the memory doors of the trauma track.

Because traumatic memory is stored differently, it's not

236 ◆ EMOTIONAL UNAVAILABILITY

available to the person on a daily basis. When it emerges, it not only feels frightening and overwhelming, it also feels foreign and unfamiliar, making it all the more threatening. It also may feel completely unrelated to what the person is consciously aware is happening to him.

Let me give you an example. I was seeing Doris because of her feelings of victimization in her relationship with her husband Barney. This being Minne*snow*ta, she was on her way to a session in the middle of a March blizzard when she was involved in a car accident.

Over the next three weeks, her PTSD symptoms emerged and became almost unbearable. Doris was having nightmares, flashbacks, body memories, bouts of unexplained sobbing and anger. She was afraid to leave her home, afraid to drive, afraid of the dark, and deeply depressed. She told me a number of times that suicide was the only way she could imagine to escape all the raw pain she was feeling.

The car accident had accessed the trauma track and thrown open all the old trauma memories, jumbling them together in a confusing and overwhelming way.

She began to have memories of being sexually abused as a child by her maternal grandfather. Now she had to work not only on this terrible abuse but also on the date rape she'd experienced in college, the physical abuse by her mother and her first husband, and a mugging.

Instead of being able to work on one item at a time, we were forced to throw everything into the emotional kettle and try to deal with whatever boiled to the surface. Meanwhile, Doris went from feeling relatively safe in her world to feeling victimized by an avalanche of memory and emotion. Doris's response to this heightened emotional state was to shut down. She was trying to find some way to feel in control of this out-of-control flood. This is not uncommon with people who have several old traumas.

Once someone has worked through his or her traumatic memories, the memories still seem to exist on the trauma track—that's the old safety valve built in from the cave-dweller times. But gradually the traumas seem to lose most of their emotional punch. And, better yet, they also seem to get mixed in with the nontrauma memories and become a part of life. People who have worked through their traumas are able to talk about the experiences without feeling retraumatized or frightened.

This normalization of traumatic memory into the daily working memory is what PTSD therapy is about. Things you see every day tend to be less terrifying and out of control than memories that emerge suddenly and with great intensity attached from traumatic experience.

A person whose emotional unavailability is based in past victimization and trauma needs to do the extra work of processing the trauma or traumas in a safe setting as a part of connecting with his or her emotions.

## Connecting Emotions and Body Feelings

The emotion-body connection is an important asset for someone who is learning to feel his or her feelings. Emotionally unavailable people have lost the link between the body emotion and the mind emotion. The mind emotion is there, but it's buried or concealed.

Your body can help you connect with your emotions. When you have a body feeling, stop and experience the rest of the brain-body connection—the emotional end. Ask yourself, "What am I feeling in my body? What am I feeling in my emotions?"

At first this process may feel awkward and slow. It takes time to assess what you are feeling in various parts of yourself and what those feelings might mean, so don't try to go too fast. Take time to experience the feeling, then assess it to connect it with the emotion.

Remember the example of being alone in a dark unknown house with no flashlight? For a moment imagine you are there.

- What do you feel in your body?
- How intense is it?
- How long will it last?
- Which effect lasts longest?
- Which of the basic four emotions do you feel?

This would fall into the scared category. Now you have developed a template for scared. You have a clear understanding of the body response and how you experience it. You have connected it to an emotion you would feel in that particular situation.

The next time you encounter something that makes your heart race, your breathing accelerate, your stomach knot, and your knees wobble, you'll have a template in your memory bank with which you can compare the experience.

The good news is that you can identify it as either love or fear! That's where your intellect comes into play. If you're feeling all those things and you're in a romantic spot with the object of your affection, it's probably love. If, on the other hand, you're sliding on a patch of black ice toward the trunk of a very large oak tree, you can assume you are feeling scared.

## Connecting to Other People

The ability to connect body and mind emotions is an essential part of getting connected to other people. If you are unable to assess your own emotional condition accurately and interpret what those emotions mean to you, you will be unable to interpret the feelings of another person.

When you are able to interpret and assess your own feelings, the emotions of others will become much more clear to you and will function as a guide to help you choose respectful, loving responses to your partner or someone else.

# Developing Values and Beliefs

A second key to developing an internal feedback system is to be clear about your own values and beliefs.

- What do you believe in?
- What do you hold as a value?

I'm talking not about the value of something in terms of monetary worth, but your values as a person. Values are those beliefs we hold that guide us.

For example, part of my value system is that I believe in being truthful with people. In response to this belief—this value—I am careful when talking to others to be truthful and convey information in a clear and nondeceptive way. This value would also include being truthful about my feelings with others.

Other values people hold are family unity, upright community connections, financial morality, including paying all bills on time and not victimizing others financially, being a good parent, being a loving spouse, honoring your commitments, being on time, being religious, etc.

The values a person holds come from deep in his or her personal past and are enduring.

If, however, you missed the installation of values in adolescence, you may have a limited internal moral code against which to judge your own or others' behavior. All you can do in that case is cast judgment and react according to the reactions of those around you.

This reactive position is fine if you are always in the company of people whose values are strong and positive. But if you are in the company of people who have negative values or unclear values, you will have no reliable frame of reference.

The double bind here is that since you don't know your own values, you may not be able to judge whether or not another's values and beliefs are positive. It's for exactly this reason that adolescents sometimes get themselves into intense, negative relationships so quickly. It's not simply that they choose the wrong people; it's that they have some difficulty judging which people are healthy and which are not. They are reacting more to external cues because their own value systems are still forming.

Like emotions, which are present in the emotionally unavailable person but not accessed or acknowledged, the value system is also present. It's often hidden from view to the emotionally unavailable person because of the chameleon-like quality he or she has adopted over the years to be acceptable in all situations. It goes back to the external locus of control: If you always look outside yourself for feedback, you get very good at matching what you think you need to match in order to stay present in the world. What you don't get good at is identifying where you are and what you believe.

The values are in there. You learned your family's values, those of your community, your religious affiliation, your school, and your neighborhood. Now you just have to identify them. So here's an exercise to help you.

---

## VALUES IDENTIFICATION

1. Divide a piece of paper into eight columns. Head each column with one of the following:

   Family
   Community
   Business
   Religious/Spiritual
   School
   Neighborhood
   Nation
   Ethnic Community

2. List as many of your values as you can think of for each category. You might do this over several days or weeks as you think about what you believe.

3. Examine each of your beliefs and rate yourself from 1 to 10 on how much your behavior reflects your values and beliefs in each category, 1 being not at all and 10 being always. Then add up your score in each category and divide by 8. The closer you are to an average of 10, the more clear you are about your values and beliefs and the more you live by your beliefs.

4. On those values you rated at less than an 8, consider why you believe it if you don't live it!

## Building Trust

Once you know what you believe and let your behavior reflect it, you will be more emotionally available to yourself and to others. You will be emotionally visible and consistent—not a chameleon. The change will make it easier for other people to trust you. Good emotional relationships are built on trust.

The ability to be trusted and trusting is a major part of developing an internal feedback system. Many people who are emotionally unavailable have had violations of their trust earlier in life, either by victimization, emotional abandonment, or other trauma.

From this experience the emotionally unavailable person has given himself the mandate not to trust anyone in the belief that if he doesn't let anyone into his self, he won't ever be betrayed again. Unfortunately, it seems to work in exactly the opposite fashion. Rather than being protection, the barriers provide only isolation, which seems to open the door to betrayal and abandonment.

It may seem a difficult task to learn how to trust, but it is actually quite a simple process. Start with one small, focused attempt. Choose a person and a situation in which you would usually pull back from trusting and do precisely the opposite. You will be very uncomfortable, but you can help ease this discomfort a bit by telling the person, "I'm uncomfortable with trusting, but in this situation I'm trying to learn with your help." Most people will empathize with your feelings and cooperate.

As you become more able to experience having your trust validated, you will find it easier to trust in new situations. It's the same basic process you use to create emotional memories on which you can draw in the future. If you are unfortunate enough to be betrayed in this attempt to trust someone, try to have the courage to try again.

Part of the process of learning to trust is learning how to judge whether or not someone is trustworthy, and that sometimes takes practice, especially if you have been cut off from yourself and others for a long time.

The other side of trust is to be trustworthy yourself. The development of trustworthiness comes from being emotionally predictable. In order to trust others, we must be able to predict accurately how they will behave, how they will react, and how they will position themselves emotionally.

If you extend trust to someone, you must also be trustworthy in return. Otherwise you are taking the power away from the other person and creating a burden for him or her.

To demonstrate emotional trustworthiness, you must be willing to take a risk and be emotionally vulnerable to another person. In this way you both build trust. The nice side effect is that you also begin to trust yourself and your ability to make judgments about other people.

Katie and Susie had been friends in their office for about a year before the new manager arrived. He began harassing each of the young women, aggressively and sexually. The bond between the two of them became closer under duress and they decided to become roommates.

Each of these women had been victimized in childhood and had a lot of trouble being emotionally available, but they both treasured the friendship.

As time went along, Susie became engaged and wanted to move in with her fiancé. Katie was crushed because she saw this as a rejection of herself and an end of the friendship.

Both women were in tears as we talked about this issue. Susie wanted very much to keep Katie's friendship and to move in with her fiancé. Susie wished Katie well but feared they would never see each other since they had both quit working at the office with the abusive boss and had taken new jobs in separate companies and towns.

Each needed to learn some trust with the other. I encouraged them to make a schedule to do something together. This schedule was to build predictability. They also set up a schedule of phone conversations and a plan to have breakfast together once a week. Both Katie and Susie had to be willing to take the risk to trust the other party emotionally and both had to demonstrate constancy.

In other words, each woman had to be both trusting and trustworthy. Each had to have the courage to take an emotional risk that could have led to abandonment or rejection by the other.

The two friends learned that emotional intimacy comes from the willingness to be vulnerable to hurt or rejection. It was a valuable lesson for both women, as they learned how to develop their internal feedback systems using trust.

At the risk of stating the obvious, let me add the caveat that some people will be glad to betray you. Unfortunately, we each have a mixture of trustworthy and nontrustworthy people in our lives. Having access to your trusting self, however, makes you better able to choose trustworthy people for relationships and to predict and avoid people who are not trustworthy.

It takes time and the willingness to take risks, but remember what my wise old friend Charlie Jones once observed: "There can be disruption without change but there can be no change without disruption!" Disruption and change are uncomfortable, but then again, being alone, isolated, and unhappy is pretty uncomfortable too!

There's one more thing people need in order to develop an internal feedback system: the ability to be compassionate—to feel what others feel. Compassion and empathy are essentially the same idea. They are the result of being connected with your own emotions and working to interpret the feelings of others. To achieve empathy, you must not only interpret the feelings of others, but embrace those feelings so that you can experience them firsthand.

It's not as intrusive as it sounds, nor as difficult. Let me give you an example. Jason was fifteen when I first began meeting with him and his parents in an effort to mediate the escalating disputes they were experiencing.

Jason seemed incapable of focusing on anything but his own needs, regardless of the needs and wants of anyone else, particularly his family. He was loud and aggressive about his demands and behaved like a jerk to everyone—parents, teachers, cops, adults in stores, and me.

We worked hard in therapy, confronting each behavioral issue as it arose, and each time it came down to Jason digging in his heels and refusing to understand his parents' position or to empathize with them in any way.

Jason wanted to be allowed to stay out with his friends after midnight, for example, and he wasn't able to hear that this was not only impractical and potentially dangerous but it was also against the law in their community where there was a curfew for people under eighteen years of age.

Jason said he didn't care. He wanted to stay out and skateboard until he was ready to come home. We negotiated and reasoned and talked. Jason would finally agree to a curfew, then would go off and stay out as late as he pleased. He shrugged off getting arrested, dismissed being grounded and other punishments, cursed his parents, and was verbally abusive with me even when his folks and I both told him how inappropriate his assaults were. This battle went on for months with everyone involved getting frustrated except Jason, who stayed seamless and unreachable.

I was contemplating suggesting a hiatus in therapy, as we didn't seem to be getting anywhere. But then one day Jason paged me with a *911, which is pager code for an emergency.

Jason asked to come in for a special session on his own. His first gesture on arriving was to give me an exuberant hug—very unusual. He then proceeded to tell me, with tears in his eyes, what a jerk he had been to his parents, his siblings, his teachers—and especially to me. I'm cynical enough not to fall for this kind of quick turnaround, but I supported his intention to apologize to his parents, siblings, and teachers.

Over the next few months, Jason demonstrated over and over his ability to recognize and empathize with the emotions of others. He still made some adolescent choices, but he was able to connect with his mom when she was upset with him and it was clear he empathized. He was uncomfortable, not with the situation of being confronted but with the choices he had made and the pain he'd caused with his choices.

Finally one day I asked him what had helped him make the change to being more compassionate. He told me it was "the amoeba story" I'd told. I had to search my brain, but then I remembered suggesting to him that to understand with his heart what his mom was feeling, he needed to be an "emotional amoeba" and spread himself out to encompass the perspective and feelings of others. I'd told him that until he could do that he would never be a complete person. Apparently that single image was vivid enough to make a life-changing impression on Jason.

## Developing Empathy

Connection with compassion requires the person making the connection to reach out with his heart to another person, embrace that person's emotional state, and offer support from that perspective. Don't confuse *empathy* with *sympathy*.

- *Empathy* is making emotional contact with good boundaries. A person who is empathic is able to say, "I know how it feels to feel sad and if there is anything I can do, please let me know."
- *Sympathy*, on the other hand, is more "I feel exactly what you feel and I'll fix it for you and try to make everything all better."
- *Sympathy* takes the other person's power away and gives it to the person who is being sympathetic.
- *Empathy* allows both parties to keep their power—their choices—open and in their possession.
- *Sympathy* is intellectual.
- *Empathy* is emotional.
- *Sympathy* is external.
- *Empathy* is internal.

So how do you know how others feel? Obviously this is going to be different from reading your own emotional cues because you won't have the internal process (body emotions) to rely upon. When trying to discern what others are feeling, you use visual cues, experience, and careful listening.

## Visual Cues

Visual cues are body language. You might remember that body language analysis was a fashionable pop psychology movement in the mid-1970s that focused people's attention on carefully observing others.

You get a general impression from the way the person is standing or sitting—relaxed, tense, leaning forward and listening, or all closed-up with arms folded and legs crossed—from the expression on the person's face, and from his or her tone of voice.

Body language is an important way of reading another

person emotionally. The longer you are in a relationship, the better you become at reading your partner's cues. You also can become more accurate at interpreting them, providing your partner is emotionally available.

We often misread our partners because we haven't connected emotionally and we haven't checked in with them on emotional issues. Without connecting and checking in, neither side has a foundation of experience on which to draw conclusions.

## The Template of the Expected

Experience goes hand in hand with visual cues. The trap that experience can sometimes lead us into is prejudging and expecting a person to react in a particular way.

Have you ever steeled yourself for some emotional response you expected from a partner, a boss, or a parent, only to be caught completely off guard when the response goes the other way? You're braced for a battle and instead you get cooperation. Then you wonder if you've missed something or if the person is just fooling with your head. In either case, your expectation has planted self-doubt.

Experience without prejudging and without a set of expectations can be a very helpful tool in interpreting the emotions of others. The more you have stored in your memory about a person, the more likely you are to be able to interpret how he or she is feeling, based on what you see and hear.

It would be great if each of us were a perfect listener. Communication problems would virtually evaporate. However, most people are not perfect listeners. Things distract us, both internal and external. The television, the stereo, the traffic, the blue-light special, the kids, other people around us, and our own thoughts all get in the way of clear listening.

There has been some interesting research lately about how we see. What researchers have found is that our eyes don't have anywhere near enough nerve receptors to perceive in the sort of detail we see things. The theory these researchers are putting forth says that our brains make a template of the expected—a sort of mental paint-by-numbers—and that what we actually see simply fills in the template of the expected with details. You can apply this theory to emotions. When you are accustomed to someone's emotional patterns, you make an emotional template of the expected and operate from there.

If you use experience to prejudge, don't clarify your partner's visual cues, and operate out of a template of the expected, you can imagine the potential misinterpretation of emotional states.

You want to learn to observe differently, setting the template aside and paying attention not only to content (what your partner is saying) but also the intent (the emotional load of the content).

The combination of these three things, then, is the key to understanding what others feel. You will have varying degrees of success depending upon how well you know the person with whom you are communicating, how much experience you have, how carefully you are listening, and how sensitive your own emotional filters are. As you become more conscious of where someone is coming from emotionally, you will also become more able to interpret what he or she is feeling.

In summary, developing an internal feedback system has four steps:

1. First you must learn to identify feelings, both emotional and physical, and how to connect the two.
2. You must know the value system and beliefs you hold as your code of life, and your behavior must reflect your beliefs.
3. You must learn how to trust and be trustworthy.
4. You must learn how to be empathic or compassionate with another person.

By developing each of these individual skills, you will develop an internal feedback system that will free you of having to depend upon others to tell you how you feel and how you should react to the feelings of others.

## Goals and Structure

One element common to emotionally available people is that they have personal goals that guide them in daily life. Most people who are emotionally unavailable tend to be reactive to life and do not have a strong forward plan.

In Chapter 17 we looked at the goal-setting process in the context of relationships. These rules also apply to personal goals. Short-, medium-, and long-term goals can be set for personal achievement along with relationship goals without any contradictions at all.

Remember, I'm not talking about vague intentions or wishes such as "I want to be rich," "I want to be president," or "I want to be a professional baseball player." These are, for most people, fantasies. Living in a fantasy world contributes to emotional unavailability because it keeps you at a distance from the realities of your life. You are at arm's length from your emotions.

Realistic goals, however, help you to stay connected because they require an internal feedback analysis of what you want and what you feel. If you can't connect with who you are, it's pretty hard to decide where you're going.

In relationships emotionally unavailable people often can't make a commitment because they are not clear where life will take them.

Setting goals involves soul searching, even for short-term goals. The commitment to the goal is built when a person has thought carefully about the goal, exploring both the means of getting to the goal and the timing involved in achieving it.

A good example of goal setting without commitment is the annual New Year's resolution. Millions of people set themselves huge goals but usually without a plan of action or a timetable—and without much commitment. As a result, the average New Year's resolution lasts only six days!

When you're deciding which goal to set, consider your objectives. Ask yourself what you want to accomplish.

It may be a personal goal—losing weight, quitting smoking, getting in shape—or it may be a relationship goal—better communication, closer connections. It can also be a financial, educational, career-oriented, or any other sort of goal.

## Setting Achievable and Realistic Goals

The trick is to create a contract with yourself to achieve something within your reach in an appropriate amount of time. It is most important that the goal is achievable and realistic. I've always wanted to be 5'9", but that's neither achievable nor realistic and I'm very clear about that. Still, if I do find that magic lamp. . . .

The factors to consider are your own gifts and abilities, which will enable you to get where you're going; the costs in both financial and psychic terms; the practical applications of the accomplishment; and the ways in which your goal will improve or enrich your life.

## Making a Plan of Action

After you've decided on the goal, the next step is to make a plan of action to reach that goal. This is where structure comes in. People who have clear goals with clear plans of action are most likely to be successful. The plan is the foundation on which you build the results you want to achieve. The plan dictates the structure.

For example, you decide you want to finish your college degree. You call your school and find out that when you dropped out, you had 30 credits left to take. Nine of those required credits were to be in math, six in a language, ten in science, and the rest in electives in your major. The decision to finish your degree is a medium- to long-term goal. The courses you still require are part of the plan to achieve the goal. You know you can't take all the requirements at one time, so one of the first steps in creating the plan is to assess the amount of time you have available to devote to attending school and to studying, the amount of money you have to invest in the courses, and the date on which you would like to graduate.

Once you have that information, the next part of the plan is to decide how many credits you must take per quarter to achieve the goal of the graduation date, and how you should mix those courses so you won't be either bored or overwhelmed.

Once you have decided these questions, you can construct a master plan with timetables, schedules, financial solutions, and expected outcomes. Now you have the structure on which you will hang the various parts of your goal until you are able to achieve them.

## Creating Structure

Structure—the framework of a person's operations—also helps give boundaries and definition to a person's life. It is this quality of guided, structured focus that gives a person an emotional home base from which to operate. It also lends a definite note of safety and comfort to a person because it makes the world seem more predictable.

If you are pretty secure in your world—you feel pretty safe and able to control and predict what will happen around you, you feel you know who you are in the context of that world, you are clear about your beliefs and values, and you know where you're going and have good goals—then it's not so difficult to allow yourself to be vulnerable and reach out to someone else emotionally.

The tasks of setting goals and making plans may seem tough and complex, but remember, simplicity is at the core.

Which of the following seems more complicated?

1. Constantly having to be on guard and watch every movement and change of the world around you, armoring yourself against threats, real and imagined, and having to protect yourself against those threats from all sides
2. Accepting the world as it comes to you because you are clear about who you are, what you believe, and where you are going

Obviously, the better choice is 2, and that's what being emotionally connected and available is all about.

## Unloading Old Baggage: Attachment, Abuse, and Abandonment

People are emotionally unavailable for good reasons—or what seem like good reasons to them at the time. Often the decision to retreat is not made all at once but results gradually from a series of betrayals of trust by significant persons.

Abuse of any kind, abandonment, and attachment problems can all contribute to a person's withdrawal from the emotional arena. What begins as a protective device becomes a destructive habit, which perpetuates itself because a person who is emotionally withdrawn from himself and others has no connection. People without connections continue to be abandoned and isolated from others.

As people work to find their emotional selves again, they encounter not only the good feelings that have been stuffed into the Gray Zone but also some of the uncomfortable feelings that got them to withdraw in the first place.

For many, the instinct at that point will be to turn tail and run back into the safety of the numbness that has served so well for so long.

Unfortunately, what they usually find there is not refuge but further discomfort. Oliver Wendell Holmes said it best:

"Man's mind, stretched to a new idea, never goes back to its original dimension."

If your mind has been stretched to a new idea—experiencing your emotional self and living in a connected way—it will be uncomfortable and difficult to return to numbness. Once on a connected path, you might as well keep pushing forward. If you're going to be uncomfortable anyway, you might as well find some rewards for your discomfort.

If you have issues of abuse, abandonment, or isolation, healing can be accomplished with the help of a therapist. The progress of therapy is often surprisingly quick—not like the old image of deep psychoanalysis, which entailed a daily hour on the couch and was apt to drag along for years.

With the advent of solution-focused therapy and the push—primarily by insurance companies—to keep the process short, therapists and clients have become problem-solving teams that work together to help the client experience his or her life in a more comfortable and productive way.

If you choose to form a partnership with a therapist, finding a therapist and knowing what you want to work on are vital parts of healing. In the next section, I'll give you some suggestions about how to find and evaluate a therapist and how to focus your healing so you get what you want out of the experience.

## Choosing and Using a Therapist

Therapy is the subject of many misconceptions. It's also the butt of *lots* of bad jokes and the foundation for quite a few television and movie scripts. I'm often amazed at what people think is going to happen when they come into my office. So let me take a few minutes to tell you what therapy is and is not, how to find a therapist, and what to expect in therapy.

People find therapists in many different ways. One fairly reliable method is a referral from a friend who has worked with a particular therapist. You can always use that old ruse of "I have a friend who is looking for a therapist," if you don't feel comfortable coming straight out and admitting the therapy is for you. You can also check with your doctor or your pastor, both of whom may have professional relationships with therapists whose work they know and trust.

In the world of managed care, your insurance company may have a list of approved providers. These are therapists who have presented their credentials and liability insurance and have been accepted as in-network providers.

Your insurance company may provide you with a list, written or verbal, of providers. Or you may be required to see someone in the insurance company's own clinic system. Your cost will usually be a copayment of $10 to $25 (or more) per visit. The advantage is convenience. You will never have to fill out forms or pay in advance then wait for reimbursement, and you will be assured that the provider has the proper licensure and education.

The disadvantage is twofold. First, most insurance policies limit the number of sessions you may have with the therapist and you will probably not have much choice within the clinic setting of which therapist you are assigned.

The second disadvantage is that your issues will be recorded in the insurance company's computers in order for you to receive ongoing care. You shouldn't be paranoid about this, but you do need to be aware that the privacy of your therapeutic relationship extends one ring outward from you and the in-network therapist.

There are other alternatives, even if you have insurance. There are many fine therapists working in the managed-care world, but there are also many excellent therapists who choose not to participate within the limitations of managed care. They operate independently and frequently will work on a sliding scale based on your income.

You may have out-of-network benefits from your insurance, in which case you will be able to recover a percentage of the costs of out-of-network therapy, often after a deductible has been met. Or you may choose not to access your insurance benefits and seek a provider who works on a sliding scale. What you want to be sure of in any case is that the provider is a licensed practitioner (psychologist, social worker, family therapist, etc.) who has maintained his or her education through continuing accreditation.

There are also community-based providers that operate in various low-cost or no-cost clinic settings in various communities. Sometimes therapists there are working to get their hours toward their licensure or are interns working under supervision. These providers often have waiting lists unless you are in crisis or are a danger to yourself or others. But the price will be low and there will be few limits to the number of sessions you will be able to have.

Connecting with a therapist is sort of like a blind date. Sometimes you meet the right person on the first try. Other times, it takes a few attempts. Make sure you are comfortable with this person. You should feel as though the therapist would provide a safe environment in which you could talk about difficult subjects without feeling judged, ignored, or dismissed.

This doesn't mean the therapist has to be warm and fuzzy. Many are not. Many are reserved and maintain very tight boundaries, particularly at first when they are getting to know you. This relationship is not designed to be a friendship, and you should be wary of therapists who want to make it that way. To be effective, therapists need to maintain a distance from the client. Therapist distance does not mean coldness, however. If that distance is not maintained, you are not getting what you're paying for—instead you're getting a *very* expensive pal who gives you advice.

*Therapists do not give advice.* Friends, lawyers, medical doctors, dentists, nurses, hygienists, tax accountants, gardeners, interior decorators, real estate agents, waiters, store clerks, talk-show hosts, bartenders, barbers, and cab drivers give advice, so the field of professional advisers is pretty crowded. A good therapist creates an environment in which *you* are able to give *yourself* advice. After all, can you think of a more valid source? You need to find someone whose personal style complements your own.

Convenience is another consideration. Therapists set their own hours. If you can't take time off from work and need an evening or weekend appointment, make sure the therapist you want to see can accommodate those hours.

As you go along through therapy, you will develop a sense of trust with your therapist, and as that grows, much of the real work of healing is done.

Your therapist will listen not only to what you say but to how you say it and will then give you feedback or ask you to clarify or confront your thinking to help you see the world differently. Therapists also teach people skills. As this happens and you acquire new tools to do the work you need to do, you will grow to feel more comfortable in the world, which is, after all, the whole idea.

## What Therapy Is Not

- Therapy is not magic. It takes work on the part of the client and the therapist. Change happens as a result of the work.
- Therapy doesn't fix people because people are not broken.
- Therapy doesn't change who people are in their core but addresses how they interact with others.
- Therapy is not about blaming or judging or shaming or put-downs. If you experience those things from your therapist, confront him or her immediately. Shame, blame, judgment, and abuse are not healing techniques!

Therapy is tough. It requires a commitment and a lot of work. It also requires laughter and tears and talk and a willingness to learn new tools. It is one of the most difficult, most exciting things you may ever do in your life and I highly recommend it.

One more thing: it's important to remember that you cannot turn the clock back and simply erase your life experiences. That's what someone who buries things or stuffs them has done.

Everything that has happened to you—good, bad, and indifferent—has been significant in building the unique individual you are. I believe that even our most horrific experiences can give us a gift in the form of a lesson that helps us to lead better, more fulfilled lives.

## Victims and Survivors

Some people have a terrible experience and spend the rest of their lives focused only on that experience, allowing it to define them and shape the way in which they live. In a sense, that means everything in their lives comes down to one experience.

My belief is that when something terrible happens, it comes with both good and bad attached. It is our duty to find the good in those experiences that are the most horrible—to seek the lesson that will help us grow beyond the victimization.

This is the essential difference between a victim and a survivor. The victim lives in the moment of victimization and defines all else by it. The survivor acknowledges the terrible experience and honors it by finding the lesson and incorporating it into his or her life.

It is the combination of the wonderful things and the terrible things that gives our lives texture, that affords us compassion and empathy and the strength to endure whatever the future may bring.

Nietzsche, not a man noted for his cheery view of life, summed it up this way: "That which does not kill us makes us stronger." In other words, from survivorship comes strength.

## *Building Self-Esteem*

People who don't connect often cease to believe they are worthy of connections. This lack of self-worth can also be defined as low self-esteem. "Nuts to that," you're saying. "The emotionally unavailable guys I've been involved with are egomaniacs—everything is me-me-me for them." It may surprise you to know that such selfish behavior is also an indicator of low self-esteem. People who hold themselves in low regard do things to try to build that regard, including bragging or being self-absorbed.

Other hints of low self-esteem are alcohol or drug use, constant need for reassurance or reinforcement, self-deprecating remarks, promiscuity, an external locus of control, and other types of externally focused behavior, including violence.

The underlying message is, "I'm not good enough to earn your attention just for who I am, so I'm going to push you away so you won't know I'm vulnerable even though I need your love desperately."

Low self-esteem comes from the person's belief that he or she is not good enough. The message came from parents or teachers or other significant adults who would say things like, "That's nice that you got straight A's, but . . ."; unfortunately, the part of the sentence that sticks is what follows the "but," which is not usually something supportive and reinforcing. Often what the person remembers is something like, "you can do better," or "be sure they don't become B's," or "be sure you don't get a swelled head." I think it stems from not wanting our kids to be egomaniacs. In the process, we give them low self-esteem that lasts a lifetime!

As parents or others who interact with kids, we can prevent low self-esteem by skipping the qualifying "but" when we offer praise or reinforcement. Let the compliment stand on its own: "Sam, you are a great kid!" If you need to correct him, do it in a separate sentence or at a different time. You can say, "Sam you are a great kid. I really love you and I'm so glad you're my kid. You might want to work on being a little less rowdy when we're in the store. I'd like that." At no point does Sam hear an implication that he's not good enough for you, so his self-esteem will remain intact.

If you need to make a big correction, you could say, "Sam, I love you. Your behavior in the store, however, could use a change. The consequences of not changing will be _____." This way Sam is getting a clear message that the problem is his behavior, not his personhood. Remember, *but* erases everything that comes before it.

## Confront Negative Self-Talk

Adults can help themselves build self-esteem by working to counteract those old negative messages: "I can't learn how to _____." "I'm not smart enough to _____." "I'm no good at _____." These are the kinds of negative old messages seeping through to present-day consciousness.

You'll know when one of those old messages comes up because when you hear the thought, you'll feel like the little kid who heard the messages when they were stored.

When you hear a negative message coming from inside your own head, contradict it. People forget that they are in charge of their minds. You don't have to think anything you don't want to think. So if an unwelcome thought comes into your consciousness, aggressively push it aside. You can do that aloud—if you're either alone or *very* secure—or internally. Don't let negative thoughts linger even for an instant because they are powerful and, unfortunately, contain familiar messages. They will take root and grow without much provocation.

## Acknowledge Your Talents and Gifts

Another technique to build self-esteem is to make a list of your talents and gifts and acknowledge—to yourself—the contributions they make to your life and to the lives of others with whom you are in contact.

Knowing your strengths isn't being egocentric. Instead it's reinforcing those gifts and talents, which gives you a foundation for healthy good feelings about yourself.

## Learn to Be Alone

It's also important to learn how to be alone. People who are secure with themselves are comfortable being in their own company.

One way to practice being comfortable alone is to take

yourself out for dinner as though you are taking yourself on a date. Choose a nice restaurant, dress up, have a drink if that's your pleasure, order something you enjoy eating, and be present with your thoughts. See how much you enjoy your own company. You can also go to a movie or sporting event alone and enjoy the experience of doing something you enjoy in the company of a person you value—yourself.

## Learn New Things

Learning and knowledge bring the power of independence. When you gather knowledge, you are gathering personal power through the ability to understand and do new things.

## Associate with Positive People

If you're around negative, problem-focused people, you will be negative and problem focused. If, on the other hand, you seek out positive people with an optimistic outlook, you will reflect that optimism. Optimism is part of good self-esteem.

## Let Go of Control

People who have low self-esteem and have difficulty connecting with others often need to be in control of other people and of the situations in which they find themselves. It's a way to feel safe. It's also a cruel illusion. As I've said before, it's impossible to control other people. Most of us have a tough enough time controlling ourselves.

Once you have developed an internal feedback system and have a clear vision of your goals and belief systems, you will find that your need to control other people disappears. You will be concerned with controlling yourself and with feeling connected to yourself and will feel safe to let other people control themselves.

It sounds simplistic, but most solutions really are simple. Culturally we value the complicated because we think if something is complicated, it's significant. In reality, if something is complicated, it's probably been put together by a committee!

Letting go of the need to control other people gives you the energy to increase your self-esteem, feel more comfortable in your world, and, best of all, connect with someone else on an intimate emotional level.

Healing and growing and changing are part of a lifelong process. We learn daily lessons from our lives and the people in our lives. The outcome of these lessons may not always be what we expected, but if we're open, we learn from each experience. The process of change is exciting. You can learn to celebrate not only the change but also the process of bringing about the change.

# Chapter Nineteen

# DUMPING THE TOXIC AND MOVING ON

*E*veryone has some appropriate degree of emotional distance from others. It's a natural way we have of protecting ourselves emotionally from people and situations we don't know—or people we know to be dangerous to us. The emotionally unavailable person falls outside the range of normal reserve in the degree of emotional distance he or she keeps from others.

People who are emotionally unavailable exhibit a wide range of behavior, from somewhat distant to completely unconnected. When you completed the rating scale at the end of Chapter 16, you determined where you fall on the continuum of emotional unavailability.

Many people who are emotionally unavailable can make changes in the way they connect with themselves. Only by connecting with themselves can they learn how to connect with others.

We've spent most of our time in the preceding chapters looking at emotionally unavailable persons who are able and willing to change and those people who choose to be in relationships with them.

Beyond this group, there is a small but downright dangerous group of persons whose emotional unavailability is a part of other, greater issues. The constellation of all these issues generally makes these people a real threat to the physical and emotional safety of anyone with whom they come in contact.

I'm not talking about your average emotionally unavailable person who is unwilling to work on issues at a given moment. Toxic people are *unable to change* and are *extremely manipulative* of others to get what they want. They are people who should have a warning label identifying their dangerousness and personality disorders!

## Personality Disorders

Let me clarify the term *personality disorder*. A *personality trait* is an element of a person's personality that is consistent over time and is incorporated into that person's approach to the world. An example of a trait would be a person's blunt manner of speaking his or her mind.

Someone who is blunt may be unlikely to change, but the trait usually doesn't get in the way of the person's relationships with others. Others who know the person know that the personal style of that individual is to be blunt. They either accept it and the person or they distance themselves. In the global world, however, traits don't get in the way of the person having a full and connected life.

When traits get in the way of relationships, however, we in the psychobusiness refer to them as *personality disorders*.

*Personality disorders* divide into behaviors that have severe negative impact on others and behaviors that have severe negative impact on the self. Obviously, those personality disorders that impact others are the ones with which we are concerned at the moment. Those include the following:

- *Narcissistic personality disorder* encompasses those who believe the world spins on their personal axis. They tend to be manipulative, cold, and distant. They use other people for their own pleasure or to fulfill their goals without concern for anyone's feelings but their own.

- *Histrionic personality disorder* includes those people who make a drama out of everything. Their emotional stage is so large that other people can never be certain how pervasive a problem really is. This overdramatization pushes people away.

- *Dependent personality disorder* includes people who are unable to live without being told what to do by someone else. This is a Velcro person who attaches to the significant other with terrified tenterhooks, unwilling or unable to make an independent decision or take an independent action.

- *Borderline personality disorder* includes people who are terrified of being abandoned and will manipulate and badger others to keep this from happening. They tend to be vengeful when they don't get what they want and are desperate in their attempts to stay connected with a love object. They are unstable in their view of themselves, changing constantly and often engage in highly destructive activities—spending sprees, promiscuity, addictions, suicide attempts, or other self-harming behaviors—which are designed to keep the partner engaged in the only way the person knows how to hook with others—through chaos.

- *Antisocial personality disorder* persons include criminals and others who routinely victimize others. About 85 percent of prison inmates have antisocial personality disorder. These people are perpetrators of the coldest variety; they objectify and victimize everyone around them. They are as distant from their emotions as Pluto is from the sun. They rarely have any interest in making an emotional connection with anyone, although they may have a large number of sexual partners or even spouses. These are not love connections, but patterns of abuse and victimization.

- *Sociopathic personality disorder* is a term we no longer

use—the diagnosis has been split between antisocial and narcissistic—but I think it should be returned to use because persons who are sociopathic have no humanity about them—no soul—and use others like objects, exploiting them in dangerous and damaging ways. Sociopaths have far more social skills, in general, than the average antisocial person. This allows them to have much more impact on their victims because they *appear* to be connecting. They are the ultimate manipulators and absolutely the most dangerous persons around.

Only a small percentage of the general population has a diagnosable personality disorder, so it's relatively unusual to find someone whose personality traits have become a problem. If you do run into such a person, it is important to recognize that personality disorder is an enduring element of the person, one that is very unlikely to change to any degree.

No matter how diligent or persistent you might be, you will not be able to change another person's essential Self. The problem for you is that it's so tempting to try.

Let me also stress, everyone has *some* of the traits that make up the personality disorders to *some* degree. These traits are what give people texture. When the trait becomes a personality disorder, however, the texture becomes roughness. That roughness seals the emotional unavailability and takes away any potential for positive change.

When dealing with people with personality disorders, it's imperative that you remember: you didn't break them, you can't fix them.

## The Truly Toxic

Let's take a look at some of those people who should have a warning label. I've included some examples to help you imagine what this personality disorder would look like in real life.

# The Most Toxic People:
# Con Artists, Criminals, and Serial Killers

About twenty years ago, Ted Bundy attracted the interest of the nation for a number of reasons: he was a serial killer who had been captured alive, he was responsible for a nation-wide murder spree that had focused on college-age women, he was very smart, and he seemed so *normal*. When we saw pictures of Bundy, he looked like the guy down the street who'd always help you push your car out of a snowdrift.

For me, Ted Bundy represents the end of my innocence as far as toxic people are concerned. I had always assumed a monster would look like a monster—just like in the movies. This monster looked like a guy I'd dated! I remember being shaken by this at the time, but I also have come to appreciate the lesson it taught me. I now am much less likely to make assumptions about people based on how they look.

Ted Bundy represents the most extreme of toxic people—those sociopaths who have no spark of humanity at all. Into this category we can put a number of other legendary sociopaths who have come to be part of the popular culture and whose names are synonymous with evil.

Accompanying Ted Bundy and other sociopaths near the extreme end of toxic persons are those people who may not be murderers but who have little or no ability to recognize others as anything but objects. While it is unlikely that any of us will have the terrible luck to encounter a serial killer, we are more likely to encounter other cold, very distant manipulators.

Let me give you an example. Connie came into therapy because she was having trouble with her three adolescent kids and their relationship with her husband of three years, Max.

Connie is a bright, college-educated, middle-class woman from Dallas. She was certain she was the problem because she had been unable to get her kids and her husband to even be civil with one another. Max had told her she was a poor mother and wife because of it. He told her she needed to get help because *she* was the problem.

Connie came into my office wanting me to tell her how she could be a better wife and mother. Instead we began to look at her relationship with Max and with her sons. She had met Max shortly after her divorce from Ted, the father of her children, who was a high-powered salesman and very focused on his career.

Max had seemed caring and interested in Connie and her kids. He had offered to help her change careers and had worked on repairs on her house. He had taken her kids places and they had thought he was super. He'd told her about his sad previous marriage to a woman who had died of cancer and his fears about leaving the Air Force after his career in the military. Connie had fallen in love with him and they had married.

Right after they married, he suggested private military school for the kids and told Connie he thought they were out of control. He also took a job in Minnesota, hundreds of miles from where they were living, without consulting Connie, then simply announced that they were moving. Connie had been able to dissuade Max about the military school but was powerless about the move.

Two of her kids decided to stay with their father, but one came along to Minnesota. He soon began to have conflict with Max, who was a real dictator in their home. Max kept Connie on a very tight leash, following her and checking up on every aspect of her life.

Connie told me that Max had gone through her purse, checkbook, mail, and drawers many times and had installed a wiretap on their phone so he could listen to all her conversations.

Then Max lost his job. Connie had been saving money throughout her working life for her kids' college and had nearly $100,000. When Max lost his job, he asked to borrow some money from her savings.

He was more than willing to sign a promissory note and offered to pay interest as well at a rate far greater than she could get from a bank. After thinking about it for a while, as Max pressured her, Connie decided to trust him and gave him $40,000. The next $55,000 seemed easier, she told me, as Max made it sound as though they would profit enormously from his investment of her money.

Max would tell Connie he planned to come to therapy with her, but each appointment brought a new excuse as to why he could not appear. As we worked, Connie began to realize what had happened with Max and her money and she finally asked him what his plans were to pay her back.

Max told her about money he had coming from the investments he'd made, but the market wasn't quite right to liquidate the stocks. When she asked to see the stocks, he told her it was all on computer and his computer was down. He told her he was expecting cash from the sale of an apartment building he owned in Indianapolis and had money coming as soon as the estate of his late wife was probated. When I asked Connie if she believed him, she said she wasn't certain but that she wanted to.

Connie asked Max weekly about the progress of repayment, and his excuses were always elaborate—and plausible. Meanwhile he was becoming more and more aggressive with her son and there were several physical confrontations between them.

Connie was reluctant to file for divorce because she feared Max might kill her or her son and because she believed she would never get the money back if she put him out. She was also afraid to be around him since he was so unpredictable and seemed to be increasingly violent. She was miserable.

Finally, after he had beaten her severely enough that she needed to be hospitalized, she could bear no more and served the papers for divorce on Max. He was furious and stalked and threatened her for a couple of months, but finally faded and left town.

Emboldened and empowered with the promissory notes Max had signed, Connie decided to try to collect on them after she'd heard he had a good job in Seattle. She felt confident that the distance would protect her and that she might be able to get a lien on his bank account.

Several months after filing the promissory notes with the court in Washington, Connie got a letter from the federal court in Seattle. Max had filed for bankruptcy, listing her promissory notes along with many thousands of dollars of other debt.

Connie wrote back to the court that he had the stocks, his late wife's estate, and the apartment house. She was stunned at the reply. Max owned nothing. Furthermore, he had been married *eight* times—all of his ex-wives were alive and each of them had been attempting to collect on promissory notes from him.

Connie came back to therapy devastated. She was most upset by the fact that she had been so naive as to assume Max had told her the truth. She talked often and at length about the feeling of having been a fool for not having seen through what he was doing.

I'm not sure how many of us would know a con man if we encountered one. First, we don't expect people to treat us in that way. Second, we're taught by our culture that it's bad manners to believe negative things about people we supposedly trust. To most people, you'd seem paranoid if you checked into your spouse's background.

What Connie really learned is the terrible lesson that no one is immune and no one is exempt. Anyone can be victimized, but that doesn't make the victim a bad person. Connie continues to work hard to recover her trust in herself, which in the end was the most important thing Max stole from her.

Con artists, criminals, and serial killers will not change the way in which they connect with others. They survive in the world by tricking other people and stealing from them and they believe this is how all people act toward one another. Anyone who doesn't act this way, they believe, is a fool who deserves to be victimized.

Into the category of dangerously toxic people we can also put those folks who deal drugs; people who routinely, even after treatment, solve problems with violence; and people who are doing time for criminal activities.

I'm not saying that all people who have made mistakes and served prison sentences are bad risks for relationships. I do believe, however, that being in prison changes forever the way a person sees the world. I encourage people to be very cautious when dealing with someone who has a prison record.

## Toxic Critics and Toxic Controllers

Another toxic group is composed of those people who want to take over the life of anyone with whom they have a relationship. These toxic controllers will do anything, including be violent, to stay in charge. They are unwilling to negotiate or compromise and they will frame you as the problem if you try to change the balance of power.

I remember seeing a couple on a talk show who were a perfect example of this. He firmly stated that his marriage certificate contained a clause that said his wife was his property. He held firm to this belief despite the best efforts of the host and audience to change his mind. His wife reported that he had told her that she was to do anything he asked— even including the most personal of personal hygiene. This man was a toxic controller.

Linked with toxic controllers are toxic critics. These people go far beyond the normal range of appropriate, helpful criticism when they criticize every aspect of their partners' lives. The objective of this intense criticism is control. The victim of the criticism begins to doubt his or her own abilities to make any sort of reasonable decision. The victim becomes emotionally frozen. The critic then can tell the victim exactly what to do and how to do it.

## Extreme Narcissists

These are not the average self-centered narcissists who sometimes are able to make an emotional connection with someone else. Instead these are the pernicious and dangerous narcissists who believe other people are just objects to be used and disposed of at will. These are the people who steal your life and then tell you it's not good enough. They are unwilling to make any kind of change and will simply abandon anyone who suggests that change might be appropriate.

This sort of narcissism is a bottomless pit into which you could throw your entire life. And it would still not be enough. It's not that you are not good enough but that you are too good, too intimidating, too able, and the toxic narcissist can't tolerate the feeling of inferiority this generates. To protect their very fragile egos, toxic narcissists attack you to bring you down.

Meanwhile, however, what you hear from them is that you are not good enough, that your efforts are not good enough, and that you are disappointing to them. Toxic narcissists often choose people who are success oriented and who can't stand the idea of not being good enough. The result of the narcissist's badgering is that the victim becomes self-victimizing as he or she attempts to rise to the impossible demands of the toxic narcissist.

The ultimate objective of the victim is to be loved and the message of the toxic narcissist is "If you're perfect, I might love you." Unfortunately, the operable words are "perfect"—an unachievable goal—and "might," which guarantees nothing while promising everything. In addition, the toxic narcissist will never define what "perfect" might mean, nor will he or she reveal the expectations. If expectations and rules *do* get verbalized, the toxic narcissist will instantly change them. This is a great example of a no-win situation.

## Toxic Liars and Toxic Cheaters

These people base their relationships with others on a foundation of lies, half-truths, and deflections. They put a great deal of effort into concocting plausible stories and scenarios, then build further lies on what others have believed of the first lot. Eventually little of reality is reflected in their presentation.

Oddly, the objective of all this untruth is to make the

toxic liar feel better about himself. He wants to be exotic or unusual or exciting. In the process he deceives others so much that there is nothing to connect with and the partner spends vast amounts of energy trying to make a connection with nothing but lies.

Let me give you an example. A friend of mine, Melissa, met Chuck in a bar. He was older and swept her off her feet with tales of his bravery in Vietnam as a helicopter pilot. He told her he'd worked for Air America there. Melissa excitedly told me he was a *spy*! Chuck went on to tell her that he was now flying special missions for the CIA and hinted at Latin American runs from Florida. She was captivated. When I told her I was concerned that spies usually don't tell new friends that they are spies, she was quick to defend him.

Eventually Chuck and Melissa moved in together. He chalked his sexual dysfunction up to a war injury, explained that his shaky financial status was due to lack of access to his Swiss bank accounts, told her he couldn't work a regular job because he needed to be on call for a mission, and told her she was lucky to be able to supply him with a home, food, and entertainment because it proved she was a loyal American.

Periodically, he would disappear for days at a time and would reappear filled with new tales. Melissa was working two jobs, getting very little sleep, and becoming increasingly angry with Chuck's lack of contribution to their lifestyle, when he abruptly disappeared once again.

This time he didn't resurface for six months and then only by accident. Melissa happened to run into him in a neighboring town; he was walking with his arm around a very pregnant woman who introduced herself to Melissa as Chuck's wife. Colombian drug lords and war wound my foot!

Toxic cheaters fit into the same category because their lives are also built on a foundation of lies but these lies are an attempt to cover up their multiple liaisons from their primary relationship.

A quick comment about affairs. Unfortunately, people sometimes make the choice to go outside their primary relationship to have a secondary relationship. This choice rarely has anything to do with the primary relationship even though the primary partner may be blamed by the person who wanders.

In general, an affair is a bad problem-solving technique for addressing feelings of fear or confusion or inadequacy in the person who has the affair, but it's a problem-solving technique that creates a lot of emotional debris.

Here's the good news. The majority of people who stray from their primary relationship never make that choice a second time because they see the damage it does. This insight helps the wanderer clarify the issues and make a commitment to the primary relationship.

There are people, however, who have affairs because they are completely unable to make a commitment to anyone and are much too scared to be alone. In a sense, they use people to medicate their loneliness while keeping a primary relationship that guarantees they will never have to be alone.

The core of these people is a hollow shell that can never be filled no matter how many affairs they have. Instead, they repeatedly hurt and sadden the people who love them. They have little or no regard for the feelings of others.

There is nothing that will change their behavior because there is nothing as powerful as the hope of feeling something. If you suggest therapy, however, they will angrily declare that there is nothing wrong with them that would require therapeutic intervention. A perfect double bind!

## Danger Signals and Warning Signs

Although these people should come with warning labels that would make them much easier to avoid, what they do come with is certain behaviors that can serve as a warning label.

The following list of toxic behaviors does not include all the possible permutations. But any of these behaviors can serve as a warning for you to pay attention to the rest of what is going on in your relationship.

## The Baker's Dozen of Toxic Warning Signs

1. *You are the problem.* In this case, the toxic person is unable or unwilling to own any part of the problems he or she may have created. Instead, you are told repeatedly that if you were only better, richer, prettier, taller, thinner, or smarter, then there would be no problem. Toxic people are so outwardly focused that they are unable to see that they own any part of the problem.

2. *Controlling behavior or extreme jealousy.* If your partner wants to run every moment of your life or is extremely jealous of anyone or anything else that takes your time or interest, beware! This person wants to own you and absorb you.

3. *No boundaries.* Having no boundaries himself and ignoring any boundaries you try to set are another sign of a toxic person. Once again, the desire is to so completely destroy the lines between the two of you that you will no longer exist as a separate entity. People who lack boundaries believe they have the right to do anything they wish because you are indistinguishable from them.

4. *Violence.* Do not tolerate any violence in any relationship for any reason no matter what. Period. There is no excuse, explanation, rationalization, clarification, or justification for interpersonal violence of any kind. If your relationship includes violence, it is not a relationship. Leave and press charges.

5. *Conning or criminal behavior.* If you are in a relationship with someone who is engaging in criminal behavior, you could come under suspicion even if you are not involved. If you are being conned by someone, speak to the police or your local district attorney to find out

options, and follow their advice. In neither case should you get in any deeper in hopes of recovering what has been lost. That misguided philosophy is what keeps Las Vegas a booming town.

6. *Addictions.* If a person is unable to break an addiction to drugs or alcohol, you need to make the decision to end the relationship. The person's relationship is with the drug, not you, but you will pay for it if you stick around. If the addicted person wants the relationship with you bad enough, he or she will be willing to get clean and stay that way. Making this clear to him or her is your only weapon—don't hesitate to use it.

7. *Cheating/affairs and/or unusual sexual practices.* People who demand acceptance of unusual sexual behaviors, including affairs, as a prerequisite to being in a relationship are a bad bet unless you subscribe to exactly the same set of rules. I'm not talking about the occasional foray into Frederick's of Hollywood garb, but rather practices like S&M or bondage or other destructive behaviors. If you tell your partner you are not comfortable trying something and he or she persists, be warned that this behavior is possibly toxic.

8. *Commitment phobia.* If your partner of long standing still is unwilling to commit to the relationship in a formal way, you may consider this a warning that they may never be able to make a commitment.

9. *Put-downs, insults, and teasing.* A little loving teasing is not a bad thing, but if your partner persists in saying hurtful things to you in public or teases unrelentingly, this toxic behavior is designed to put you in a one-down position. If you have been repeatedly teased and insulted and put down, confront your partner. If the teasing persists, your alarm bells should be ringing.

10. *Black-and-white thinking.* Lack of flexibility in your partner's thinking can spell trouble for you. If he or she is unable to see any gray area, then you have very little room to make mistakes before you are condemned as wrong, wrong, wrong, bad, bad, bad. This means your partner might very well be toxic, toxic, toxic!

11. *Yes, but . . .* If you hear more excuses than explanations and if every confrontation is deflected with the words "yes, but . . . ," you are dealing with a person who is unwilling to own his or her behavior. A person who needs someone to blame for everything is unlikely to be a good candidate for a partnership.

12. *Double binds.* Just as a refresher, a double bind is a situation in which, no matter what you do, you will be wrong. Everyone experiences some double binds. A good example might be that you hate your job but if you quit you will have no money. If the double bind always comes from your partner, however, it is a toxic behavior designed to keep you always off balance and always wondering.

13. *Lying.* Everyone lies once in a while about small things (and they're lying if they deny it!). If your partner routinely lies or if the lies your partner is telling result in your getting in some sort of difficulty, that's a clear indication of toxic behavior.

None of these signs is a stand-alone indicator that you need to send your partner packing instantly, but any of them or groups of them should tell you that you need to take a very close look at what's going on in the relationship and at least be cautious about any further involvement.

Anyone can make a mistake. But if these behaviors are part of a pattern then the pattern should serve as a warning that you are in a relationship in need of a careful assessment.

## HOW TOXIC IS MY RELATIONSHIP?

Rate each statement from 1 (not at all) to 6 (perfect match) by comparing it to your relationship. Write the number in the blank to the left of the question.

_____ 1. My partner has hit or pushed me.

_____ 2. My partner calls me names, puts me down, teases me too much.

_____ 3. My partner lies to me.

_____ 4. My partner has had more than one outside relationship.

_____ 5. My partner cheats people out of money or material goods.

_____ 6. My partner steals.

_____ 7. My partner abuses drugs or is an alcoholic.

_____ 8. My partner threatens me with violence or abandonment.

_____ 9. My partner is unable to make a commitment to our relationship.

_____ 10. My partner demands his/her way without willingness to compromise.

_____ 11. My partner can't hold a job.

_____ 12. My partner has huge, unpredictable mood swings.

_____ 13. My partner violates my boundaries.

_____ 14. My partner and I do not communicate on any issues.

_____ 15. My partner clings tightly to me and doesn't allow me time to myself or friends of my own.

_____ 16. My partner is jealous.

_____ 17. There is no trust in our relationship.

_____ 18. My partner has rages.

_____ 19. My partner tries to control my life.

_____ 20. My partner has no self-control with food, money, or alcohol.

_____ 21. My partner is a chameleon. I never know who to expect.

_____ 22. My partner tells me, directly or indirectly, that I'm not good enough.

_____ 23. My partner is a black-and-white thinker. There is no middle ground.

_____ 24. My partner has no close friends and is not close to his/her family.

_____ 25. My partner has spent time in jail or prison.

_____ 26. My partner greets suggestions with "yes, but. . . ."

_____ 27. My partner tries to keep me away from friends or family.

_____ 28. My partner is cruel to my pets/children/family.

_____ 29. My partner has few emotional reactions to anything.

_____ 30. My partner brings up everything from my past and acts as though I'm the only one with problems.

Now add up your scores:

| | |
|---|---|
| Under 54 | Your relationship is open and connected. Needs a tune-up every so often. |
| 55–79 | Some problems, but workable without intervention. |
| 80–109 | Consider a therapist. There's lots of room for improvement. |
| 110–134 | Get a therapist and get ready for a long haul. |
| 135–159 | Your relationship is probably not workable. |
| Over 160 | Caution! This relationship is toxic. |

# Why the Bad Ones Are So Appealing

In general, then, although most people are able or willing to make some changes, there are some who are toxic and who will not or cannot change. So why get involved with them?

If you've ever asked yourself, "What was I thinking?" welcome to the human race! Most of us have gotten ourselves into at least one of these toxic, distant relationships only to find ourselves trashed and doubting our ability to make any kind of choice.

Our choice to get involved has to do with a couple of things. First, people who seem to need repairs to their essential Selves are terribly tempting. After all, the mythology goes, a good relationship can change a person.

The actual situation is that a good relationship can enhance people and expand them but it cannot change them. The only thing that ever changes a person is his or her own choice to change. If a person is willing to make a change in how he or she processes and experiences the world, you will know that fairly early in the relationship. The battles will begin, however, when he or she wants you to change in unhealthy ways or to function in a less fully emotional way.

The seductive thing about this process, however, is the hint that if you change a bit, your partner will match that change. This is where the dance begins as you make the choice to surrender parts of yourself to the hope that your partner will live up to that unspoken promise.

Meanwhile, the objective of the toxic person is to keep you dancing at a distance as he is able to get all his needs met while you keep trying to find the magic formula that will turn everything around.

*There is no magic formula.* As long as you are working hard to make everything perfect, the toxic person is getting what she wants. You can ask for what you want, make a firm stand, or push for change, and if that works, bravo. If it doesn't, you need to be prepared to end the relationship.

This will be a very painful process because you have been doing all the work in the relationship to begin with so you have a huge emotional investment in the outcome. These are the relationships that make us wistful and leave us snuffling into a tissue for a long time because they are so unresolved.

Remember, *you didn't break them so you can't fix them.* You're better off using your time to work on strengthening yourself so you'll choose healthy relationships in the future.

## Healthy Choices

Nobody is perfect. There is not a person in the world who will come without baggage to a relationship; and there aren't very many who couldn't afford to make some changes to be more connected or more emotionally available. People change all the time. A good relationship will foster and support healthy changes as the two of you work to match and join with each other to make the relationship stronger.

So how do you identify the healthy, able-to-change people who will make good partners?

1. *Listen.* Listen carefully to what people say about prior relationships, the way in which they connect with their families, and how they feel about themselves.
2. *Feel.* Express your feelings not only about the relationship but about life in general. If the other person is able to talk about feelings *and* able to demonstrate them, you have the makings of a healthy relationship.
3. *Take time.* Getting to know someone takes time. You can't assume that just because something feels right it will take the direction you want if you don't give it time to grow and strengthen on its own.
4. *Use your common sense.* If your alarm bells go off, stop and listen to them and assess what is setting them off. If you have been in negative relationships, a positive one might feel odd so you don't want to dump out too quickly. Use your head and look at the situation without the filter of your prior bad experience.

5. *Listen to your friends.* If your friends support and encourage a relationship or try to tell you this one doesn't seem right, don't dismiss them. Listen to what they are observing and take it under advisement in making your own decision.

6. *Be true to your Self.* If a relationship feels right in your deepest self, it probably is. Give your innermost voice credit for being able to know the right thing when it comes along.

Remember that dinner party we began with? It's my hope that instead of going to that party, you might decide to stay home with a good book and wait for the right thing to come along!

Good luck and happy relationships! Remember, you not only deserve to be invited to the party, you deserve to be the guest of honor!

# READING LIST

The following list of books might be helpful to your further study of some of the issues we've looked at. There are many valuable books available that can help you. Don't stop with this small list. Your librarian, your friends, or your therapist can make suggestions as well.

## *Conflict Resolution*

McKay, Matthew, Ph.D., Martha Davis, Ph.D., and Patrick Fanning. *Messages: The Communication Skills Book*. Oakland, CA: New Harbinger Publications, 1983.

Scott, Gini Graham, Ph.D. *Resolving Conflict with Others and Within Yourself*. Oakland, CA: New Harbinger Publications, 1992.

## *Recovering from Abuse*

Elgin, Suzette Hardin, Ph.D. *You Can't Say That to Me! Stopping the Pain of Verbal Abuse—an 8-Step Program*. New York: Wiley and Sons, 1995.

Engel, Beverly, M.F.C.C. *The Emotionally Abused Woman: Overcoming Destructive Patterns and Reclaiming Yourself.* New York: Ballantine Books, 1990.

Evans, Patricia. *The Verbally Abusive Relationship.* Holbrook, MA: Bob Adams, Inc., 1992.

Forward, Dr. Susan, with Craig Buck. *Toxic Parents— Overcoming Their Hurtful Legacy and Reclaiming Your Life.* New York: Bantam Books, 1989.

# Growth and Change

Burns, David, M.D. *Intimate Connections.* New York: William Morrow & Sons, 1985.

Forward, Dr. Susan, and Joan Torres. *Men Who Hate Women and the Women Who Love Them: When Loving Hurts and You Don't Know Why.* New York: Bantam, 1986.

Norwood, Robin. *Women Who Love Too Much: When You Keep Wishing and Hoping He'll Change.* New York: Tarcher, 1985.

Redfield, James. *The Celestine Prophecy.* New York: Warner Books, 1994.

Rosen, Carol. *Maybe He's Just a Jerk: Find Out How to Spot Him, Stop Him and Get Him Out of Your Life.* New York: St. Martin's Press, 1992.

Wetzler, Scott, Ph.D. *Living with the Passive Aggressive Man.* New York: Fireside, 1992.

# Boundaries

Katherine, Anne. *Boundaries: Where You End and I Begin.* New York: Fireside, 1993.

# Self-Esteem

Burns, David, M.D. *Ten Days to Self-Esteem.* New York: William Morrow & Sons, 1993.

Jeffers, Susan. *Feel the Fear and Do It Anyway.* New York: Ballantine Books, 1987.

# INDEX

Solvers, 193, 204, 206, 207
  characteristics of, 184–86
  open-ended questions and,
    209–210
Spies, 28–31, 131–32
Spock, Benjamin, 172
State-dependent learning,
  234–35
Stoicism, 136
Structure, 223–26, 249–52.
  *See also* Goals
  creating, 251–52
Submission, 114
Substance 'holics, 19, 21–22
Surrender, 114
Survivors, 257
Sympathy, 246

Taking care, 192
Tango metaphor, 94–95
Teasing, 276
Template of the expected,
  247–48
Tens, 13–15
Therapy
  choosing and using a
    therapist in, 253–56
  cost of, 254–55
  misconceptions about,
    256–57
  privacy in, 254
Three-way connection, 203
Toxic balloon, 73–76, 136
Toxic cheaters, 272–74
Toxic controllers, 271
Toxic critics, 271
Toxic liars, 272–74
Toxic relationships, 263–82
  appeal of, 280–81
  personality disorders in,
    264–66

quiz, 277–79
warning signs of, 274–77
Tracks metaphor, 91–93
Traumatic memory, 78–79,
  235–37
Trophy hunters, 14–15
Trust
  in attachment theory, 66
  building, 241–45
Trustworthiness, 242
Truth, honesty vs., 31,
  127–28, 130–31
Twelve-step programs, 161

Unattached people, 65, 66–67
Unconditional love/
  acceptance, 16

Values, 239–41
Velcro babies, 64
Verbal abuse
  lies as, 128
  refusal to tolerate, 212
Victims, 257
Violence, 124, 275
  Fixers and, 193–94
  intellectualization and,
    108–110
  power imbalances and, 116,
    117
Visual cues, 246–47

Why questions, 221–23
Worry, 37–38

Yes, but . . . , 141–46, 277
  catastrophizing in, 143–45
  Players and, 196
  self-esteem and, 142, 145